the
natural
kitchen

Deborah Eden Tull

the
natural
kitchen

Your Guide to the Sustainable Food Revolution

process self-reliance series

Process Media
1240 W. Sims Way Suite 124
Port Townsend, WA 98368
processmediainc.com

Cover design by Lissi Irwin
Interior Design by Bill Smith
Illustrations by Jess Rotter
Edited by Jessica Hundley

ISBN 978-1-934170-12-0
Printed in the USA on recycled paper
10 9 8 7 6 5 4 3 2 1

THIS BOOK IS DEDICATED TO MY FATHER,

ROD TULL (1941–1985),

AND MY NIECE, OLIVIA ROSE TULL,

FOR MODELING JOY AND TEACHING ME WHAT MATTERS MOST.

*"Those who dwell among the beauties and the mysteries of the earth
are never alone or weary of life."*

—Rachel Carson

ACKNOWLEDGEMENTS

THIS BOOK IS LIKE A POT OF SOUP THAT HAS BEEN SIMMERING SLOWLY for many years. Many ingredients went into this book and many hands helped to stir it. Its creation has followed me from city to farm and back many times and I thank everyone who has shared any part of the journey. This book was a project inspired by community, written in community, and I was supported by community along the way.

First, I wish to thank my students and clients here in Los Angeles who have moved me so much by their sincerity and willingness to embrace change. I thank my mom Tanya and stepdad BJ for their solid and unwavering support throughout the writing of this book and for being such heroic editors. I thank my sister Rebecca for getting what I was trying to say when I was beyond words and for being my best friend; my brother Dani and sister-in-law Yvonne for their love and for embracing the sustainable food revolution in their lives so fully; and my brother Jim for his support from afar.

I would also like to thank: Process Media for being so enjoyable to work with, Jessica Hundley for helping to get things in order, Jess Rotter for her artistic wizardry, Jane Gould for helping me "bring it all together," Chuck Hurewitz for invaluable advising, Nichole Dowlearn for being ready to help with anything, Maryam Henein for sharing her honeybee wisdom, and Julia Russell for her inspired library.

This book would not have been written without the powerful encouragement of Walter Makichen and Ramada, whose guidance I am forever grateful for. Many teachers and colleagues in the field of sustainability have inspired this book, including Penny Livingston, Helena Norberg-Hodge, Debra Lynn-Dadd, and Dr. Vandana Shiva. Their support and contributions have been priceless.

I would also like to thank Amanda Bramble for years of collaboration, gardening, play, and for sharing the path of sustainability, Caverly Morgan for being a part of every turn since this journey began and for sharing the path of practice, Tamar Krames for her endless creativity, compassion and inspiration, and Sky Mantis for the heart-opening conversations that fed this book and a journey across oceans.

I would like to acknowledge the contribution of all of the communities mentioned in this book: The Zen Monastery Peace Center, Ampersand, Green Gulch Farm, Earthaven, Arcosanti, Free Farm Stand, L.A. Eco-Home, and the farms and communities who haven't been mentioned, but have made a huge impact on my life. I would also like to thank Terry and Greg Hargrave, Michelle Durand, Laure Redmond, Kim Colwell, Gabrielle Newmark, Amely Greeven, Deema Dabis, Peter Youngblood-Hills, Natalie Friedberg, Kevin Gruenberg, Kairyn Godoy, Anne Albrecht, Serge Berliawsky, my housemates on Micheltorena St., Project Butterfly, and my larger community.

Lastly, I offer a special thanks and deep Gasshō to Cheri Huber and the monks, for the practice of compassionate awareness and the inspiration that it feeds me every day. The ideas in this book were illuminated for me in your presence.

This book is printed on recycled paper. I acknowledge with humble gratitude all of the resources that went into this book and the resources that sustained me throughout its creation.

The Gulf of Mexico oil spill occurred in the final editing stages of this book. I acknowledge the tremendous suffering this disaster has caused to so many forms of life, and I hope that this book is one part of our collective commitment to compassionate action and an Earth-centric revolution.

CONTENTS

HOW THIS BOOK CAME TO BE...

THERE I WAS, FRESH FROM THE SIERRA FOOTHILLS—LAND OF DIRT roads and blue skies, tall pine trees and, yes, the occasional roaming cow. We lived simply. We grew much of our own food. We made our own bread, soy milk and granola and ate meals in silence. We lived by the energy of the sun and in the winter we rarely used lights after the sun went down. We chopped our own wood and built everything with our own hands.

We were Zen monks.

For seven years I had lived in a tiny hermitage in a forest, on 80 acres of silent sanctuary for people, plants and animals to live together in peace. At the monastery, summers were hot, winters were wet and freezing, the sunsets were riveting and a million stars shone in the sky every night. In the cooler months, I would rise each morning to fresh misty air, build a fire on a tiny woodstove and trek up the pathway to the main buildings, a rustic yet elegant earthen villa that had a dining hall on one side, a meditation hall on the other side and an archway and bell in between.

Unexpected circumstances had called me back to Los Angeles, the place I had grown up in and called home years ago. It was the day before Thanksgiving and I was in line at the market to find a turkey alternative for the vegans in the family. In the parking lot, people honked anxiously at one another for a space and, once inside, the atmosphere seemed even more unpleasant—lines of people toting tons of overly-packaged prepared foods, drinking beverages in disposable cups and buying turkeys.

Having spent the past decade (and beyond) living in some form of sustainable community, it was a little overwhelming to arrive in Los Angeles for my spell out in the "urban jungle." At the monastery, I used to think to myself, 'you can hear the earth breathing'... and I could always feel myself breathing. Now I was in a place where (unless you woke up and walked the streets at 5 a.m. while the city was still sleeping, as I sometimes did) a restaurant with music playing in the background was considered quiet. There was a constant "buzz" and beyond the audio distraction, the streets were also lined with visual distraction—billboard advertisements and neon lights.

At that time, it was rare for people to have a backyard food garden (though things are changing quickly!) and impossible to find a restaurant that used biodegradable material. Sprinklers sprayed sidewalks and roads wastefully, public trashcans overflowed, giant homes and buildings had lights shining throughout and very few customers at Starbucks brought their own mugs. At the time, I was often the only one in a market who brought my own bags and jars. And that's just some of the waste you could *see*....

Then there was all that went unseen about the impact of this type of lifestyle—impact on the environment and impact on the people who lived there. L.A. was a mix of beauty and tragedy to me.

I have always been aware of having a city girl and a country girl inside of me. The city girl can appreciate a city as a melting pot of culture, art, language, religion, a place where there is so much "edge" in the meeting of different worlds that it is a vortex of creativity and possibility.

The country girl loves fresh air and ancient trees over anything "human-made," and the amount of concrete and overconsumption in the city depressed her. I always felt that a city with so much "edge" would be an amazing environment in which to sow the seed of sustainability. But when I left L.A. in the early '90s, there didn't appear to be soil for that seed.

In my late teens, there had come a time when a craving for the natural life simply appeared and I had to follow. I exited L.A. and spent the next 15 years exploring sustainability in places that felt full of hope. For years I would do a spiritual comedy routine (more like a drama) every time I came to visit my family: "Oh, this city is overwhelming," "I wish there were more awareness here," "Someone has got to do something about this." And then I would step back, see myself getting caught up in my frustration and let go... until it started again.

So...back to the market and the day before Thanksgiving...

I looked around me, realized that the people I was surrounded by hadn't had an education in sustainability and that most people did not even have a conceptual framework or an awareness of how their actions impacted the world. And this time, when I heard the voice of "someone's got to do something," I remembered that I'm a "someone" and if I had anything to offer, it seemed that now was the time.

I found myself with a humorous and grave challenge, and at the same time, a riddle: How was I going to transfer my practice of peace, simplicity and sustainability to an environment like L.A.? I like a good "spiritual challenge"—so I guess I had found one.

Along with a large trunk I brought down with my personal items (yes, only two pairs of shoes had been needed in that life), I carried these things with me:

A passion for both spirituality and food

A LOVE of cooking and doing anything crafty with my hands

An enthusiasm for "we can absolutely change the world we live in for the better, so why don't we?" (a symptom of being born into a family with a long lineage of women who knew the power of one person to make a difference)

The knowledge that changing our minds (letting go of limiting beliefs) is not only the most important change we can make, but perhaps the most fun a human being can have

Years of experience in how to live simply and close to nature (and NOT a whole lot of experience driving on city streets or operating a cell phone!)

The ability to get a group of people together and to facilitate a transformative conversation that takes us from limitation to possibility

So I offered what I had brought with me, a down-to-earth education in sustainable living, conducting workshops where people could get together and start to unravel and demystify sustainability in a way they could understand. From open discussions to hands-on organic gardening classes, the point was to get "real" about sustainable living and to do so in the belly of the beast.

Both personal and planetary health have always been important to me. When I found myself living in a city with contaminated water and polluted air, the quality of my food became even more important than ever, and it became more vital to me to share my knowledge with others. Food for me is an experience of connecting to nature. I often experience the sacred while harvesting a sprig of rosemary, sorting through barley grains, or kneading soft fresh dough while baking bread.

The Sustainable Kitchen workshop became one of my favorites to teach, I think because the ritual of food is one that all people everywhere can relate to and it was one way to share the sacredness of nature with city folk, regardless of how "green" they might be.

In the workshops I teach, people get the information, but they also get to experience me personally providing the information. As I don't have the opportunity to do that with each of you, I wanted you to know a bit about me and where I'm coming from. I'm grateful to Process Media for inviting me to share this perspective with you. I met Jodi Wille while on a walk around the Silver Lake Reservoir one day and, as she had recently exited the city too and was enjoying her own renaissance of growing food and living more simply, we both agreed this was a timely topic.

At times this book will read like a linear guidebook and you will read through lots of lists and some disturbing news/statistics (although I try to go easy!). But I focus on inspiring *solutions* and break things up with stories, questions and exercises to get you thinking—because really the whole point of this book is to help you to be successful in making long-lasting change and to enjoy your life and the wonder of nature more fully.

Thank you for your efforts to help humans live in better harmony with our planet and with each other.

In Peace and Passion,
Deborah Eden Tull

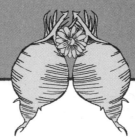

Introduction

"How we eat determines to a considerable extent how the world gets used."

—Wendell Berry

THIS BOOK IS NEITHER A COOKBOOK NOR A CALL FOR A particular diet. Instead, this book invites readers to experience greater health, well-being, joy and satisfaction in their lives by incorporating the principles of sustainability into the ritual of mealtime. The aim of *The Natural Kitchen* is to raise awareness about what it means to adopt a conscious, responsible and eco-friendly relationship with food, and transform our practices and habits in the areas of shopping, cooking, eating and working in the kitchen.

Drawing from years of experience as an organic gardener/farmer, a green activist, a monk and cook at a Zen monastery and as a sustainability coach in the city of Los Angeles, I will take readers on an educational and introspective journey that will enrich the way they relate to the food on their plates, to the environment and to their daily lives.

For the purposes of this book, **sustainability** is defined as *an approach to life that views long-term environmental, human and economic well-being as one and the same.* Sustainability honors life and the interconnections in the web of life as far into the future as one can imagine. A system is only sustainable if it is designed to take care of all components of that system—now and into the future.

Despite the gravity of the environmental crisis we are facing, there is a peaceful food revolution gaining momentum around the globe, and I will share living examples from inspiring communities whose inhabitants exemplify the joy of a sustainable relationship with food.

This book was inspired by a sustainable living workshop series I created called "Sustainability from the Inside Out," designed to help people understand how care of the environment relates directly to their personal day-to-day life and care for themselves and how to smoothly transition to a more sustainable frame of mind—inside and out.

These workshops help people let go of old belief systems that no longer serve them and realign themselves with a more compassionate and sensible approach to life. Throughout this book, there will be exercises to help you explore these issues experientially, along with general information and fresh ideas to help you green your kitchen. As one of the solutions offered to the challenges presented, this book will inspire you to ask a lot more questions. What you receive from this book will match what you put into it.

We live in a society today where people both expect and take for granted the conveniences of modern life. We flip a switch and expect electricity, turn on the tap and get all the water we need (and more), and pick up both fresh and processed foods from all over the world at the supermarket, with the mentality of "whatever we want, whenever we want it."

It is only in the past 60–75 years that Westerners have been living this high quality of life, which most of the world does not have the privilege to experience, but we have come to both expect it and take it for granted. At the same time, we often do not have the time or the peace of mind to enjoy this quality of life that is available to us.

We have begun to open our eyes, however, to the myriad social and environmental implications of this modern lifestyle and are beginning to realize that it is far from sustainable. In terms of food, we've become driven by shortsighted convenience rather than real quality, health and ecological sustainability.

None of this is our fault. We have simply been doing what we've been taught; however, if we are lucky, we may have glimpsed the alternative and realized that there is actually much more vitality and fulfillment available to us when we embrace a more sustainable way of life.

In my own experience, I have learned that my capacity for peace and well-being is completely intertwined with the degree to which I live in alignment with the principles of sustainability. The degree to which we are living in alignment and harmony with our environment reflects the degree to which we are living in alignment with ourselves and our deepest values.

Part of the problem is that most people today still lack the education and information they need in order to live a less impactful lifestyle. There is conflicting information out there about the "right" type of diet to eat and how to make eco-friendly choices.

While food is a basic and vital part of our lives, there has yet to be a clear and comprehensive guide about how to bring the principles of sustainability to ALL corners of our kitchens. Someone with good intentions, for example, might choose organic squash from the supermarket, but it could be packaged and shipped from abroad; while shopping, that same person might also buy genetically modified (GMO) soybeans and coffee in a disposable paper cup, without thinking about it. They might then go home and cook the squash in a microwave oven and toss the scraps in the garbage bin and miss out completely on actually enjoying their meal, being driven by a time crunch, convenience, or simple lack of awareness.

My intention is to teach people specifically how to practice sustainability in the kitchen while offering a deeper context and understanding for how the principles of sustainable living apply to our entire lives. Sustainability is an attitude of mind and the kitchen can be a laboratory for cultivating this attitude of mind.

My Own Journey from Consumer to Earth Steward

WE EACH HAVE OUR OWN UNIQUE JOURNEY DURING WHICH WE become more conscious. I grew up in Los Angeles, the belly of the beast, but in a family of free thinkers who exposed me to more progressive ideals and taught me to keep the "bigger picture" in mind. My grandparents were artists/bohemians who held a deep respect for nature and packed their tents and kids every summer for weeks of camping in the wilderness. This tradition trickled down and I was aware from an early age that I thrived in nature.

My dad was the first person to turn me on to natural foods. He followed a diet of whole and natural foods long before it became popular and was perhaps the first true environmentalist I knew. My dad practiced yoga, rose early in the mornings to run in Griffith Park, and brushed his teeth with natural soap. His diet was based on whole foods and, while his kids ate plenty of sugar, we were also influenced by our dad's food choices. Even as a little girl I was aware of the connection between his simple-living approach to life and the twinkle in his eye and joy with which he lived.

In high school I experimented with macrobiotics and the degree of vitality I experienced validated my interest in moving toward a holistic way of life. I became a vegetarian, took up yoga and committed to a healthy whole-foods lifestyle. As a young adult, taking on these practices helped me to become aware of the personal impact of the "consumer" way of living versus the choice to live differently, in alignment with nature. Beyond the philosophies behind these practices, the obvious benefits in how I felt were clear to me. There was no turning back.

I left Los Angeles after high school and attended college in a rural New England community where I was able to design my own major—"Ecology, Community and Social Change: Design for a Sustainable Future." I began to seek out and spend time in **intentional communities** and projects where people were living in tune with nature. All of these communities were farm- and garden-based and their kitchens were filled with the rich smells, colors, textures and tastes of nature's biodiversity.

There was something nurturing, healing and magic in the meals I helped to harvest and prepare during that time, with people who valued slowing down, rolling up their sleeves, and doing the work of living a simple earth-based lifestyle. I connected for the first time with the joy of gardening and found that there was nothing more natural for me and fun than the experience of digging in the soil and planting seeds. Gardening felt like an effortless extension of myself and learning to cultivate healthy soil and grow my own food felt like one way of giving back to life.

As a student during this time, I studied the intelligence of sustainable agriculture in the context of the world food crisis and my eyes opened to all of the social, economic, environmental and spiritual implications of our meal (and lifestyle) choices. I studied the work of Vandana Shiva, Helena Norberg-Hodge, Wendell Berry, E.F. Schumacher and other activists whose work assured me that there was an emerging global network committed to these issues. I had the opportunity to travel the world and see firsthand the impact of Western hybrid-seed companies on traditional societies; taste home-cooked meals of people eating off their own land for hundreds of years; meet courageous villagers working to preserve their cultural traditions and save seed varieties in the face of globalization; and experience the inspiration of activists and leaders committed to finding solutions to the environmental crisis.

That trip changed my life, both because it erased any illusion that the environmental crisis was somehow separate from me and because it showed me the power of change that committed people could make. It helped me to see even more clearly the promise that living in alignment with nature had to offer humanity. It also showed me how rarely environmental issues are clear-cut and encouraged me to take a much broader approach to environmental issues.

I feel extremely grateful for the fact that green ideas are finally moving into the forefront of our culture's awareness. I hope we are willing to rise to the occasion and make long-lasting and authentic change. This will require, however, our focus, commitment, and active participation.

One of the solutions presented to me in that year of travel was **permaculture design**. Permaculture design is a holistic approach to designing our homes, gardens, landscapes and settlements in alignment with nature. What excited me about permaculture was how accessible and do-it-yourself it was and that it was more of a celebration of the incredible solutions that arise when we work *with* nature rather than fight *against* a "problem." Permaculture offered tangible ways to redesign our built environment and offered solutions we could apply in cities.

My college thesis was on Urban Gardening with Youth, and during this time I worked in urban gardens and for a nonprofit organization called The International Society for

Ecology and Culture which promotes locally-based alternatives to the global consumer culture. The question of how to green our cities became more and more my focus and I then spent one year in the Arizona desert, co-running the farm at Arcosanti, one architect's vision for a more ecological city. I spent another year doing a farm apprenticeship at a Zen center on the Northern California coast focusing on sustainable agriculture.

In each of the communities where I lived, there were mentors and teachers, showing me the simple goodness and potential of people coming together with a clear intention and passion for change. These people were living close to nature, living enthusiastically and demonstrating that something more is possible when we step out of society's patterns and limitations. Though the communities I traveled to were diverse, there was a central theme to my studies.

The question at the forefront of my awareness was: How can we live collectively in harmony with the environment and with ourselves? The sincerely curious part of me asked, "What can we do?" The riled-up part of me said "What's it going to take people to make change?!!" Again and again I learned about how resilient nature is and how easily our environmental problems could be solved if only humans would make the effort and commitment required.

During this exciting time, I was also practicing meditation. I began meditating in college and attended my first 10-day retreat the day after I graduated. Meditation practice required me to become aware of my impact on the earth on a much deeper level. I began to realize that even in the world of progressive, proactive, solution-oriented environmentalism, I was witnessing a serious irony. I saw people advocating change "out there," but living in stress, in dissatisfaction, in fear and in competition with each other.

I saw people (including myself) exhibiting self-righteousness and judgment. People who were attempting to live harmoniously in intentional communities were sometimes distracted by human drama and a lack of commitment. I saw this imbalance in others and I could see it in myself. I saw how my own, sometimes frantic, desire to make change overtook my own peace and well-being.

Seeing how much judgment I carried about the world around me, I began to understand why environmentalism was not so popular to those people who didn't identify as environmentalists and realized that the self-righteousness it brought out in me was no longer serving me. I also felt that if I was going to live in the sustainable world I was learning how to cultivate, I had to find a way to let go of the messages from the "old world" that were still running my life.

> *"When we try to pick out one thing in the universe we find it hitched to everything else."*
> —John Muir

MIDWAY THROUGH MY INTENSIVE INVOLVEMENT IN THE EMERGING sustainability movement, I picked up a book by American Zen teacher Cheri Huber and it transformed my life; I recognized her teachings as the missing link for me in my explorations of sustainability.

I became a Zen Buddhist monk at 26 and for the next seven years lived as a monk at the Zen Monastery Peace Center in Murphys, California—Cheri Huber's center for the practice of peace and sustainability. During my time as a monk, I supervised the gardens, served as the cook, facilitated workshops, and wore many other hats. In all of these roles, the primary focus was to practice an unwavering commitment to peace and conscious compassionate awareness.

To live in a community practicing sustainability in every realm was the greatest gift I have ever received and it was the first time I had experienced a community willing to do "whatever it took" to cultivate peace and sustainability. I felt that through our practice we were given the gift of experiencing the heart of sustainability.

Working in a kitchen committed to the highest degree of **mindfulness**, or present moment awareness, was a powerful experience, and monastic living enabled me to explore deeper issues around food and sustainability. Before living at the monastery, I knew all the right "green" ways to approach my diet and cooking, but I was still running on auto-pilot and was too distracted by my own issues to truly embody sustainability in myself.

My time as a monk expanded my awareness and deepened my sense of interconnection with the world around me, eventually enabling me to reintegrate the principles of sustainability into my life from the place of "what is best for ALL?" I also learned an invaluable lesson during this time: Our every action impacts our world. If the spirit of kindness is lacking in any part of a person's attempt to live a more "low-impact lifestyle," that in itself is not a "low-impact lifestyle." Kindness to a human being is like compost to soil—we cannot thrive without it.

It was so simple. In the words of Matthieu Ricard, *"Nothing goes right on the outside when nothing is going right on the inside."*

When I moved back out into "the world," I felt, and continue to feel, inspired by the opportunity we have to realign ourselves with nature and to create a kinder, more sane, world wherever we are. If the skills for sustainable living I had experienced over the past 15 years had been so successful everywhere I had lived and traveled to, there was NO reason all of this couldn't be applied to an urban environment like Los Angeles.

Step one for me was to learn quickly how to adapt the skills I had already been practicing to city life. To support my own efforts, I founded Creative Green Sustainability Coaching and began offering my services and support to others.

I offer people through Creative Green Sustainability Coaching: an integrated education that teaches the tools for living sustainably inside and out and emphasizes that as we go deeper into living consciously, our lives become richer and more fulfilling. The Creative Green approach to green living is both lighthearted and grounded in acceptance of the gravity of the situation we are in.

So… back to food…. Why is food such an important part of sustainable living? Is it really going to make a difference if we take the extra time to get our kitchens in order and green our food habits? The answer is Yes! Our attitude toward feeding ourselves reflects our attitude toward life.

This book invites you to move beyond the role of "consumer" and into the role of an engaged "earth steward." Remember, as consumers we are not held as responsible for the impact of our choices and we think of this responsibility as a burden rather than our birthright.

Creating a Kitchen Aligned With Nature

FOR DECADES THERE HAVE BEEN PEOPLE AND COMMUNITIES MODEL-ING a "back to the land" approach to living green, but how does one apply this in urban and suburban environments? How can we embrace green living everywhere? Isn't it going to cost a ton of money? How do we find the time and knowledge for such an endeavor? How do we develop the right attitude and support required for our intentions?

Though the principles of sustainability are not new and are practiced in varying degrees in cultures around the world, modern Western culture seems to have left these principles completely out of its design and our memory. This book offers a guide for realigning our kitchens with nature and letting the process impact our overall approach to life.

The process can be deeply inspiring and fun, but will also challenge you and invite you to move beyond your comfort zone. It will require you to become aware of things (about the food you eat and about yourself) that you previously did not know.

To live sustainably, then, is a movement away from a life that's insulated and focused on "me," and the bubble each of us can live in, to a life of connection and interdependence. It is an approach that moves beyond the orientation of "What is best for ME?" to "What is best for all, including me?" The important piece here is that YOU are part of the ALL. In my experience, it is so much more satisfying to live with this ALL mentality.

One thing that struck me from the first community I visited was what a good time these people were having! AND—back to the focus of this book—what healthy and delicious food they were eating.

RATHER THAN OFFERING ANOTHER "10 THINGS YOU CAN DO TO BE green," the Creative Green approach teaches the principles for sustainable living and invites you to integrate these principles into your own lifestyle. In the words of Wendell Berry, *"A change of heart and mind without a practice is just another frivolous novelty we cannot afford."*

While doing small things to help the environment is great (every effort, no matter how small, helps), if we don't change our overall approach to how we relate to ourselves and to the world, our efforts will be futile. We will end up continuing to perpetuate the same attitude of mind that created the challenges we now face. We will also be missing out on a glorious opportunity to enjoy our lives more fully by experiencing our interconnection with the planet.

People regularly ask me "How am I supposed to be successful in going green when I'm really busy and I don't have time to cook?" or "I don't have enough money." My answer is that we can integrate sustainability into our lives whatever our circumstances.

Going green in the city requires little time and little money. All it requires is a shift in understanding and a committed choice to be an earth steward, a concept I will expand on in the next chapter. Greening your kitchen will actually simplify your life, save you money, and feed you more *joie de vivre* than you have experienced before.

Country Lessons for City People

THE MESSAGE OF THIS BOOK REFLECTS YEARS OF PERSONAL EXPERI-
ence in sustainable kitchens throughout the United States, from intentional communities living off the grid, to urban permaculture projects, to organic farms and the Zen
Monastery Peace Center.

I will share personal stories and examples from these communities, as well as provide
examples from people I admire who have successfully integrated these ideas into their
kitchens. The communities mentioned vary in their focus, but are all living an alternative
to the consumer way of life.

What these groups of people have in common is that they are all committed to making a lighter impact on the planet and they are models for a fulfilling life based on interconnection, practical creativity and self-reliance to varying degrees. Their inspiration has a
lot to offer us all, no matter where we live—in the country, in the city, or in the suburbs.

We can be interested in the ideals of green living and engage in intellectual conversation about the environment, but sustainable living needs to be interwoven into the
most practical and mundane aspects of our daily lives, from how we wash our dishes to
how we perceive "trash." Sustainability grows from the inside out and we have a great
opportunity to bring sustainability to every corner of our lives if we begin with our own
relationship with food.

This book also reflects the spirit of permaculture design, an approach to designing our
human settlements in greater harmony with nature. In permaculture, we rely on observation to see how different components of a system (for instance, a kitchen and a garden)
could work together more harmoniously. We focus on what solutions might be accessible
when we simply observe and work WITH nature.

In my workshops, there is a wide range of participants, as there will be readers of this
book. Some of you might be ready to make a 100% commitment to following protocols
for a completely sustainable kitchen. Some of you are already doing the work and want
to go deeper. For you I have covered all the aspects of a sustainable kitchen—from the
practical elements to recipes and guidelines for sustainable kitchen design.

For those of you for whom this information is completely new or who are simply
curious about the topic, I hope to inspire you to actualize *one simple change* in your life,
rather than to feel overwhelmed by all of the ideas and then not do any of them. I would
much rather see you integrate at least one change into your life and appreciate yourself
for doing so, rather than become immobilized into inaction. One conscious step always
leads to another....

Before You Begin Reading:

THERE IS AN EVALUATION WORKSHEET IN CHAPTER Sixteen that you might want to look over before you start reading, and then again when you finish. It will help you to consciously relate elements of your own life to the contents of this book. Chapter Fifteen offers tools for consciousness to support you in actualizing the changes suggested in this book, and can be read at the beginning or end.

There is a Glossary and Resource List at the very end. Words and terms that are in bold upon first mention can be found in the Glossary.

Each chapter has questions for you to consider to help you to take next steps. This book also contains some recipes and sample menus. I have included both vegetarian and omnivorous examples, to help everyone apply the ideas presented in this book. My point is to help you learn how to integrate the principles of sustainability into your daily lives. The sustainable food revolution is not exclusively a vegetarian food revolution. It is a revolution for everyone who eats.

Chapter 1
THE PRINCIPLES OF SUSTAINABILITY AND THE FOOD YOU EAT

"We have lived our lives by the assumption that what was good for us would be good for the world. We have been wrong. We must change our lives so that it will be possible to live by the contrary assumption, that what is good for the world will be good for us. And that requires that we make the effort to know the world and learn what is good for it."

—Wendell Berry

G ROWING UP AS AN URBANITE IN THE '70S AND '80S, I found that most of the kitchens I entered were designed for and motivated by convenience. There was a lack of awareness about ecology, an enthusiasm for all things "instant" and "fast" (there was a 78% rise in fast food in the eighties) and a "have what I want when I want it" attitude that pervaded society.

It was typical for a kitchen to include convenient, easy-to-prepare foods (memories of Swanson's TV dinners, Pop Tarts and Top Ramen come to mind) with compromised nutritional value; excess packaging (and colorful shiny packaging being part of the appeal of some foods); produce shipped from far away and grown with pesticides; microwaves becoming all the more popular; increasing trash and an upswing in the use of plastics; and a rise in additives and artificial tastes and smells. It was typical for the tap to be turned on and left running while other activities occurred and for lights to be left on all the time.

While this old kitchen model is familiar and comfortable to so many of us and is still the norm for many people in the world, realizing that this is simply not a sustainable way to approach food might inspire us to want to learn some new tricks and habits.

What Does it Mean to Be an Earth Steward?

MOST OF US WHO GREW UP IN CITIES OR SUBURBS FROM THE 1950s through the end of the last century were not taught to pay much attention to caring for our environment. We were brought up as separate from the natural world on some level—as consumers who simply turn on the tap, flip a switch, flush a toilet and dump our trash in a receptacle without thinking about where it goes.

Can you see how this consumer mindset has operated at some point in your own life? Can you see—without judgment—a way in which it might operate in your lifestyle choices today?

In reality, we are not separate from the natural world. The repercussions of this mentality are HUGE and range from carelessness in our use of natural resources, to a lack of compassion for non-human life forms, to being out of touch with our own bodies. As a culture, the task of shifting our paradigm to a more earth-reverent approach to life is just beginning and it is one I hope we take to heart. An **earth steward** is someone who chooses to be an active participant in the world we live in by letting go of the "consumer/user" role and taking on more of a role of "steward" and "participant."

An earth steward is one who recognizes the impact of our lifestyles on the earth and who accepts passionate responsibility for both learning and modeling a more sustainable lifestyle now and for future generations.

By rolling up our sleeves and taking steps to disengage with our unconscious, never-questioned habits like switch-flipping, we can re-engage with our environment in a participatory and reverent way.

The difference between being a consumer and being an earth steward is similar to the difference between the attention and care you give your own child or dog as opposed to a child or dog you just pass on the street. When we really see something as "ours" and an extension of ourselves, as in "our world," "our soil," "our food system," we have a totally different relationship with it. We would do everything in our power to take care of it.

This approach requires more responsibility but it also provides us with a deeper sense of personal power and it is the only way we are going to make a significant change. The more I access the power in me to make a positive impact in an area that I was once asleep to, the more in touch I am with my own power. Consider that the entire grid mentality is set up in such a way to support our being unconscious and out of touch with our interconnectedness. Our power as people lies in our ability to know that we are interconnected.

Conscious choices spring naturally once you experience the joy of sustainable living.

For instance, when I share an organic, garden-picked, scarlet runner bean with a city kid who has not tasted one before, or the smell of a fresh sprig of lavender, the pleasure of the senses inspires an appreciation of the natural world in a way no school book can.

A client who always drove to work allowed me to talk him into biking to work one day instead. I had to offer a lot of encouragement, as he kept telling himself he was "too busy" to ride his bike, it was going to take forever and since he couldn't afford an energy-efficient car, he should just give up on going green. It turned out, however, that the ride reminded him of his childhood and was so much fun, so energizing and so quick, that he decided to bike to work every day for the love of biking.

This shift also encouraged him to start a small garden, spend more time cooking and begin enjoying the outdoors again. How can we care for the planet if we remain unaware of the pleasure and satisfaction that so doing can bring into our lives? How can we be excited about going green if we don't know that caring for the planet is a way of caring for ourselves?

You may already be well aware of this "secret," that caring for the planet is a way of caring for ourselves, and perhaps have been living this way for years. For those of you who are new to sustainability, here are six steps you can take to begin making this shift and cultivating the earth steward in you:

Accept the way you have been living (or were brought up) without self-judgment.

Give yourself a grounded education in sustainable living. Reading this book is a great first step!

STOP and ask yourself honestly if your current lifestyle is truly nourishing and fulfilling, or if you are letting stress and convenience guide your choices. Can you see the possibility of living in a more joyful, balanced and healthy world?

Begin learning what it means to make the choice that is "best for all." Everything is interconnected and the more we understand this, the more we can make conscious choices regarding the production, consumption and disposal of the resources in our kitchen.

Begin to access the part of you who is willing to go beyond the call of duty and engage with the world in a more active, alive, joyful, creative (yes, sustainability inspires and requires our creativity) and empowered way. This movement is only going to last if we are having fun!

Practice non-judgment as you approach change, step by step. Learning new habits can take time, but we can make the process more enjoyable by practicing non-judgment every step of the way. *There are no cops in the green kitchen.*

BEFORE I INTRODUCE THE PRINCIPLES FOR A SUSTAINABLE KITCHEN, let's look a little more closely at the big picture regarding food and consider a more sustainable perspective:

Food is a WE thing. The food on our plates comes from a web of interconnection that includes and depends upon the soil, sun, water, air, beneficial micro-organisms (such as fungi, bacteria, protozoa and nematodes), honeybees and earthworms, farmers and fishermen, oceans and animals and other forms of life we rarely think about when we glance at our plate of food. When we acknowledge all that goes into food production, we are even more appreciative of our meal, beyond the sensory pleasure and nourishment of our food and we realize it is our responsibility to honor and respect our food system.

Eating an instant or packaged meal alone while watching the TV or on the computer, we can easily forget about the web of interconnection surrounding that meal. Eating while double-tasking, with our attention not focused on our food, we can forget. When we share a home-cooked meal of local veggies from a farmer we know, flavored with herbs we have harvested ourselves, it is a lot harder to forget.

Each of us is part of this WE. So it is up to each of us to take good care of ourselves and to feed ourselves a healthy nourishing diet. It is up to each of us to become attuned to the difference between authentic nourishment as opposed to what I call "phony food." (Once we are tuned into the present moment, rather than following our form of autopilot, this is easier to do.)

All food is not created equal. There is a dramatic scale out there in terms of who is serving quality food and who is not... and it is our opportunity as earth stewards to become aware of this, rather than to blindly trust our food servers. The sustainable food movement prioritizes quality and health, and provides more nutrition from simple whole foods as the alternative to overly-packaged, irradiated, shipped and processed food that has required more energy, water and waste than necessary.

As food is a WE thing, sustainable food should be affordable and not something only the lucky few can afford. We must begin to find ways to make healthy food affordable to all.

Real food and the ritual of mealtime require time, care and attention. We don't have to buy into this idea that convenience is going to save our lives. A sustainable kitchen isn't bound to the belief that there is "not enough time for what is important," and thus a sustainable kitchen is a lot more enjoyable.

Food in general should reflect the true costs that went into it. Why not acknowledge the hidden costs of a food item that required pesticides, processing, packaging and then oil to fly it across the globe?

Sufficiency and sustainability come first. For example, rather than growing nutrition-depleted food in poor soil only to then fortify the food with minerals and use artificial supplements, why not cultivate healthy soil and therefore produce healthy food in the first place?

The quality with which my food is grown and prepared is as important as the quality with which I ingest my food. Being present to our meals has the ability to feed us on a whole other level and has the ability to bring a new kind of peace into our lives.

As earth stewards, we actively participate in creating a sustainable food system. We acknowledge the power in our role as conscious consumers and choose to execute our power.

Food security is a real issue. How is it that we have armies protecting our country but we are not taught or required to protect our sustenance? The more we learn about the delicate balance of our food security system, the more compelled we are to care for and protect it.

Food is an opportunity to experience our interconnection and interdependence with all of life, to take care of ourselves, to honor the natural world, to come together, to express our creativity and to celebrate life.

What are the Guiding Principles for a Sustainable Kitchen?

Imagine a kitchen that nourishes our bodies, our families, our community and future generations, as well as honoring our responsibility to care for the earth. A sustainable kitchen creates a foundation for finding the balance between health, environmental/social responsibility, mindfulness and *joie de vivre*!

If a kitchen is aligned with nature, it reflects health on all levels. The following principles will help you to find your own way in making the best choices you can in your sustainable kitchen. I hope that they also help you to bring more peace and simplicity into your life.

• Conscious Consumption of Resources

Consciousness comes from the Latin root "to know." Consciousness in the kitchen means that rather than choose to remain unaware of what goes into our food and the impact of our choices, we choose to know and to act accordingly. We make a commitment to become continually more aware of what is good for ourselves and for the planet in the long term, rather than just be run by "what I want right now."

A sustainable kitchen is built on the foundation of consciously chosen healthy ingredients and a focus on organic, local, whole foods. In addition, being green in the kitchen means being conscious about our use of every resource, from using the entire carrot from root to top and not wasting leftovers, to practicing conservation and reuse of the energy, water and packaging that comes through our kitchens.

• Conscious Disposal of Resources: Zero Waste

A sustainable kitchen brings the same degree of awareness to kitchen "waste" that we bring to our cooking, shopping and all that goes into producing a meal. The examples range from cutting down on waste by composting our food scraps and recycling containers to choosing minimal packaging and recycling water used for cooking and cleaning. The system I introduce in Chapter Three: Radical Recycling, is a comprehensive way to implement conscious recycling of resources.

• Awareness of our Energy Use and Carbon Footprint

The sustainable kitchen utilizes less energy than a conventional kitchen. Whether it is through bringing attention to the way we cook our rice, for instance, to baking cookies in a solar oven or utilizing energy-efficient appliances, there are countless ways to reduce our energy use and thus the **carbon footprint** of our kitchen. Consider that an organic farm uses 30–50% less energy than a conventional farm, primarily due to the huge energy savings when avoiding synthetic nitrogen fertilizer, so you are saving energy by simply eating organic.

• Commitment to a Safe, Non-toxic World

From the building products we use to construct our kitchen to the storage containers and cleaning products we use to maintain it, we choose only safe non-toxic ingredients in a sustainable kitchen. This awareness extends to what we put down the drain and what goes into the trash, as we know our waste has an impact on other life forms.

• Sustainable Food Security Local and Global

A sustainable kitchen is engaged in the mission to support future food security by being aware of issues such as soil health, small-farm welfare, water quality and conservation, awareness of federal food regulations, genetic engineering and other threatening food practices. A couple of simple ways to honor this tenet of sustainability are to make a commitment to local, organic and seasonal foods and to buy our food directly from the farmer whenever we can.

• Financial Sustainability (with Financially Friendly Strategies)

In a sustainable kitchen, we find creative, empowering and community-based strategies for living green without compromising our pocketbook.

• Connection with a Sense of Place and Community Through Food

In every cultural tradition, food is something that connects people with land, the seasons and with a sense of community. There are numerous strategies today to ensure that food connects us with the place we live and our local community, such as farmers markets, Community-Supported Agriculture (CSAs), community food-buying and food-sharing, resource sharing, community gardening, food-based service projects, and even potlucks and conscious food celebrations. Sustainability is a shared community endeavor that connects us to each other locally and globally, and there is richness, pleasure, and joy when we connect through food.

• Mindfulness

Mindfulness is the attitude of mind that is most helpful if we want to live a sustainable life.

Mindfulness focuses our attention and awareness on the present moment. This helps us disengage from habitual, conditioned, unsatisfying and unskillful habits and behaviors. Mindfulness helps us to see clearly, as old habitual ways arise, that we have the opportunity to make another choice. By bringing this attitude of mind to our kitchen, which is the center of our homes, we can begin to change the entire tone in our home and lifestyle. The more we take care in our kitchen, the more well cared for we feel and the more care we have for the world around us.

• Efficiency and Ease in Design

Sustainability exists in finding harmonious and efficient systems for humans and nature to work together and for all parts of a system—for instance a garden and kitchen—to work together. A green kitchen has to be easy and efficient for the people it is serving. We'll explore strategies for green living to be human-friendly, as well as kid-friendly and family-friendly.

• Giving Back/Generosity

Traditionally a farmer sets aside a small portion of his or her land to grow food for the needy. In this spirit, given that 1.02 billion people in the world are starving, those of us who have our basic needs taken care of have a unique opportunity to assist with the ending of world hunger if we choose to.

As urbanites, we have the opportunity to practice generosity with food by doing what we can to provide for those who do not have it. This spirit of generosity also translates to "giving back" to the soil that our food is grown in (as will be discussed in Chapter Five, sustainable agriculture gives back to the soil and replenishes nutrients while conventional agriculture leads to soil depletion) and respecting the web of interconnection that makes up our food system.

This may appear as an ambitious list and a set of high standards to those of you who are beginning to learn about sustainability; however, once we shift our perspective to that of an earth steward, it's really very simple. Instead of seeing ourselves as consumers of resources we "use," we become more participatory and rooted in interconnection, choosing to take passionate responsibility for our every action.

CONSIDER:

To bring these ideas into your own kitchen, consider the last meal you ate. Where did your meal come from? Was it a home-cooked or home-grown meal, or did you eat out? How much do you know about what went into your meal, from the soil it was grown in, or the environment it was raised in, to the plate in front of you? How much did you think about it? Considering the information you do have, did the meal reflect your values? Or were your choices made primarily out of habit or convenience?

Acknowledge the ways you are bringing the principles of sustainability into your meals already. ●

Chapter 2
RADICAL RECYCLING AND ZERO WASTE:
Transforming Trash Into
a Path of Gems

"The future belongs to those who understand that doing more with less is compassionate, prosperous and enduring and thus more intelligent, even competitive."

—Paul Hawken

A S THE MAIN TRAIL AT THE MONASTERY MEANders its way through the property, it takes you through manzanita and cottonwood trees, past green meadows and pine forests and past the rustic hermitages and structures of the monastery. As one walks along the path, one begins to notice that there are magic gems scattered amongst the stones and earth of the ground—specks of blue and white and green adding color to the path as it curves its way through the hills and forest.

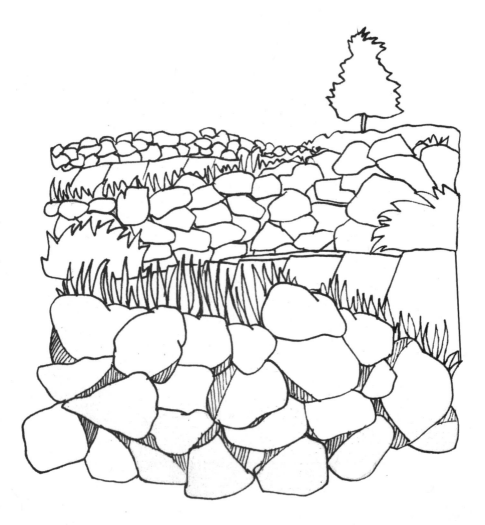

Well, these are not exactly "magic gems," but over the 20-plus years the monastery has been in existence, every ceramic dish, mug, or bowl that has broken has been smashed into pieces and scattered along the path, creating a lovely organic mosaic of color worked into the ground.

Walking the trail at the monastery, I always appreciated that the ceramic pottery, handmade from the earth by a member of the community, was being returned to our land in such a simple and artful way. This was one of many ways of creating a "**closed cycle**" on the monastery property. I appreciated that rather than dumping one more "useless" object into a landfill, a purpose and place on the property could be found for even broken pottery.

When we begin to see our "trash" with fresh perspective and apply the principle of creative reuse, everything we might otherwise toss begins to appear as a useful or artful resource. Consider this: even broken ceramics from your kitchen can be put to reuse, for creating a mosaic or adding a special touch of magic gems somewhere unexpected.

A natural kitchen is committed to the principle of **Conscious Disposal of Resources: Zero Waste**. This is the foundation for a natural kitchen and, in my experience, an area that provides opportunity for the most creativity and new ways of seeing things. Because we are so trained in our society to view waste as inevitable, this principle serves as the starting point for a sustainable kitchen. We begin to see all of our perceived waste as a valuable resource when we adopt this principle. I easily turn cereal boxes into artistic file folders, tea boxes into recipe cards or holiday decorations, yogurt containers into protective collars for garden transplants, colored bottles into bottle walls for raised beds and more. By putting this principle to action, I save money and cut down on the need for new "stuff" by reusing what I have in inventive ways.

When I first moved back to Los Angeles after years of living as a Zen monk, I was alarmed by the amount of trash I seemed to create here even living a "simple life"—not purchasing unnecessary items and trying to leave a low carbon imprint each day.

I immediately decided to challenge myself by committing to one month of zero waste. What I found was that it was very easy as long as I did a little homework. I had to find out where I could get everything I needed in bulk or with minimal packaging, let go of a few things I didn't need (for instance, because I could not find cheese wrapped in a way I felt good about, I eliminated it from my diet) and equipped myself with an urban eco-kit (to be explained further in this chapter).

Other than toilet paper, I was able to produce zero trash—though I did end up with a tiny bag of non-recyclables from which I created a unique piece of art. (We've got to give ourselves a little leeway in our efforts.) The process required me to look at how far I was willing to go. It also required me to find companies that shared my values for EVERY item I purchased and it felt good to be putting my money only towards companies that I respected for their green business practices.

Why Take On Radical Recycling and Zero Waste?

ACCORDING TO THE ENVIRONMENTAL PROTECTION AGENCY, THE average American produces about 4.4 pounds (2 kg) of garbage a day, or a total of 29 pounds (13 kg) per week and 1,600 pounds (726 kg) a year. This only takes into consideration the average household member and does not count industrial waste or commercial trash.

As a nation, though we only make up five percent of the world's population, the U.S. produces 30% of the world's trash and consumes 30% of the world's resources. If these numbers sound staggering, you would be surprised to know that 80% of all the products produced in the U.S. are used only once and then discarded. In helping people to green their homes, I have learned that most people live with a degree of queasiness or resignation about the amount of trash they send to the dump each week. People feel that they do not have enough time to address one more detail in their lives and often feel powerless to change the situation. Or, because they choose to cut corners and create extra waste consciously, they are followed around by a little voice that acknowledges, "It doesn't feel good to be creating so much trash. I don't want to be creating so much trash, but I'm too busy to address it and everyone else seems to be resigned to this, so I am too."

Consider: What is your relationship with trash? Do you think about the amount of trash you create each week? Are you already taking steps to curb it? Are there things you throw out rather than recycle because it's easier? What is the most obvious way you could cut down on your trash output?

Obviously, recycling saves natural resources and saves landfill space. Recycling also reduces pollution, saves water, energy and taxpayers' money and creates employment; however recycling also requires a lot of energy, water and money. Please do not do yourself or your environment the disservice of believing that "as long as I'm recycling, I'm doing my part." It is a step in the right direction, but recycling unconsciously is as unhelpful as doing anything unconsciously.

Remember that "reducing" our use of resources and "reusing" the resources we do use is as important as "recycling" our resources. If we can come up with a creative reuse for something (for instance, a glass bottle or brown bag) to extend the life of the object for as long as we can before tossing it in the recycling bin, we are being a much stronger part of the solution. If we can find ways to live well with fewer new purchases and invest in long-term products instead of disposables, this is even better.

You can easily cut your waste output by setting aside some time on the weekend to create your own household Radical Recycling Center. The result of doing this is that you will be making conscious reuse of resources an easy, convenient and almost automatic part of your daily life. The way you see trash will shift entirely and you will also save money and ignite your creativity by engaging in this approach to the waste. Practicing this mentality in our kitchens naturally begins to extend into our home and entire lifestyle and we will never see trash the same way again, but will see endless opportunity to reduce, reuse and recycle.

Radical Recycling in Nature

In nature, there is no such thing as "waste." Waste or trash is something that human beings invented on our own. Picture a forest: In a forest eco-system, when leaves fall from a tree they offer mulch for the ground and decompose into carbon, feeding the soil and the mycelia beneath the soil. If a tree falls in a forest, it quickly becomes shelter for squirrels and other small animals. Every part of a forest eco-system recycles back into the forest. Every eco-system—from wetland to prairie to ocean—demonstrates the same thing. Nature is a radical recycler.

On a sustainable organic farm, the farmer works to mimic this concept of radical recycling through composting, feeding plants from the nutrients naturally growing on the site, recycling water and using animal waste as manure. A truly sustainable farmer seeks to create a **closed cycle** where the least amount of nutrients and materials are shipped in from afar, the food is sold locally and the farmer is making the very best use of every single resource on the land.

Human settlements and cities today have veered a long way off the path of nature's radical recycling. We ship our water, food and energy in from far away. We throw away tons of useful resources daily and haul it as waste to faraway trash dumps, which pollute the land, air and ground water. How can we avoid this by creating more of a closed cycle in our own lives?

Obviously, there are steps that need to be taken by cities and by countries globally to address the issues of waste and recycling and we need to actively support local, national and global initiatives promoting sustainable practices. However, we should also be more proactive about promoting radical recycling in our personal lives and we can do so by beginning with our kitchens.

As simple as this may seem, developing a closed cycle in our own lives can dramatically reduce the amount of trash we create, water we use, gas we use, money we spend and our overall carbon footprint. In addition, finding ways to connect the dots and better utilize the resources on our own property is fun and stimulates human creativity.

How to Set Up a Radical Recycling Center

Organizing Your Kitchen for Creative Reuse

First, you need to have a good working system for the basics: trash, compost and recycling. It makes it much easier to do these things if you have a setup that is efficient and easy for you to access. While you can use a simple cardboard box, trash can, or old crate, I have found that people are more likely to recycle and consider their recycling system smooth and efficient when they have a bin designed specifically for this. It is harder when something is hidden and messily stacked in a cupboard or a too-small space. For a list of recycling bins that are good for city folk who may not have much space, visit the Resource List.

Next, set up a place for creative reuse for the rest of the materials that come through your kitchen and home. You need a place for:

- Reusable one-sided paper
- Reusable envelopes
- Reusable magazine pages that can be made into envelopes… easy!
- Reusable cardboard, such as from cereal boxes, that can be turned into file folders, recipe cards and collars for your garden
- Reusable packaging for gifts and special events
- A jar for twist ties and rubber bands
- A place for string
- A place for bags (of all kinds)

If you have a well-organized space for each of these things, you will be amazed at how much reuse can come from kitchen items. I recommend a set of stacked drawers, if you want to commit to reusing everything creatively. Creative reuse is something that you can take on as a project and see what works best for you and your family, given the kinds of projects you have going on.

Normally, people put a lot of attention into all of the "production" aspects of their kitchen and very little thought to the "waste" aspect of the kitchen. In a sustainable kitchen, we are cultivating a completely different attitude of mind. We are as mindful of our waste system as we are of our production and consumption.

Some Basic Ideas to Get You Started With Creative Reuse

GLASS JARS/BOTTLES —Can be used for safe food storage and water storage.
ONE-SIDED PAPER —Can be reused as scrap paper or printing paper.
ENVELOPES that come in the mail —If opened neatly, ideally with a letter opener, these can be stowed for easy reuse.
MAGAZINES—Before recycling, these can be gone through quickly, a stack made of "pretty pages" and delightful, easy-to-make envelopes can be made. I have done this for years and send the majority of my mail in homemade envelopes. Kids love this project too!

NAPKINS/PAPER TOWELS—If you use unbleached paper towels and napkins, they can serve as carbon for your compost.

PLASTIC CONTAINERS—Can be used as storage for office supplies, cleaning supplies, or to serve as reuse in the garden. (See below.)

OLD SPRAY BOTTLES —Can be cleaned and reused for cleaning or for the garden.

General recycling can be used for art projects (I've led fun reuse art projects at schools using cardboard, glass, cereal boxes, paper bags, etc.) and, in addition, a section can be created for gift wrapping and making homemade cards, with paper, ribbons, fabric, etc.—so that when it's time for a birthday or the holidays, you have all you need.

How to Make a Homemade Envelope— Kids Enjoy This Activity Too!

I like to collect magazines and periodically go through them, pulling out pages I am drawn to, recycling the rest and making envelopes out of the pages I have removed. I keep a traditional standard-size envelope on hand and use it as a guide for sizing the new envelopes. (If they are too small, they may not make it through the mail system to their destinations.) I fold the bottom of the page to form the body of the envelope and then fold the top down to form the flap. Next I fold both sides in and cut them to size with scissors, leaving enough to glue them to the body of the envelope. Leave the flap open until you've stuffed the envelope and then glue it down. I glue the sides down first, stuff it and then glue down the top. Glue sticks make the job easy and mess-free and the plastic containers can be recycled when empty. If the page I chose from the magazine happens to be dark, I use a label to create a place for the address (the label can just be a scrap of paper). When feeling particularly adventurous, if you find a thick enough paper to recycle into an envelope, you can even hand-stitch the edges closed with a thick thread. This weekly ritual takes about 10 minutes, I never have to buy new envelopes and I get to put something more artistic in the mail than a boring old store-bought envelope.

Ways to Incorporate the Garden Into Creative Reuse

If a family has a garden, one project parents and children can do together is to build beautiful garden beds by creating "bottle walls," in which used glass bottles are placed side-by-side and set with **cob** or plaster. Gardeners can also collect old plastic containers to use for seed propagation or pots for transplanting (just remember to poke holes in the bottom for drainage). **Reclaimed** plastic, glass, cardboard and even newspaper can be used to make garden supplies. Here are some ideas:

Plant protectors can be made from used containers.

Yogurt or cottage cheese containers can be turned into "collars" for new seedlings to protect them from pests.

Large clear plastic containers, such as gallon water jugs, can be cut into transplant covers for cold weather (using the idea of a "cold frame" to protect plants from cold weather in the wintertime).

Compost tea (see Chapter Ten for more information) can be stored in large plastic containers to "steep" before being applied to plants.

Scoopers, for applying amendments such as compost or soil fertilizer, can be made out of leftover plastic or glass containers.

Seeds can be stored in leftover glass jars or plastic containers.

Plant pots can be made out of newspaper with the Pot Maker by Richters—a great tool for any home gardener!

If you have construction projects on your property, there is even more opportunity to get creative with reuse. At Earthaven Community in North Carolina, colorful glass bottles, bottle caps, broken ceramics and mirrors are used to decorate earthen plaster in every home and community structures.

For plywood construction, Earthaven uses oak pallets that they buy for $1 from the company that sells them juice. The company would otherwise throw all of these pallets away. Finding a use for resources that someone is throwing away is how we begin creating a closed cycle in our homes, on our properties and in our communities. It's that easy.

Plastic Recycling

Consider that at this moment in time, 95% of plastic beverage cans are thrown away rather than recycled.

A sustainable kitchen is free of plastics, to the best of the cook's ability. Most people I meet continue to be confused by the world of plastics, though they tend to know by now that plastic is something to move away from. To make it easy, all plastic containers that are manufactured today are stamped with a symbol on the bottom. These symbols identify the type of resin or resin mix used in the container.

It is important to familiarize yourself with the regional recycling guidelines for your area. In many cities, only two types, PETE and HDPE, are typically collected for recycling. PETE (Polyethylene Terephalate Ethylene) plastic is most typically used to bottle water, juice, soft drink, detergent and cleaners, as well as nut butter and other cooking items. HDPE (High Density Polyethylene) is typically used for water and milk jugs, shampoo, detergent and bleach bottles, plastic bags, household cleaners, butter tubs and motor oil bottles.

Here is a summary of some of the unfortunate impacts of plastics in our lives:

• Toxins leaching into soil and water.
• Overflowing landfills. Some plastics, like #1 and 2 PVC, cannot be recycled, creating 1.23 million tons of waste per year.
• Birds and sea creatures being killed by plastic packaging or bags that they eat or get snagged in.
• Plastic food packaging and water storage that is considered so unsafe that it is banned in other countries.

Here is the breakdown of food-grade plastics in relation to our health. The toxins contained in these plastics have been proven to leach from packaging into food or water: PVC (polyvinyl chloride) is the most toxic plastic for our health. It is found in food packaging with the number 3 on the bottom, but is also in shampoo bottles, shower curtains, water pipes, and medical equipment.

PHTHALATES are contained in food packaging and detergents (I think also shampoos and some other cosmetics) and adversely impacts the endocrine system. Research shows a link to reproductive abnormalities, reduced sperm counts, and liver cancer.

BISPHENOL A (BPA), also found in plastic water bottles, baby bottles, plastic wraps, and food packaging, (including the lining of much canned food) can adversely affect the brain in fetuses and young children and has also been linked to breast and liver cancer.

In Chapter Six, I will discuss the notion of the "**toxic barrel**." It is difficult to know how much exposure to plastic causes damage, so it is truly up to consumers to be conservative and limit their exposure as much as they possibly can. To further the problem, plastics give off gas for many years, which means that they can have ongoing impact on our health and on the environment. The reality is that plastics in our furnishings, our house construction, and sitting on our shelves are continuously releasing gas in the form of chemical toxins into the air we breathe. This is part of why the EPA considers indoor air pollution as Number 5 on the list of human health hazards.

The rule of thumb is, the older the plastic, the more gases it has released, and the fewer toxins it continues to release. So in essence, older plastic (20-year-old Tupperware, for example) is certainly safer than newer plastic containers. If you do use old plastic for storing food, never put it in the microwave. Always pay attention to what kinds of plastics (and products in general) you are purchasing. If you have to purchase plastic, then look for labels that say "free of BPA and phthalates."

Bottom line

A sustainable kitchen is not reliant on plastics and utilizes plastic only where NEEDED, if at all. ●

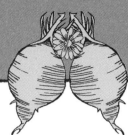

CHAPTER 3
FOOD WASTE AND COMPOSTING
There Is No Such Thing As "Away"

I ONCE WORKED AT A SCHOOL IN MASSACHUSETTS WHERE the students were being raised with an inspiring degree of eco-awareness. Some of the kids came up with the idea of posting signs on all of the school's trash cans that said "THERE IS NO SUCH THING AS AWAY." Consider the impact such signs could have in your own house! What might you do differently in your kitchen and home with this daily reminder? How would we relate differently to the food we cook and consume with this daily reminder?

The key elements in bringing the practice of zero waste in cooking are:

• Shopping responsibly.
• Making it a habit to cook with the whole vegetable.
• Preparing vegetables and fruit mindfully, using techniques that create less waste.
• Turning all the food waste we do create into useful nutrients (as in stock or compost).

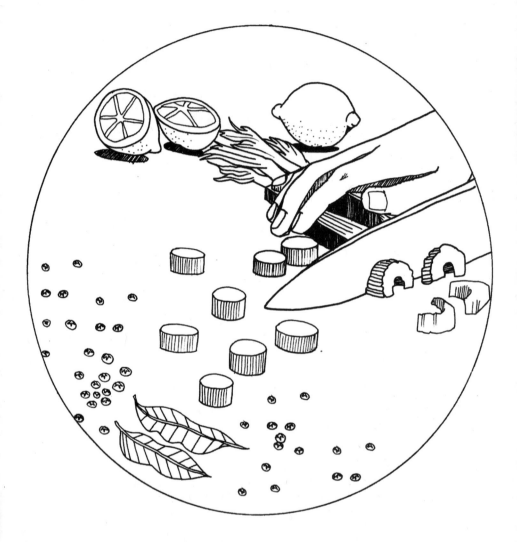

Shopping Responsibly

REDUCE FOOD WASTE BY SHOPPING RESPONSIBLY. ALWAYS CHECK OUT dates on what you purchase, store food by placing the newest food at the back of your pantry and the oldest at the front, store food appropriately regarding temperature and sun/shade needs and clean out your pantry and refrigerator weekly.

Here are more tips for how to reduce food waste in your kitchen, starting with your shopping trip:

- Buy food for just one week at a time.
- Follow conscious menu planning and the recycling of leftovers into meals as discussed in Chapter Six.
- Choose to eat what needs to be eaten over "what I want to eat right now," if reducing waste is truly a priority.
- Pay attention and keep an eye on your inventory.
- Instead of putting produce scraps into the compost, consider making stock when you have time.
- For families, consider the value of teaching your kids this attitude of mind to train them to be stewards of sustainability.

Using the Whole Vegetable

YEARS AGO, I SPENT TIME IN A MACROBIOTIC COMMUNITY WHERE I was taught to appreciate and use the whole of every vegetable I consumed. In the practice of macrobiotics, it is acknowledged that different parts of a vegetable—for example, the turnip root and the turnip stem—offer different nutrients and forms of energy.

This awareness is honored by cooking with every part of every vegetable—rather than using just the florets of broccoli, for instance—and tossing the rest. This practice ultimately provides the base for creating zero waste in cooking.

Using the whole vegetable requires creativity and might include using carrot tops for stock or decorative garnish, using broccoli stalks to peel and steam with your dinner, or saving lemon and orange peel to use as zest for salad dressings and baking (orange and lemon peel bring a special zing to so many recipes).

Consider that if you currently tend to buy bagged, pre-prepped vegetables, such as broccoli florets, it may be time to give up this habit. What happens to the stalk from the broccoli that gets pre-prepped and bagged? If we are serious about sustainability, it is a necessity to address this waste.

Follow these suggestions for preparing vegetables:

BROCCOLI—Peel the stalks carefully with a peeler, slice or chop the stalk and serve it raw, steamed, or in a soup. Chop the leaves and sauté them just like chard or kale. Prepare the florets for steaming or serving raw. Odd-shaped pieces of broccoli can be set aside for a blended soup or to chop up into a salad. You might also cook all parts of the broccoli into a creamy blended soup.

CAULIFLOWER—Follow the idea for broccoli and cook both the leaves and head.

CHARD or other greens—Prepare the leaves by washing and chopping them, then separately, finely chop the stems and steam or sauté them either with the greens or separately. The greens can even be served surrounded by the edible and colorful garnish of the stems.

BEETS (roots and greens)—Wash and prepare the roots and greens separately. Either gently peel the roots or scrub them well and leave the skin on. You can also boil the root, with the skin on, to soften it and peel it off by hand. The stems and greens can be finely chopped and steamed or sautéed. Consider serving the beet roots on a bed of greens.

TURNIPS—Follow the suggestion for beets and prepare both roots and greens. There is no need to peel turnips if you scrub them well.

CARROTS—Wash and prepare the roots and tops separately and either add the carrot tops to soup or stew or serve them as a garnish. Consider, for the dish you are preparing, is it necessary to peel the carrots?

After you have prepared your vegetables, there are also many reuses for food scraps before they get composted. These range from making stock to creating garden amendments to making homemade paper. Here are some ideas to get you started:

Creative Uses for Food Scraps

- Egg shells and coffee grounds are great in the garden to deter pests.
- Orange and lemon peels are good for deodorizing your countertops and cutting boards.
- Lemon, lime and orange strips can be used as decorations in drinks (or grated and used for cooking and baking).
- Potato and avocado peelings can be used to reduce eye puffiness.
- Beet ends make amazing ink stamps for kids (and adults) to use for art projects.
- Daikon root can be prepared for dinner, while their tops are used to turn your bathtub into a natural cleansing spa. (This is one of my favorite things. Visit minadobic.org/externalremedies.php to learn how to do this.)

To Make Stock:

I like to keep a bag of scraps for stock in my fridge, where the scraps will stay fresh (just a few days at a time) until I can make stock. I include garlic/onion peels, veggie scraps and seeds from squash/pumpkins I have cooked (seeds make a delicious nutty-flavored stock!). I leave anything that is particularly dirty or aging for the compost.

Wash all of the scraps, place them in a large pot and fill it with purified water until the scraps are covered, cover the brew with a lid and bring it to a boil. After it boils, simply turn it down to simmer, gently lift the lid a bit and let the stock cook for the next hour. When finished, let it cool a bit, strain it, compost the scraps and use the stock to make soups, cook rice, veggies, stews, etc. You can store the stock in glass jars in the fridge for up to four days.

Mashed Vegetable Medley

I like to collect scraps such as broccoli stalks, the leaves of cauliflower and other vegetable scraps I need a use for, then cook them up in a little water and simmer for about 10 minutes with garlic and herbs. After, they should sit covered for a few extra minutes. Sometimes I add one chopped potato or root vegetable for a more creamy consistency and I then blend the mixture up into a soft colorful mashed potato alternative, adding a little sea salt and olive oil, coconut oil, or butter if desired. This is a delightful, nourishing and nurturing treat and an easy way to use all of the vegetable. It has the softness and savor of mashed potatoes, with even more flavor and more vitamins.

The Final Stage: Composting

ONCE WE HAVE USED THE WHOLE VEGETABLE, BROUGHT ATTENTION to how we prepared the vegetable and brought awareness to creative uses for scraps, we can take the final step and compost our food waste. As a fourth grader discovered at a composting workshop the other day, "Wow! We can turn our trash into something useful! I want to do that!" Yes and beyond that, we can turn our waste into something beautiful, practical and nourishing.

Why Compost?

Composting is a fundamental part of radical recycling and the ultimate "giving back." Composting is easy, free and the reward is phenomenal… a reduction in your trash output by 50–75% and beautiful, rich, organic matter for your soil and plants. Compost feeds the soil vital nutrients, aids in water retention and encourages earthworms in your soil.

How Does the Compost Ecosystem Work?

Composting creates a mixed balance of nitrogen, carbon, air and water, which forms a decomposition process that feeds new life. How wonderful that we can take our old food and waste scraps and use them to feed new food! All we need to do as the composter is to follow simple steps to keep these elements of nitrogen, carbon, air and water in balance and to monitor the decomposition process. Here is an in-depth explanation of how to compost:

What Can I Put in My Compost?

If you set up a conventional compost system (either an outdoor hot pile, an underground pile, or an actual compost bin), you can put in everything from vegetable and fruit scraps, grains, dairy and pretty much all foods except for meats and heavy oils. If you have a worm bin, you can put in fruit and vegetable scraps (except for a few kinds I will mention later) and if you use the bokashi system, which I describe below, you can actually compost meat scraps as well.

What Makes a Good Compost Bin?

A good compost bin has proper aeration, is well-protected, is easy to turn and easy to harvest from. I personally like the Garden Gourmet for an urban/suburban household first-time compost bin, because it is easy to put together, easy to use, and is made of recycled materials. At the time of this book's writing, the city of Los Angeles offers a compost bin for half the price (about $20) but I tend to choose products made of recycled material whenever it is an option.

Other designs you can consider are a barrel composter, which has a bar that turns the compost, rather than having to use a pitchfork to stir things up. You might also build your own compost bin. My favorite is a three-tiered bin with one section for throwing in scraps for the first part of composting, a second section for transferring the partially composted material when the first bin is full, and a third section to transfer it into again, with a special sifter to perfect the final product. This kind of bin is ideal if you have a larger amount of food scrap to compost.

How Do I Get Started?

First, decide what kind of system is best for you. For a four-person family that cooks regularly, I recommend a simple standing bin, along with a worm bin, or perhaps a hand-made three-tiered bin if you have a large backyard. The most important features for a standing bin to have are sufficient air flow, a sturdy cover to protect the bin from animals, and an easy design for attending to the compost process, aerating and collecting the finished product.

For someone living in a small apartment alone, I recommend a worm bin that can fit in your kitchen or on your balcony. For anyone who eats meat, I recommend a Happy Farmer. The Happy Farmer is a system similar to composting that can be used indoors and can process all food scraps—meat included—through an anaerobic fermentation process, which is different than the conventional composting process. This system is called **bokashi**, which is a Japanese term meaning "fermented organic matter."

If you are a meat eater who cooks a lot, you may need to also have a hot pile or bin that sits in your backyard. I also recommend a Happy Farmer if you are the "neat and tidy" type who finds the idea of composting repelling.

If you have a large backyard or a plot of land, then you can compost the old-fashioned way and build a **hot pile** and simply build more piles as needed for the amount of food waste you have. A hot pile is an intentional heap of compostable materials created outdoors in such a manner that generates all of the heat required for the process of composting. There is an appropriate composting system for every situation and new designs make it easy for everyone to compost today, whether you live in a tiny apartment or on a large homestead.

Composting As a Daily Practice

FOR ME, COMPOSTING IS A DAILY PRACTICE OF COMPASSIONATE SELF-discipline. I've been composting for almost 20 years and, even though I love the composting process, still, every now and then, when I'm in a hurry, I hear a voice say, "but I don't want to take that extra step… I have no time." I hear that voice and use it as a flag to check in with myself. Am I really about to choose laziness (face it, that's all it is) over making a conscious choice to take care of the world in which I live? Becoming aware always energizes me. Rather than letting laziness control me, I remember that I have another choice, and that is to remain true to my commitment to be an earth steward. And, the reality is, it only takes a second!

What Do I Need To Begin?

- A compost bin!
- A sunny spot for a conventional bin or a shady spot for a worm bin
- A pitchfork
- A starter, such as already-made compost (from another batch of compost you have made or that you buy at the store) or Compost Inoculant (i.e. Dr. Earth compost starter). Manure, such as chicken droppings or bat guano, as well as green comfrey leaves, also serve as compost starter. Note that while starter is not a necessity, I have found that it improves the process and is especially helpful for the first month of the composting process.
- A scissors or pair of shears
- A closed container to store kitchen scraps in before delivering them to the compost, which can be placed on your kitchen counter, in a drawer, or in the fridge
- A source of "greens" or nitrogen and a source of "browns" or carbon. (It is smart to have a space set aside next to your bin for collecting carbonaceous materials.)

"Greens" or Nitrogen includes:

- Veggies, fruit, grains, dairy, all food scraps other than heavy oils and meat… so adding a little oil is OK but if you are a heavy fryer, don't dump huge amounts of oil into your compost. Leftover lasagna, soup, salad, bread, all of it can go into your compost.

- Coffee grounds (include the filter if you use unbleached)
- Tea bags (without the tag unless it's eco-friendly) ·
- Grass clippings
- "Browns" or Carbon includes:
- Napkins and paper towels that are unbleached and not dyed
- Leaves (disease-free only)
- Branches
- Stems
- Shredded newspaper
- Weeds (but watch for seeds)
- Wood chips (use sparingly, high carbon)
- Sawdust (use sparingly, high carbon)

Neutral

Things which go into your compost and can be added to your food bucket, but are neither "greens" nor "browns."

- Eggshells
- Laundry lint

What Else Can I Add?

- Dr. Earth Compost Inoculant
- Bat guano, rabbit droppings, chicken manure
- Manure
- Ready-made compost
- Seaweed

More on Coffee Grounds:

Coffee grounds can be an excellent addition to a compost pile. The grounds are relatively rich in nitrogen, providing bacteria the energy they need to turn organic matter into compost. Used coffee grounds, approximately 2% nitrogen by volume, can be a safe substitute for nitrogen-rich manure in the compost pile.

What Cannot Go In:
- Anything that takes longer to decompose, e.g., coconuts. Put these in your green bin.
- Large seeds like avocado seeds. How about planting them instead?
- Any kind of meat
- Dog or cat droppings
- Food peels containing pesticides

For a Worm Bin, What Do I Need?
- All fruits and vegetables (including citrus and other high-acid foods)
- Vegetable and fruit peels and ends
- Coffee grounds and filters
- Tea bags (even those with high tannin levels)
- Grains such as bread, crackers and cereal (including moldy and stale)
- Eggshells (rinsed off)
- Leaves and grass clippings (not sprayed with pesticides)

All You Need to Do:
All you need to do is to lay a few inches of carbonaceous bedding, such as dried leaves, at the bottom of your compost bin. Then each time you dump your "greens" or food scraps in the bin, you add a sprinkle of inoculant or ready-made compost, you cover the greens with an equal amount of browns, so they are well protected, you turn your compost with your pitchfork to aerate it, and you monitor. Every now and then check your compost to to see if it needs moisture. It should ideally feel slightly damp like a wrung-out sponge.

The Ideal Balance:
The ideal balance that creates fertile, sweet-smelling compost has a C:N ratio somewhere around 25 to 30 parts carbon to 1 part nitrogen, or 25–30:1. If the C:N ratio is too high (excess carbon), decomposition slows down and you might notice your pile drying up or "just sitting." If the C:N ratio is too low (excess nitrogen) you can end up with a stinky pile.

Different ingredients we put into the compost bin have different C:N ratios. Our job is to pay attention and adjust what we are adding to keep things in balance. For example, adding manure or grass clippings may lower high C:N ratios. Adding wood chips, dry leaves, or paper may raise Low C:N ratios.

Below are the average C:N ratios for some common organic materials found in the compost bin. For our purposes, the materials containing high amounts of carbon are considered "browns," and materials containing high amounts of nitrogen are considered "greens."

Estimated Carbon-to-Nitrogen Ratios

Browns = High Carbon	C:N	Greens = High Nitrogen	C:N
Ashes, wood*	25:1	Alfalfa	12:1
Cardboard, shredded	350:1	Clover	23:1
Corn stalks	75:1	Coffee grounds	20:1
Fruit waste	35:1	Food waste	20:1
Leaves	60:1	Garden waste	30:1
Newspaper, shredded	175:1	Grass clippings	20:1
Peanut shells	35:1	Hay	25:1
Pine needles	80:1	Manures	15:1
Sawdust	325:1	Seaweed	19:1
Straw	75:1	Vegetable scraps	25:1
Wood chips	400:1	Weeds	30:1

*Please note that ash is not helpful for acidic soil, so be aware of the pH of the soil you are working with before applying this to your compost in large amounts.

How Long Will My Compost Pile Take?

While the amount of time it takes to make compost varies, depending on the balance (of nitrogen, carbon, air and water) in your pile, in my experience regular composting can take from 3–6 months to produce a finished product. A worm bin may take 1–2 months to fill and then 3–5 months to fully compost. The bokashi fermentation system takes two weeks for the initial breakdown and then at least two more weeks to be compost.

Do I Need to Add Water?

Ideally your compost will have an equal mix of nitrogen additions which provide moisture and carbon materials that are dry, so that it will be a nice crumbly consistency. If it's not, you can add water as needed. An easy way to do this is to use the leftover water from rinsing out your food scrap bucket.

What's the problem if my compost smells?

Too much nitrogen and not enough air will make the compost too acidic and this results in a foul smell. In this case, just add carbon and aerate your compost.

What Do I Need to Know to Create a Healthy Worm Bin?

To get started, you will need about 500 g. of worms or 2000 worms. They can be purchased online or through an organic gardening source and typically cost from $40–$50. Worms like a diet of veggies and fruit, plus 30% carbon (shredded newspaper, paper towels, envelopes, etc.) Worms don't like bread, onions, garlic, meat, dairy, or large amounts of grass or leaves. If you take on worm composting, it is your job to take care of the vermiculture ecosystem in order for the worms to thrive. I have suggested books and websites on vermiculture on the Resource List, and I recommend that you read up for more information.

Here is some advice from my own experience: If you notice fruit flies forming around your worm bin, add a nice sprinkling of lime and wait a day or two. Additional carbon (shredded newspaper, paper towels, envelopes, etc.) can be helpful too. A handful of lime of gypsum once a month also assists the decomposition process.

Worm tea is so potent that it can actually be harmful if not diluted. Dilute it about 1:10. Worm castings don't have to be diluted. They can be mixed with potting soil or applied directly to soil and plants as you would apply regular compost.

But I Don't Have a Garden. What Will I Do With My Compost?

Feed it to your indoor plants. Feed it to your trees. Give it to your neighbors. There is never a shortage of uses for good compost. As we will discuss in Chapter Four, our soil is desperate for nutrition. Creating compost out of food scraps is one way of giving back to the soil, reducing trash and creating more of a closed system on the land you live on. ●

CHAPTER 4
WHERE YOUR FOOD COMES FROM
The Real Deal

"The passive American consumer, sitting down to a meal of pre-prepared food, confronts inert, anonymous substances that have been processed, dyed, breaded, sauced, gravied, ground, pulped, strained, blended, prettified and sanitized beyond resemblance to any part of any creature that ever lived. The products of nature and agriculture have been made, to all appearances, the products of industry. Both eater and eaten are thus in exile from biological reality."

—Wendell Berry

"Strawberries are too delicate to be picked by machine. The perfectly ripe ones bruise even at too heavy a human touch. Every strawberry you have ever eaten has been picked by callused human hands. Every piece of toast with jelly represents someone's knees, someone's aching backs and hips, someone with a bandanna on her wrist to wipe away the sweat."

—Alison Luterman

IN 1994, I HAD THE OPPORTUNITY TO PARTICIPATE IN A "SEED SAVERS exchange" in the foothills of the Himalayas in northern India. Men and women from villages throughout northern India had gathered in one village to share the seeds of all kinds of vegetables, fruits, grains and medicinal plants they had been saving. The display was an unbelievable array of colorful seeds of different shapes, sizes and patterns that held the tastes and traditions of thousands of years and afterwards we sat and shared a delicious meal of rice, dal and curried vegetables like none I had ever tasted, served on banana leaves and eaten with our hands.

The seed savers explained that where there were once thousands of varieties of rice seed grown there—all different colors, textures and tastes—at that point there were less than 100 varieties. Western companies had begun introducing hybrid seeds to indigenous farmers worldwide as part of the **Green Revolution**. Because the hybrid seeds did not reproduce, the villagers then had to rely on rebuying the seeds each year from the companies who controlled the rice seeds.

The Green Revolution was the movement to introduce high-yielding seeds, pesticides and Western irrigation techniques to Third World countries, beginning in the 1960s. While India once had 20,000 varieties of rice, the varieties promoted under the Green Revolution were literally a handful. About 3000 varieties of rice have been rescued and conserved by Naydanya, an NGO based in India, founded by Dr. Vandana Shiva.

Not only did this make the people dependent upon those companies for seed, but the seeds were also not appropriate for the climate and landscape of the area. Additionally, the companies introduced pesticides for the first time... with often disastrous results for the health, water supply, wildlife and soil of that region.

As an American, this visit with the villagers was a moment when I first "got it" that with every food choice I made, the difference between ignorance and education had a major impact on some people and some land somewhere in the world. For the first time I realized that there is a major difference in buying locally grown organic rice, full of vital nutrients and grown by conscious farmers, versus buying white hybrid rice brought to us by Monsanto all the way from India, at the expense of traditional cultures (around the globe).

But more importantly, perhaps, I began to get a sense of how the world food crisis might be connected to me personally as a consumer in more ways than I had been previously aware of. If consumers were aware of what really went into their food production, would they still be making the same food choices?

I realized that even as a conscious consumer, I had been inadvertently supporting companies and practices that, had I known better, I would not choose to consciously support. I realized I hadn't been fully exercising my power to participate and that as a collective of consumers, our participation and power were urgently needed. Meeting the actual villagers on their own land, and considering the impact of my choices on them, made a lasting imprint on me. I became committed to overturning every stone I could in my food choices, so that what lay beneath the labels was no longer a mystery to me.

If we all (or more of us) understood the global implications of conventional agriculture practices and the vital importance of small-scale local organic agriculture, we would see very different products on store shelves. (Maybe this is a clue as to why most people still do not have the information.) Many people still need a basic understanding of what makes agriculture sustainable. Food security is an area where we truly want to make sure that people don't make sloppy decisions without considering the long-term impact.

Most of us need help navigating wisely through all the information out there. It can be overwhelming to keep ourselves updated on the specifics of every ingredient we buy, from coffee to sugar to grapes to rice, but if we educate ourselves about the primary issues challenging our food production system, we will be prepared to make knowledgeable choices. And as long as we're prepared, it's easy. The following is a brief overview of the major threats facing our food supply stemming from conventional agribusiness today:

- Global topsoil loss due to conventional agricultural practices
- Depletion of nutrients from our food due to poor farming practices
- Loss of biodiversity
- Genetically modified (GMO) seeds and foods
- Pesticides and their runoff
- Use of fossil fuels for transport
- Over-packaging of food
- Depletion of honeybee population
- Dependence on foreign, rather than local, food production

This list does not include issues such as food safety, nor does it go much into the plight of small farmers. This is not to undervalue the importance of those issues. It is simply to not overwhelm the reader with too much information all at once, and at the time of this writing, these issues are becoming more commonly known. For people who want to further investigate sustainable agricultural methods, I offer a Resource List at the end of this book.

We depend on labels for everything in the world of food. "Organic," "natural," "farm-raised," "conventional," "pesticide-free"—but do we really know what we are buying, even with the labels? Do we really know what they mean? Until there is more widespread understanding of the real meaning of sustainability, it is a RELIEF to me that no one has come up with a label or certification for "sustainable." Why? Because, while one day this could be an effective way of making sure that our food is grown and treated the way we want it to be, right now buyers use labels as just another way to "pass the buck" and make quick, "convenient" decisions, while ultimately remaining uneducated and passive, avoiding taking larger responsibility for our food system. The reality is that there is too much unknown when we just view a finished product with a label. We cannot know if the company producing the food operates in keeping with the principles of sustainability.

Rather than demand honest and thorough information so that we can support the growers and producers who truly hold sustainability as their priority, many people barely glance at what they are buying and rely on advertisements targeted at gullible consumers. My hope is to help people learn to navigate the complex web of issues around agriculture (ranging from environmental to political to economic) and empower people to learn to trust their intuition and put more thought and inquiry into what they are buying, rather than just going for the "right" label out of convenience. It is possible for us to live in alignment with nature, but being inattentive is not going to get us there.

Digesting This Information

THERE ARE MORE EYE-OPENING BOOKS AVAILABLE THAN EVER EXPOSing the world of conventional agriculture and corporate farming, but we have a way to go in terms of making a change on the larger scale. As a writer, my challenge in this chapter was to acknowledge that to learn where our food comes from, "the real deal," is to receive some bad news. It is crucial that we use the *bad* news to empower ourselves as consumers and to give our full-fledged support to all of the natural farmers and conscious companies out there who are spearheading the solutions. I have included solutions and ways you can help throughout the chapter. My intention is to help readers to understand three KEY POINTS:

There is a difference between organic agriculture and sustainable organic agriculture. Organic is a set of standards. Sustainability is a frame of mind or set of principles. We are going for "sustainable organic agriculture" or agriculture that is in alignment with the principles of sustainability.

As food consumers, it is vitally important that we bother ourselves with the matters of agriculture (and NOT entrust this aspect of planetary well-being in the hands of a few), because the issues involve us directly and our food security depends upon it. Take the recent example of the **honeybee disaster** to be discussed later in this chapter.

We can keep ourselves from feeling overwhelmed or getting disheartened by redirecting our attention to powerful solutions and following practical guidelines for our food choices.

The Intelligence of Sustainable Agriculture

People who learn to garden for the first time find it miraculous to watch a tiny seed sprout and grow into a giant tomato plant, forming succulent fruit for them to pick. Likewise, people tend to feel deeply empowered when the veil is finally lifted and they have a more solid understanding of where our food comes from and what part they play in the food system.

In Wendell Berry's words at the beginning of this chapter, our food should *connect* us to biological reality or nature, rather than feed the illusion that we are somehow separate from it. When I learned how to grow my own food, I felt connected to the natural world in a deeper way. The food growing process was demystified and I was finally invited to participate in what seemed a natural extension of my role as a human being. Part of the importance of the act of growing food is that it puts us in direct contact with the miracle of plant and soil life and, if we are not already nature junkies, these become things that we cherish and want to take care of to a degree we may not have before.

Food is a basic aspect of our survival; however, most of us living our lives in cities and suburbs are more or less disconnected from our food production and hold numerous misconceptions about where our food comes from and the political-environmental issues around the foods that we eat. We are not taught to think about the soil, the bee, the earthworm, the water, or the farmer who (together) grew our food. If we care about the earth and our health, we have to become deeply interested in where our food comes from. A first step is for people to be educated about the differences between conventional agriculture and sustainable agriculture.

One of the major differences between conventional agriculture and sustainable agriculture, in my perspective, is that there is an inherent intelligence to sustainable agriculture that works with and respects nature and relies on techniques that have been practiced for thousands of years. These include the idea of the closed cycle we discussed in Chapter Two and the spirit of giving back.

Meanwhile conventional agriculture too often tends to disrupt the cycle of nature in a way that we have yet to know the full impact of. One of the downfalls of our society is that we make decisions to move forward with technologies and chemicals without being able to foresee the impact they might have long-term. Though there could be grave consequences down the road, we dive in, distracted by human cleverness and driven by instant gratification. Agriculture is a perfect example of an area where the impact of interfering with nature has had grave consequences.

"The frog does not drink up the pond in which it lives."
Native American Proverb

One of the principles of the sustainable kitchen is "giving back," and this is a core characteristic of organic food production. Giving back to what? To whom? We should give back to every part of the production system: from the bees that pollinate our food, to the soil that must be replenished, to the watershed by keeping it clean, to the farmer who grows our food by making sure s/he gets paid a fair wage. Where traditional agriculture techniques are based on the concept of giving back to, or respecting nature, conventional agriculture's approach has caused major problems through its focus on controlling nature and prioritizing human convenience—i.e., through a mentality of "let's see how we can grow miles of monoculture broccoli on one tract of land" rather than an approach based on how nature really works.

City dwellers are so far removed from the food production process that by the time the food gets to us—processed and packaged—we are unaware of the quality of agriculture (or lack of) that produced it. We think only of "this bag of chips" or "this packaged soup" we are sitting down to eat, with little thought about where it came from' or how it was produced.

From my perspective, the solution comes down to expanding community awareness and participation in our food system on the local level and recommitting to organic sustainable agriculture without exception globally. As a collective of consumers we have tremendous power that we are just beginning to tap into. Learning more about some of the vital issues we should be concerned about regarding our food production will hopefully begin to engage you in the process.

An Example of Sustainable Agriculture: A Closed Cycle That Gives Back

IN THE LATE '90s A FRIEND INVITED ME TO CO-OPERATE A **COMMUNITY Supported Agriculture** (CSA) project in the middle of the arid desert of Arizona. It was a land of intricate canyons and rock formations, an endless blue sky and cottonwood trees, but very little water and hardly any shade. The circumstances were much more hot and dry than any I had grown food in; yet with the inspiration of traditional agriculture techniques as the guide for all our choices, we managed to grow thriving and abundant vegetables, fruits and herbs in rich fertile soil with minimal water and minimal work.

Crop rotation was practiced religiously. The fields were designed in a brilliant maze of berms and pathways, which allowed water to slowly filter in just once a week and to be directed exactly where we wanted it or shared evenly throughout the field with no water waste. In the garden, beds were sunken in order to serve as receptacles for water or to receive the full benefits of monsoonal rains we did get from time to time.

I learned to sow corn seeds the way the Hopi traditionally do in that region: planted 12 inches beneath the soil, to protect the seeds from the intense heat, while we waited patiently for the rains to naturally water them. In the next act of giving back, the Hopi encouraged us to sing to the seeds, because in their tradition this kind of loving attention is what would inspire the seeds to grow up out of the soil into tall elegant stalks. In the final act of giving back, every ounce of plant scrap was decayed into compost for the soil, thus starting the cycle again.

What You Can Do to Give Back:

Get to know the farms you are supporting personally. Talk to the farmers at the farmers market and learn about their techniques, practices and challenges. If you join a CSA, sign up for one of its farm tours or go out and volunteer. Schedule a visit to your favorite farm and support it at the farmers market. Learn firsthand how these farms are practicing sustainable agriculture, how they have created a closed cycle, how they are giving back, and how you can support them.

Topsoil Loss

MOST PEOPLE TAKE DIRT FOR GRANTED, SO IT'S HARD TO GET PEOPLE excited about taking care of our dirt, let alone seeing soil as "sacred"; however, it is important for all of us to consider the global implications of topsoil health in terms of food security. Just as it takes hundreds of years for a clear-cut forest to return to an old-growth state, an inch of topsoil can take 500 years to form and at least six inches of topsoil are needed for crop production.

Think of topsoil as "the shallow skin of nutrient-rich matter that is used for crop production." Consider that we lose 7,000 tons of topsoil each year through erosion due to conventional agricultural practices, land development and degradation. That accounts for 1% of our topsoil every day. On average, the planet has little more than three feet of topsoil spread over its surface. Today, this soil is washed away 10 times faster than it is replenished in the U.S. and 40 times faster in China and India.

As a result of erosion in the last 40 years, 30 percent of the world's arable land has become unproductive. Essentially, we are outstripping the earth's natural rate of restoring the precious topsoil we depend on though modern agricultural practices. Quality soil is loose, clumpy, filled with air pockets and full of vital minerals and microorganisms. While sustainable agriculture honors soil health and is focused on building and rebuilding healthy soil, agribusiness leaves the soil out of the picture and focuses on growing "the most, the cheapest."

The assumption that there's enough "dirt" to grow food on this planet long-term without taking care of it is an illusion we can no longer afford to entertain. In addition, when we work *with* the soil, we can grow healthier crops that attract fewer pests and create soil that retains water much more efficiently than when we grow conventionally. Healthy soil is our greatest asset as farmers.

How You Can Help:

- Support sustainable organic farmers who give back to the soil.
- Support sustainable land development and sustainable land stewardship.
- On your own property, in your own garden, take care of your soil by mulching it and protecting it.

Depletion of Nutrients From Our Food Due to Poor Farming Practices

"WE ARE WHAT WE EAT," LITERALLY. SO THE NEXT TIME YOU ARE FEEL-ing depleted or think you need some vitamins, consider what you have been eating and remember that human nutrition is directly related to soil nutrition. If a vital mineral is missing from our soil, then it is missing from the foods we eat and will impact our health. Add to that the food processing and the refining our foods undergo to prepare them for the market and the nutritional value of our foods is further depleted. You have probably noticed the incomparably better taste of organic produce. In its natural state, a tomato is allowed to ripen slowly and some of the sugars and nutrients do not reach the fruit until this critical time; however, mass-produced tomatoes are typically harvested green and shipped away to be disinfected, washed, and waxed. The end result: they taste like a pale version of a properly ripened tomato!

Consider that there are more than 70 trace minerals necessary to produce healthy, nutrient-rich crops, but most conventional farming methods routinely put back only three to five of them. In addition, inorganic fertilizers and pesticides kill the precious microorganisms in the soil that are essential to the creation of organic complexes—which further depletes the nutritional value of our food. We have gone beyond simply using up the available trace minerals in our soils (those in the form of organic complexes) to also destroying the means of replenishing these soil-based microorganisms. This impacts both topsoil health and human health.

Since the 1800s, modern, economic-based agriculture has replaced virtually all of the critical organic complexes with inorganic fertilizers, which also cause toxicity in water runoff and further imbalance the delicate nature of our soils. In the 1930s, when farmers began to add inorganic fertilizers to the soil, it was thought that biological organisms could assimilate minerals in any form. This is not the case.

We are now discovering that inorganic minerals and trace minerals simply cannot be easily assimilated by plants. The result is that not only are our bodies not receiving these minerals from our food, but because our food is lacking them, they are unhealthy and attract more pests, thus calling for more pesticides. How does this translate to your dinner tonight?

Linus Pauling (twice awarded the Nobel Prize in medicine) said to the 74th Congress of the United States, "Every ailment, every sickness and every disease can be traced back to an organic trace-mineral deficiency." It has become alarmingly evident that we are severely deficient in one of the most basic components necessary to sustain health: organically complex trace minerals. Furthermore the use of chemicals eventually sterilizes the soil and reduces the microorganisms that keep the soil balanced. As the good microorganisms in the soil are wiped out, the vegetation loses its ability to gain the proper balance of minerals from the soil. The end result: Our bodies take in these deficient foods and become depleted and imbalanced.

A 2002 study at the University of Missouri showed that smaller organically grown oranges contained 30 percent more vitamins than bigger conventionally grown oranges. Nutritionist Virginia Worthington found that organically grown produce contained more than 27% more vitamin C, 29.3% more magnesium, 21.1% more iron and 18% more polyphenols. She found organic produce also contained fewer nitrates and heavy metals than conventional foods. Salicylic acid, an important plant compound and major anti-inflammatory agent, has been found in quantities as high as 1,040 nanograms in organic soup as compared with 20 nanograms in the average nonorganic soup.

What You May Not Know About Seeds: Biodiversity vs. Genetic Engineering

IN HINDI, THE WORD FOR SEED IS "BIJA," WHICH MEANS "CONTAINER for life." Our seeds contain the memory and genetic pool for plant life for thousands of years. Today genetic diversity is eroding at an alarming rate. About 75% of agricultural diversity has been lost within the last century. Today Monsanto and nine other seed companies produce over 50% of the seeds we use.

Ask Americans if they have ever eaten genetically engineered foods and two thirds will say no. Really? It has been estimated that 70–75% of processed foods on supermarket shelves—from soda to soup, crackers to condiments—contain genetically engineered ingredients. Consider that 75% of all food crops grown in the United States are genetically modified, including 80% of soybeans, 68% of cotton and 26% of corn crops.

The main reason companies began to use GMO seeds was to protect crops against pests. The idea was that if we insert the gene of a bacterium that eats pests into a tomato plant, for instance, the tomato would carry its own built-in pesticide; however, altering a plant in this way is not without consequence. If we simply focused on practicing the techniques of sustainable agriculture, which is founded on the creation of healthy soil, pests would be less of a problem. Scientists from the Pesticide Action Network state that GMO soybeans don't reduce the need for pesticides, but actually increase it. For example, in 1997

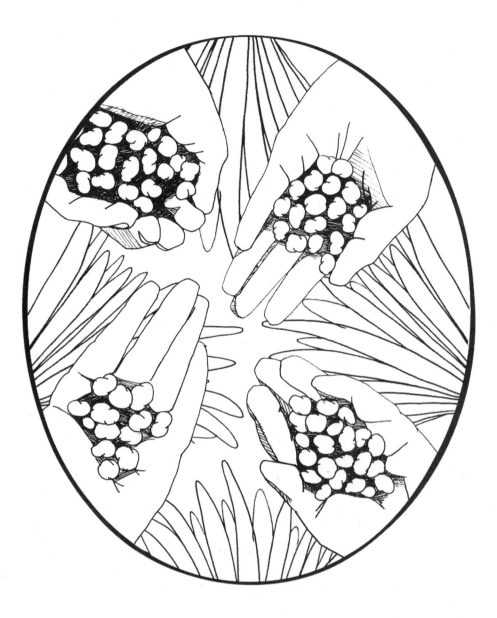

USDA statistics showed a 72% increase in the use of Roundup due to the expanded use of the GMO Roundup Ready soybean.

What is the problem with genetic engineering in foods? The first problem is that there is a great risk of allergies, which compromises the human immune system. Another problem with the genetic modification of seeds is the possibility of gene transfer (i.e. gene transfer to cells of the human body upon digestion) and of outcrossing. **Outcrossing** is the potential for non-GMO crops to be affected by GMO crops. In my perspective, genetic engineering is a shortsighted and dangerous "solution" to an issue we should be addressing with sustainability in mind. For me, this is a place where the phrase "don't mess with nature" comes to mind.

The Terminator Gene

One particularly potent issue in the world of genetic engineering is the "terminator gene." The terminator gene, owned by Monsanto, is a technology that prevents crops from producing fertile seeds, meaning it makes farmers dependent so they have to buy new seeds each year, rather than saving part of their harvest to plant next year's crop. The gene is inserted into a seed's DNA and once activated by a synthetic chemical catalyst of the manufacturer's choosing, the terminator gene makes the seed and the crop it produces sterile.

The terminator gene has no agricultural or economic benefits for farmers or consumers. According to Monsanto, the only motivation behind the gene is to protect intellectual property rights. The company claims the gene allows them to be able to recover investments on research and produce profits from their technology, as planters must repurchase seeds every year. Opponents claim that corporations will use this to squeeze more money out of dependent farmers and begin a monopoly of chemically saturated seeds we can think of as "suicide seeds."

To learn more about the terminator gene issue, please visit Friends of the Earth International, at: **foei.org/.**

Biopiracy

In her book *Biopiracy: the Plunder of Nature and Knowledge*, activist Dr. Vandana Shiva argues that genetic engineering and the cloning of organisms are "the ultimate expression of the commercialization of science and the commodification of nature…. In the era of genetic engineering and patents, life itself is being colonized." Farmers and indigenous peoples are outraged that certain plants that they developed are now being "hijacked" and patented through biopiracy.

Patent monopolies on plant and animal varieties, on genes and on new medicines, threaten to harm developing countries in three ways: first, by raising prices so high that most citizens have no access to these new developments; second, by blocking local production when the patent owner so chooses; third, by forbidding farmers to continue breeding agricultural varieties as has been done for thousands of years.

How You Can Help:

- Support local organic farmers.
- Always purchase seeds from smaller organic reputable companies such as Bountiful Gardens, Renee's and Seeds of Change.
- Save seeds in your own garden and join the Seed Saver's Exchange, **seedsaversexchange.com**.
- Avoid GMO foods. For a detailed list of GMO foods and how to avoid them, please read Chapter Five.
- Become interested in plant biodiversity in your own area. Enjoy the tastes of heirloom varieties and seek out new varieties and choices of produce that you have not tasted.

Pollution and Waste Caused by Agriculture

THERE ARE, OF COURSE, MULTIPLE OTHER REASONS TO SUPPORT SUStainable agriculture. The pollution and waste created by conventional agriculture is far greater than the organic alternative. While sustainable farming seeks to create the closed cycle we discussed in Chapter Three, the principle of radical recycling and zero waste is left out of conventional farming practices. The result is that when we are growing food through large scale agribusiness, we tend to waste vast amounts of:

FOOD—The new study, from the University of Arizona (UA) in Tucson, indicates that a shocking 40–50% of all food ready for harvest never gets eaten.

ENERGY—A study done by Dr. David Pimentel from Cornell University found that organic farming systems used only 63% of the energy required by conventional farming systems, largely because of the massive amounts of energy requirements needed to synthesize nitrogen fertilizers.

FOSSIL FUEL—According to the Worldwatch Institute, our food travels 2,000 miles on average to get from the field to the dinner table.

Conventional agriculture also creates more trash and pollution, in forms that range from pesticide runoff to the trash that over-packaging creates once it gets to us.

Dependence on Foreign Food Production

INCREASINGLY, THE FOODS AMERICANS CONSUME ARE IMPORTED AND these foods are not monitored as highly as they could be. There has been a general upswing in average import shares for both crops and animal products since 1980. Bananas, coffee, chocolate, fish and shellfish, spices, cashew nuts, apple juice and other popular foods are produced in greater quantity or less expensively abroad or, in certain cases, just cannot be produced in the U.S. By volume, import shares are highest for fish and shellfish, of which 79% is imported, versus fruits and nuts, 32% and dairy products, which is only 3%. Tropical fruits from Central and South America (i.e. bananas, mangoes and pineapples) account for more than 50% of total U.S. fruit imports.

Mexico dominates the market for vegetables, with tomatoes being the number one export, followed by Canada and the Netherlands. Just for comparison, lettuce, onions, tomatoes and broccoli are the major vegetables that the U.S. exports. In 1997, just 1.3% of imported fish, vegetables, fruit and other foods were inspected—yet those government inspections regularly reveal food unfit for human consumption.

How You Can Help:

- Commit to a 100-mile or 50-mile radius diet (locally grown foods), when possible.
- Support your local urban organic gardening movement.
- When you do buy foreign foods, choose organic and fair trade options.

The Honeybee Crisis

IN THE YEAR 2007, MORE THAN A QUARTER OF THE 2.4 BILLION HONEYbee colonies in the U.S. were lost, approximately tens of billions of bees, according to an estimate from the Apiary Inspectors of America, and this crisis continues today.

Honeybees are a pollinator species that hold vital importance in terms of world food security. One in every three bites we eat is dependent on the honeybee. In America alone they are responsible for 15 billion dollars' worth of crops. Apple pie, guacamole, fresh melon and of course honey wouldn't be possible without the honeybees, and they affect 25% of other species. The primary factors contributing to the honeybee crisis are pesticides, systemic pesticides and monoculture.

Here is a basic education about the honeybee situation: In the past the pesticides we used were foliar sprays (overhead sprays applied to the leaves of plants) and it was

easy to see the degree to which bees would be affected, but today the pesticides we use are primarily soil-drench chemicals that get uplifted by the plant root system, so the bee takes the nectar back to the hive without it being visible to us. The nectar doesn't affect the adult population, but in the winter the bees dig into their storage of pollen and it affects the entire next generation of babies with symptoms of CCD (Colony Collapse Disorder).

At the time of this writing, commercial beekeepers have grown savvy to the need to preserve bees and are introducing an artificial queen bee to create two beehives in the place of one to quell the problem. This effort, however, is NOT sustainable over the long term. In an effort to preserve and promote the sustainability of the earth's bee population, there has been a strong rise in amateur beekeeping among people who are knowledgeable about the problem.

If you are able to join in this movement, even on a small scale, there is tremendous value in doing so. You will receive the benefits of having your garden pollinated and you will be helping the bees that most people consider to be pests. At this time it is vitally important to provide safe habitats for the pollinators. There are other pollinator species to pay attention to, hummingbirds, bats and other bees besides honeybees, who are also dwindling.

If any good comes from disasters such as the honeybee crisis, it is that it finally opens our eyes to the delicacy and inherent value of a species that we took for granted and reminds us of the web of interconnection that is our food system. In keeping with the principle of "giving back," it invites us, once again, to consider how our choices can positively impact another species, and allows us deeper gratitude for how this species positively impacts us.

Maryam Henein, co-producer of the film *The Vanishing of the Bees*, encourages people to take these steps to support the end of the honeybee crisis:

• Beekeeping—yes, in your own backyard!
• Organic home gardening
• Shopping at farmers markets
• Buying pure honey, rather than honey blended with milk, corn syrup and rice syrup
• Buying honey that is organic, raw, unfiltered and local. If you can't find local honey, look for New Zealand honey. New Zealand doesn't use any pesticides.

Sustainable Agriculture and the Solution

LUCKILY, ALL OF THIS BAD NEWS CAN BE ADDRESSED BY SIMPLY SHIFTing our priority to organic sustainable agriculture. We can trust that organic foods are free of most conventional pesticides, synthetic or sewage-derived fertilizers, genetically modified organisms, ionizing radiation (irradiation), antibiotics and growth hormones. There are also a lot of farmers out there who cannot afford the organic certification but are practicing a pesticide-free sustainable agriculture.

2005 marked the first time that there was certified organic farmland in all 50 states, with over 4.0 million acres of farmland, including 1.7 million acres of cropland and 2.3 million acres of rangeland and pasture involved. California has the most certified organic cropland, primarily dedicated to fruit and vegetable production.

The International Federation of Organic Agriculture Movements released a report in February 2008, "The World of Organic Agriculture: Statistics & Emerging Trends," which estimated that worldwide in 2006 there were 30.4 million hectares managed organically by more than 700,000 farms in 138 countries; the United States ranked fourth, with 1.6 million hectares in 2005 (latest available statistics).

For a long time, we have been told that conventional agriculture and pesticides are the best and only way to go in order to feed the planet, but we need to challenge this belief because ultimately conventional agriculture is not sustainable or aligned with nature. Are we willing to reach higher and envision a world where all of our food is produced healthfully, locally, sustainably and pesticide-free? Are we willing to approach food production and food security in a way that ultimately benefits both personal and planetary health?

The Process—Becoming an Earth Steward

RATHER THAN BLINDLY SUPPORTING A SYSTEM THAT DOES NOT WORK for the common good, an earth steward acknowledges the importance of healthy soil and recognizes that seeds are "the container for life" and not to be treated as a commodity. Once we become aware of the issues of world agriculture and choose to use the information to empower ourselves, our personal diets can become a reflection of the world we choose to create and live in.

I once had the opportunity to work with international activist Helena Norberg-Hodge and she shared a notion that has been with me ever since. While many people worry about overpopulation and argue that it is the primary cause of the environmental crisis, trying to justify that it is necessary for us to engage in conventional agriculture and other unsustainable practices to simply supply the resources for so many people, Helena argued that all we really need is "more eyes per acre."

The more attentive people we have in every neighborhood, community and region advocating for "what is best for all," the more we will be able to find solutions for sufficiency and sustainability rather than having to combat over-consumption and inefficient design. All we need is more people who care. In cities, every time one person commits to becoming an earth steward, consider the dozens or hundreds (or more) people who will be inspired by that one person's choice, creating a ripple effect.

The Sustainable Farmer As Modern Hero

The more we allow ourselves to become educated about sustainability, acknowledge our feelings about the predicament we are in, and deepen our personal connection to the earth, the more we choose to take passionate responsibility for the world we live in. I don't see much need to use doom and gloom to motivate us to care for the earth. I do feel, however, that the more aware we become about the state of the world, the more we are equipped to make informed choices and to respect the web of interconnection on this planet.

When I first began to visit small, sustainable, organic farms that were practicing age-old agriculture techniques and permaculture design, there was a deep sense of relief. After so many years of sensing that there was something terribly wrong in how the urban landscape was developed and treated, and sensing the deeper implications of our approach to land stewardship or lack of it, I felt relieved by the sanity and simplicity I witnessed at these farms. I recognized the integrity in how the land was being treated, the sweet smell of health in the soil and the sanity of the farmer who shows up and takes care of this sacred eco-system day in and day out. I tasted the undeniable difference in the fruit and vegetables I was fed from these farms and recognized the fact that my cheeks became naturally rosy and glowing in a way they simply do not when I'm living the urban life.

Eating meals can be a way of connecting to nature while living a city life.

Throughout the world, traditional farmers are dying off and their kids are leaving the land, with no interest in continuing the often hard life of a "lowly" farmer. Images romanticizing the West have impacted the lives of people around the world through TV, billboards, products, advertising, the Internet and the incessant promotion of the unsustainable super-modern way of life. Meanwhile, in the Western world, people are starting to become aware and to want to make a difference. It is starting to become "cool" and "hip" to grow your own food. There are many people who have been inspired by the economic crisis to grow their own food. Today the heroes of our culture (the ones that little boys and girls want to grow up to be) are celebrities and sports figures. I look forward to the day when children, boys and girls alike, want to grow up to be farmers!

Summary of Steps We Can Take in our Own Lives and Ways we can Teach the Next Generation to Value Sustainable Agriculture:

- Begin to investigate where all of your food comes from.
- Follow the simple shopping guidelines suggested in Chapter Five.
- Grow your own food and share with your neighbors!
- Commit to a 50- or 100-mile radius diet.
- Learn the art of beekeeping—yes, in your own backyard!
- Shop at farmers markets or join a CSA (Community Supported Agriculture).
- Get to know the farms you are supporting personally. If you join a CSA, sign up for one of their farm tours or go out and volunteer. Schedule a visit to your favorite farm to support it at the farmers market. Learn firsthand how these farms are practicing sustainable agriculture, how they have created a closed cycle and how they are giving back.
- Commit to zero packaging by shopping at the bulk bin.
- Practice zero waste in your own kitchen.
- On your own property, in your own garden, take care of your soil by mulching it and protecting it.
- Purchase seeds from smaller, organic, reputable companies such as Bountiful Gardens, Renee's and Seeds of Change.
- Save seeds in your own garden and join the Seed Saver's Exchange, **seedsaversexchange.com.**
- Avoid GMO foods. For a detailed list of GMO foods and how to avoid them, please read Chapter Four.
- Become interested in plant biodiversity in your own area. Enjoy the tastes of heirloom varieties and seek out new varieties and produce that you have not tasted.
- Support the honeybee population. Buy pure honey that is organic, raw, unfiltered and local or practice beekeeping in your own backyard.
- Experiment and see if you can learn to listen to your sensitivity and taste the difference between healthy food and "phony food."
- Allow meals to become an opportunity to connect with the natural world through healthy local organic food.

Taking the Next Step:

Pause for a moment and think about all of the information in this chapter.

Take a few minutes to acknowledge the ways you are already participating in the solution and appreciate yourself for your efforts.

Now take a moment to recognize and appreciate the collective efforts going on around you: farmers markets, CSAs, local community food initiatives, community gardens, efforts on the part of schools and restaurants, etc.

What is the next immediate step you see yourself taking as part of the SOLUTION? ●

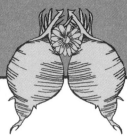

CHAPTER 5
GUIDELINES FOR SHOPPERS

KAREN, ONE OF MY CLIENTS, IS A TYPICAL LOS Angeles mother who fits in the family grocery shopping between a busy work schedule, picking up the kids at school and dropping them off at soccer practice, and trying to juggle numerous errands. She drives through traffic, tries to remember to bring her own cloth bags, and attempts to make choices that somehow fit everyone's nutritional needs.

These needs are: family health, preparing meals that are QUICK and convenient, watching her weight (face it, a primary motivator for many women and men), watching her pocketbook, and being sensitive to everyone's taste palate. Add to that the often higher price of organic foods and all the new information about "how to be green"—from where tomatoes should come from to what food containers must be AVOIDED—and this single shopping trip can become overwhelming.

Most people don't have a 24/7 "green coach" to call every time they have a question and want to do the right thing, nor do they have time to do all the research themselves. Most of my new clients admit that they either don't have the information they need OR they have the information but don't have the time or money to give the necessary attention to make the right food choices.

Some of my clients may not cook even one meal for themselves in a typical week, relying solely on takeout and snack foods. Others report that they are very used to a feeling of subtle sense of guilt after each shopping trip, a feeling that they could do better, while others report feeling annoyed because the "right foods"—those that they know are better for their health and for the health of the planet—are so outrageously expensive.

Earth-friendly shopping doesn't have to be that complicated. Once you have a basic set of guidelines for sustainable shopping, you will be empowered to make choices that you feel great about, and that guilty feeling after shopping will slowly melt away.

Remember: Sustainability is NOT a set of rules. It is a frame of mind that we carry with us into every situation, a frame of mind that asks sincerely "what is best for all?"—and that ALL includes ourselves. When we understand the basic premises of sustainability and we see ourselves as part of the web of sustainability, we understand that the choice that is best for all does not always look how we think it should, but it always feels good.

....

The basic questions for green shopping are:

- Is it organic? If on a budget, is it a food deemed OK to not buy organic?
- Is it locally grown or shipped overseas? If so, do I support the production of this food?
- Can I find it with the least amount of packaging, i.e., can I buy it in bulk?
- Is it a GMO-free food?
- Can I support the farmer directly in some way?

If it fits none of the above, ask yourself these questions:
- Do I really need this?
- Can it become a "sometimes treat" rather than a "regular" in my diet?

These questions are easy for anyone to adopt and apply to every shopping trip, wherever you are on the path of sustainability. The purpose of these questions is to help you find the choice that is best for all in each situation you encounter. There will be times when it seems unclear, so simply do your best, gather as much information you can about the impact of the choices on hand, and if you find yourself stuck in your head about which choice to make, simply turn to your heart for the answer instead. You will know you are making the choice that is best for all by the way you feel.

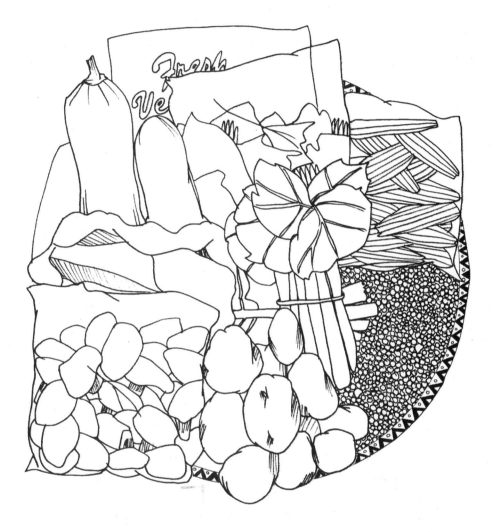

Is it organic?

More than ever before, Americans are buying organic. Most people choose organic for personal health reasons and this is of vital importance. Our number one priority as shoppers today should be to make sure we are supporting an organic food supply in the long term—free of pesticides, herbicides, and fungicides.

At the same time, it would be shortsighted to say that valuing organics for human health reasons alone will ensure a long-term sustainable food supply. Today we are required, as food consumers, to become aware of what goes into food production and to, in fact, become active advocates for healthy sustainable agriculture worldwide, as I have explained in Chapter Four.

Some questions we need to ask as food buyers today are: Are large-scale organic farms truly sustainable if they are practicing **monoculture**? Knowing that pesticides travel through water, air and pollution, are we doing enough to protect our food supply by cutting out pesticides used in non-food crops, like cotton, which are high polluters as well? Are we protecting our pollinator populations (such as honeybees) by outlawing chemicals that we know are disastrous for their health?

When I first learned to garden, I was taught to think of gardening not as "growing food" but as "growing soil." Most traditional cultures have intricate systems for sustainable agriculture, built into their lifestyle, that prioritize soil health. "Organic" is supposed to be an alternative to the unconscious use of pesticides, monoculture, low wages, dependence on fossil fuel and industrial farming structures, but the market has changed and is continuing to do so.

Some people fear that the organic certification is becoming too lax in its restrictions and diluting the purpose of the movement, and this is certainly a risk anytime we are depending on a "label." I personally know a number of farmers who are growing organically and who used to be certified organic, but can no longer afford the label OR do not currently support the shift in direction that the organics movement has taken.

While choosing organic food should be our number one priority, we want to go a step further and make an effort to support small-scale sustainable farms that honor the values of the original organics movement. Doing so also supports soil health, health of pollinator species, energy conservation, minimized packaging, and small-farm welfare.

The best way to do this is either to grow our own food or to pay attention and to buy produce directly from a farmers market or Community Supported Agriculture (CSA). We can know that we are supporting a sustainable farm if it is organic/free of pesticides, and if the farm does not package produce or ship it far away, and supports soil health and biodiversity. Rather than have to investigate and rate every farmer you come across, it might be easiest to find a few reliable farmers who are verbally doing the above practices and simply support them.

Is this food necessary to buy organic?

People often come to me seeking guidance on how to afford an organic diet on their budget. I find it very useful to carry a list of the foods that are least important to buy organic (meaning they are the least likely to contain pesticide residue) and the foods that are absolute necessary to buy organic, so you can find the middle way that works for you if you are on a budget.

The Clean 15—15 foods least likely to contain pesticide residue:

- Avocados
- Asparagus
- Cabbage
- Cantaloupe
- Eggplant
- Grapefruit
- Kiwi fruit
- Mango
- Onions
- Pineapple
- Sweet corn
- Sweet onions
- Sweet peas
- Sweet potatoes
- Watermelon

The Dirty Dozen—12 foods to eat only if they're organic:

- Apples
- Blueberries
- Celery
- Cherries
- Grapes (imported)
- Lettuce
- Nectarines
- Peaches
- Potatoes
- Spinach
- Strawberries
- Sweet bell peppers

Consider that some crops, such as onions and garlic, do not require much, if any pesticide. These alliums (a plant family that contains crops like onions, leeks and garlic) contain natural pest deterrents and if anything at all gets sprayed on them, they have tough skins to act as a barrier. On the other hand, a large amount of pesticides are sprayed on conventionally grown nectarines, and they have only a thin delicate skin.

Always buy organic:

- meat
- dairy, including all kinds of milk, butter, and cheese
- nuts/seeds, including peanut or almond butter
- oils/fats
- grains
- rice
- coffee

You will notice that a lot of foods on this list have high fat content. Pesticides get stored in fat.

Is it locally grown OR at least not shipped from overseas?

After harvesting fresh melons from my own garden at the end of summer in Southern California, I was shocked when I stopped by a market to find the same variety of melons shipped in all the way from Israel! I am always surprised by the amount of packaged produce from afar that popular markets sell, and I urge shoppers to make every effort to choose local produce rather than just choose what's in front of you at the market because it is convenient.

Remember that for the typical American, the amount of gas you use to drive each year is the same amount of gas that it takes to get your food to you. The primary benefits of purchasing locally grown foods are that they not only conserve gasoline that might be used for distant transport, but they also provide health benefits from consuming seasonally appropriate foods. Committing to buying locally grown foods is one simple step that every household can take, and depending on where you live, you may be surprised to learn what grows locally in your region.

Can I find it with the least amount of packaging, i.e., can I buy it in bulk?

This is an area which, at the moment, is in the hands of the consumer to make a conscious choice. Zero waste is an idea that, at the time of writing this book, is slowly gaining popularity; however, it is not an idea that has been readily activated in the world at large. Living in a city, I find that one almost has to make a game out of trying to avoid the overwhelming amounts of packaging and disposable junk (from paper napkins to straws to disposable plastic cups) that comes our way every day.

Simple ways to cut down on packaging while shopping are:

- Shop at the bulk food bins available at more conscious markets.
- Bring your own bags for both produce/bulk foods AND check out.
- Pick glass jars over plastic jars when you shop and reuse them as storage containers.
- Bring your own storage containers for prepared foods at the market and ask them to weigh them for you first.

Be aware when shopping at discount stores such as Costco, etc. While you can find some products in bulk without excess packaging, other products utilize excessive amounts of packaging, particularly plastic. Wherever you shop, it's up to you to pay attention to how things are packaged and to find the product that best fits your needs in the least amount of packaging.

If you do not live near any affordable source for bulk foods with less packaging, then I recommend you do an assessment of what you sincerely need to buy and limit it to NEEDS. Read Chapter Eleven for more ways to cut down on packaging and disposables in your everyday life.

Can I support the farmer directly in some way?

Shopping at your local farmers market or joining a CSA are the most direct ways you can support the sustainable farmer. Community Supported Agriculture (CSA) is a truly important direction for these times. Community Supported Agriculture is a system in which you buy a share into a small farm for a season at a time, thus giving the farmer the up-front money that he/she needs in order to produce.

In return, you get either a weekly or bimonthly delivery to your neighborhood of fresh, locally grown, in-season produce, typically in a gorgeous farm-fresh display of delightful, healthful, colorful vegetables, fruits, herbs and sometimes even flowers. If a CSA delivery provides more produce than you can eat, consider joining with a friend or neighbor. Visit the Resource List to learn how to find one in your area. Further in this chapter we will look at additional ways to buy organic produce and whole foods affordably.

Is this a GMO food?

It is estimated that 75% or more of American foods and body products contain genetically modified organisms (GMOs). The FDA has approved widespread use of GMO ingredients in many items. Dozens of countries have banned the sale, import, use, and planting of GMOs due to the lack of testing and long-term study of human and environmental effects. The U.S., however, not only does NOT ban genetically modified foods, but manufacturers are also not required to identify or label GMO ingredients in their products.

All organic foods are non-GMO foods. Therefore, if you simply focus on buying organic foods religiously, you can avoid this issue entirely… but it gets tricky. I find it helpful to use a guide/list while shopping to give me clarity about what is GMO and what is NOT when I am shopping.

In the U.S., the percentages of crops that are genetically modified are:
- Soy 85%
- Cotton (cottonseed) 76%
- Canola 75%
- Corn 40%
- Hawaiian papaya (over 50%)
- Yellow squash and zucchini (small amount)
- Quest brand tobacco (100%)

In addition, there are food products that contain genetically modified corn products and corn oil, soy, cottonseed, and canola oil. Here is a list of all the foods to be aware of:

Salad dressings	Infant formula
Bread, rolls, pastry	Baby cereal
Canned rolls and breads	Hamburgers and hot dogs
Margarine	Processed meats
Mayonnaise	Crackers
Chocolate	Cookies
Candy	Fried foods
Frozen foods	Chips
Tofu	Veggie burgers
Soy burgers	Meat substitutes
Aspartame	Ice cream
Frozen yogurt	Tamari
Soy sauce	Soy cheese
Soy nuts and products	Processed cheese
Pasteurized cheese	Tomato sauce
Marinades	Barbecue sauce
Soups	Canned stews
Sauces	Dried and dehydrated soups/sauces
Condiments	Drinks
Protein powder	Baking powder
Alcohol	Vanilla
Peanut butter	Pasta
Enriched flour	Powdered sugar
Children's snacks	Cereals
Cake and baking mixes	Frozen pie and pastry shells
Cosmetics	Shampoo
Bubble bath	Soaps
Creams and lotions	Detergents

Other areas that might be tainted by GMO products are:

• Milk/dairy from cows who have been fed GMO corn or who are injected with genetically modified growth hormone
• Meat from animals fed GMO food rather than being grass-fed
• GMO food additives such as aspartame, flavorings, and enzymes
• Honey and bee pollen that may have GMO sources of pollen

Most often, unless it is labeled organic, you can assume your vegetable oils, margarine, soy protein/flour, textured vegetable protein, dextrose, maltodextrin, fructose, citric acid, and lactic acid are GMO foods.

So how on earth does one navigate through the rows of non-labeled GMO foods at the market?

Keep it simple… stick with whole and unprocessed organic foods.

With produce, access the Price Lookup Code (PLU code), usually affixed to food items with a sticker/tag and stick with the #9. PLU codes tell you if the fruit was conventionally grown, genetically modified, or organically grown. The PLU code for conventional produce has four numbers, GMO fruit has five numbers preceded by the number 8, while organically grown produce has five numbers, preceded by the number 9.

Find products made of the purest ingredients possible (for example, choose Maggie's Soap Nuts instead of laundry detergent, buy homemade soap at the farmers market or Dr. Bronner's Castile Soap, and follow the cleaning guidelines laid out in Chapter Two.)

Consider making your own sauces, snacks, dressings and desserts with the ideas supplied in Chapter Six.

The Most Important Question for the Conscious Shopper to Ask

If the food you're thinking of buying fits none of the above shopping guidelines, then ask yourself the following questions:

Do I really need this?
Can it become a "sometimes treat" rather than a regular staple of my diet?

This is my favorite question for the green shopper. As a society, we are conditioned to choose immediate gratification rather than to choose what would be best for the long term. Rarely do we ask ourselves these questions: Do I really need this food? Can it become something I enjoy on occasion rather than an ongoing part of my diet?

In the Sustainable Kitchen workshop, I ask people to state what they believe they'd have to let go of in order to go green, and time and time again, people admit that they think they'd have to let go of their favorite foods. Most people still believe that moving toward a sustainable world means shifting back in time or adopting a Third World lifestyle of deprivation. This is simply not so. Sustainability is not about deprivation. The call for sustainability invites us to merge our modern lifestyle with some of the wisdom of a society that has a long-term, life-sustaining vision.

The Monks and the Bananas

I recall a time at the monastery when we were enlightening ourselves about the banana industry, which has been one of the more destructive crops in terms of its environmental and social implications globally. With our deepening awareness of banana industry practices, we began to realize that buying bananas did not match our intentions to "lead not a harmful life." At the same time, however, some of our most popular desserts included bananas as a major ingredient. Creating even more of a challenge was the fact that some of the monks had a harder time letting go than others with the decision to remove bananas from our diet. The Middle Way we came to was to remove bananas in our daily diet, but to buy them organically every now and then for a special dessert during meditation retreats that were conducted periodically during the year.

This simple decision actually addressed everyone's needs: our need to feel good about our choices, our economic reality (we couldn't afford organic bananas on an ongoing basis), and our need to provide special meals for our retreat attendees. The point I am trying to make is that "letting go" of some of our favorite foods should not feel like we are punishing ourselves. If it does, then it is not "letting go." If and when you are ready to let go completely of the "bananas" in your life, you will simply do so. Until then, see what kind of Middle Way you can find. In the case of the monastery, we continued with this decision until we found a banana company that had converted to more conscious practices that we could support and afford.

Every sustainable community I have ever lived in has their own version of the banana issue. Is there a food item you eat regularly that you'd like to find more of a Middle Way with?

Considerations for Meat Eaters

Overall, can I eat sustainably if I'm not a vegetarian? While it is true that the lower we eat on the food chain, the more eco-friendly our diet is, I have clients who are not ready to become vegetarians... or who are not interested. If you are a meat eater who feels the call to become a vegetarian, begin by simply choosing one meal a day to be a vegetarian meal. Let yourself develop your palate this way and you will grow to love vegetarian cooking and gradually let go of the need for meat.

If you are an omnivore, I encourage you to be as conscious a meat eater as you can be, and to take the time to educate yourself about the environmental impact of meat, and about more sustainable sources of chicken, fish, and red meat. This is KEY for your personal health and planetary health.

Remember that a sustainable diet is a conscious diet. There are vegetarians in the world who consume primarily packaged and processed GMO foods, grown through soil depletion and shipped in from afar, and there are omnivores who eat locally grown organic produce and consciously-raised meat. The point, whether we are vegetarian or omnivorous, is to make food choices by being aware of the big picture.

In the words of Wendell Berry, *"I dislike the thought that some animal has been made miserable to feed me. If I am going to eat meat, I want it to be from an animal that has lived a pleasant, uncrowded life outdoors, on bountiful pasture, with good water nearby and trees for shade."*

For your own health and for the health of the environment, consider making a commitment to choosing organic meat, raised locally and free of hormones that are unsafe for human health. Countries in the European Union have banned U.S. beef that has been given hormones, because studies show they are complete carcinogens.

These hormones continue to cause trouble ecologically as well, ending up in huge manure pools that lead downstream, affecting fish, birds, frogs, and other animals living nearby. Over 70% of the chickens in the U.S. are given arsenic in their feed, to control intestinal parasites.

I encourage everyone—meat eaters and non-meat eaters—to educate themselves about these issues. I recommend the following resources for more information:

• John Robbins' *Diet for a New America* and *The Food Revolution*
• Frances Moore Lappe's *Diet for a Small Planet*
• Michael Pollen's *The Omnivore's Dilemma*
• **Robert Kenner's** film *Food Inc.*

For personal and planetary health, consider choosing organic meat from animals raised locally on a small farm and treated well in their lifetime.

If you run into grey areas when buying meat, poultry, or fish, I recommend the following three steps:

• Educate yourself about the issues involved with the type of meat in question.
• Ask yourself "what is best for all in this situation?" looking for the Middle Way between your well-being and that of the planet.

• If you are still unclear as to how to proceed, simply ask yourself "how does this choice feel?" We can always find the best choice inside of ourselves if we really stop to look within.

For seafood, there are no organic standards yet, so for safety, it is best to buy wild seafood and avoid farm-raised fish and prawns. Farm fishing introduces dangerous hormones into the ocean. The interests of consumers are best served if seafood continues to come from wild sources that are managed well and to make sure that fish stocks are not depleted.

It's not worth paying a premium for organic fish. It is vital for seafood consumers to be aware about which fish are abundant and fished in eco-friendly ways and which fish are overfished and fished/farmed in ways that harm the environment and other marine life. I recommend that all seafood eaters utilize the *Seafood Watch: All Season's Guide* produced by the Monterey Bay Aquarium. Updates can be checked regularly online (see my Resource List).

We also need to be extremely aware of the elevated levels of mercury now found in our fish supply. Mercury is the second most toxic substance known to humans, following plutonium. Mercury pollution comes from coal-fired power plants, mining, and incinerators and it enters the ocean through runoff, as well as rainwater and watersheds. Large fish like tuna and swordfish (which feed on other fish containing mercury) contain the largest concentrations, while small to medium-sized fish are generally safer to eat. Sardines, for example, are one of the safest fish recommended on *Seafood Watch*.

Considerations for Children

Because children are smaller, they are much more vulnerable than adults to chemicals in food. Young children are also in a particular phase of growth where pesticides can have a negative impact developmentally. Pesticides have been proven to contain damaging chemicals that can lead to endocrine imbalance and a multitude of other health problems.

For children, processed foods have been proven to be significantly lower in nutrition and higher in health risk than whole organic foods. The current issue of child diabetes is yet another reason to serve our children whole, organic foods. The amounts of corn syrup and sugar that go into our processed food supply, for instance, are major contributors to diabetes.

To take this to another level, in terms of children's health, we need to make these choices now to secure a safe future on this planet for our children. Choosing foods that are sustainably grown, transported, and packaged ultimately takes better care of our topsoil, water/air quality, food supply, and overall planetary health.

For infants, the issue becomes even more critical. If you have the opportunity to start your child on an organic diet as an infant, take advantage of it. An easy option is to purchase a baby food grinder (non-electric) and prepare your own baby food from natural ingredients. Simple instructions for how to make your own baby food are available in Chapter Twelve.

Considerations for Raw Foodists and Health Food Junkies

My experience of the health food scene is that there is always a health food fad or favorite that people enjoy in large amounts, and that the latest trendy food, while it may have great human health benefits, is not always local or sustainable in its production and use.

We tend to forget the concept of moderation and balance when we get excited about "the new thing" that is finally going to heal us, help us lose weight, or save us from aging. I bring this up because I hope that as conscious shoppers, we can learn to value both personal and planetary health, without the illusion that we can choose one over the other.

In recent years, for example, there has been a major surge in the use of the following: protein powders, coconuts, cacao, goji berries, and other foods that are a particularly helpful part of the raw foods diet, but are generally harvested in foreign countries and shipped long distances. While it is my experience that there are great benefits to these foods, and I include each of these things in my diet at times, I ask people to consider, honestly, if they are including environmental awareness in their consumption of these foods.

Perhaps you are someone who would rather adopt a purely local diet and who would feel content to give up those foods. OR perhaps you are someone to whom those foods are important, but who can certainly see bringing consciousness to how you are using them. What would finding a Middle Way look like for you in relation to these foods?

A good friend of mine has a daily ritual of making fresh coconut smoothies. It is an "addiction" I can understand because they taste so good and because coconuts do wonders for us nutritionally. To make it affordable, my friend would go to the Thai market once a week and buy a crate of coconuts shipped from Thailand and individually wrapped in plastic. After attending a workshop with me, she realized that the amount of gasoline and plastic fueling her daily ritual was not in keeping with her overall values. She just hadn't thought about it before because coconuts are so important to her.

So she found a Middle Way: Instead of having a coconut smoothie every day (and sometimes twice a day!) she made it a special treat three times a week, and she drinks fruit juice the other days of the week. She now enjoys her smoothies even more and also gets to enjoy peace of mind about her consumption of them.

I am all for the raw foods diet, superfoods diet, or any other diet that improves the quality of our lives, as long as it is executed from the place that is "best for all." Why not start by inventorying the raw foods and superfoods grown closest to you? The diet will look different for someone living in California or New York versus someone living in Florida or Hawaii.

In its purest form, the raw foods diet is very sustainable, if the food is grown locally. It comes in its own packaging (skin), which can simply be tossed to compost, and nothing gets cooked. Now that is sustainable; however, the same diet can be practiced in a way that utilizes a ton of fossil fuel and an alarming amount of packaging, not to mention no direct farm-to-consumer link. If the purpose is to be eating in alignment with nature, see what adjustments you might make to find the most sustainable expression of your chosen diet.

Here are some things to keep in mind:

There are great sources of fair trade, consciously grown cacao, coconut oil, etc... but I have also seen products that are not as conscious. Are you able to find conscious suppliers for these products?

For foods like protein powders, which are soy-based, it's important to pay attention to finding non-GMO products. I like to buy protein powder in the bulk bin section when I can, and I find it useful to rotate the protein powders I use to include different options, such as U.S. grown hemp, rice, or whey.

Have you looked into creative ways to find more local sources for the specialty foods you enjoy? You can get goji berries shipped all the way from China or the Himalayas, or you can find them grown in the Rocky Mountains here in the United States, in a climate similar to the Himalayas.

Where to Buy Organic Produce and How to Do It Affordably

Farmers Markets, Community Food-Sharing, and Other Economical Strategies

Depending on where you live, it can be easy or a major challenge to find affordable, local organic whole foods. A helpful website on this topic, with resources across the nation, is **localharvest.org**. A farmers market is one of the best places to buy organic produce, because it is more affordable and you can speak directly with the farmers about how they are growing their produce.

Not all farmers who sell produce at a farmers market are certified organic, so keep an eye out and ask questions. Sometimes farmers can't afford the certification but they still grow free of pesticides. It requires a conversation to learn from whom you are buying and what their growing practices really are.

Along with the farmers market, many food co-ops are good sources of local organic produce and whole foods and they're often less expensive than your local supermarket. Most supermarkets do have some organic produce, of course, but it is not always possible to know what types of farms the produce actually comes from, nor how it is grown. For this reason, I do not recommend buying organic produce in supermarket chain stores when you have access to a CSA or farmers market instead.

It is much, much easier to live sustainably when we are living in or involved in community. It is both easier to afford green living when we are sharing resources and buying or cooking food together and it keeps us tied to one of the primary tenets of sustainability: Our food connects us with the land we live on and a sense of community .

In Chapter Six on Green Menu Planning, we will talk about how do-it-yourself food production can enhance your life and how setting up a system of sharing (balanced with community food-buying) with your neighbors can provide a homegrown local green food network.

Here are some ways you can access affordable, healthy food in a city:

- Farmers Markets
- Community Supported Agriculture (CSAs)
- Food Co-ops
- Food Buying Clubs
- Gardening, Do-it-yourself Food Production, Urban Foraging and Community Food-Sharing

For more information on these topics, please visit the Resource List in the back of this book.

How to Make Sense of "Healthy" Food Labels

You can keep your life dramatically simple and healthy by choosing the foods that embody the sustainable paradigm: seasonal, organic, locally grown, whole bulk foods. In the next chapter on Menu Planning we will look at how to create the most diverse menu from this array of foods. Meanwhile, I also want you to have some information about how to navigate other food labels you will run into. Please remember to go beyond labeling and, where there are ingredients you don't recognize, look them up.

All-natural or naturally grown:
There is no federal regulation for natural foods and we can't even assume that foods with this label are organic. This label does generally indicate that a product was processed and packaged without additives or preservatives, but I would be careful of projecting anything more onto this label.

Made with organic:
If a food product contains between 70–95% organic ingredients, it can receive this label.

Less than 70% organic ingredients:
This may be cited on the back panel of a product.

Biodynamic:
This is an approach to organic farming that was developed in Europe by Rudolph Steiner (a brilliant philosopher who developed theosophy) in the 1920s. Biodynamic farming is true to all of the organic standards and, in addition, focuses on the natural rhythms of the sun, moon, planets and stars. My opinion is that you can trust that it is high quality if it is biodynamic.

Fair trade:
This label is given to products that tend to be grown in developing countries to signify that the growers received fair prices for their goods. This label says nothing about the use of pesticides.

Buying Eggs:
In an ideal world, we would all have access to local eggs from well-treated chickens in our own backyards or neighborhoods. Most farmers markets now have eggs available. Here are some categories for eggs you will find at the market, and remember to choose cardboard packaging over Styrofoam, and make the choice that feels best to you.

Free-range/cage-free:
Basically this means that the chickens were raised with access to the outdoors. There is no federal regulation for how long they get to be outdoors and this does not mean they are organic. Also, the USDA only regulates these terms for poultry.

Raised without antibiotics/no antibiotics used:
Livestock raised without antibiotics are not necessarily organic, but as you will recall from the last chapter, there are myriad benefits to not supporting the use of antibiotics in our food system.

Grass-fed/meadow-raised/vegetarian-fed:
This signifies that the livestock are raised on grasses and legumes. Meadow-raised are also fed grains. Veg-fed are not fed other animal parts. This label has no information about organics.

In summary, as an alternative to Karen's shopping challenge at the beginning of this chapter, imagine this: To provide healthy and nutritious meals for your family, as busy as your life might be, once a week you take a family trip to the farmers market or pick up your organic local CSA produce delivery. With the CSA, you received notice in advance of what you will be receiving, or you are paying attention to what is seasonal, so that you can plan menus accordingly.

Then, based on the menus you have planned, you might have a few items to buy during a quick trip to the co-op or farmers market, so you pack your glass jars and shopping bags and, when you arrive, purchase foods mainly at a bulk bin.

Meanwhile, you have all the fresh herbs and lettuce you need growing in your own garden, so you harvest that, saving money at the same time. Your shopping didn't take a lot of time. You don't have additives and preservatives in your food or ingredients whose name you don't recognize. Your trip to the farmers market over the weekend was an enjoyable outing with your family or perhaps an opportunity to meet some friends who were doing the same. Your food shopping costs are less than they used to be. And you are eating a primarily local organic, non-GMO diet that creates minimum waste and supports your local community and companies you like.

Furthermore, the meals you prepare do not make you feel as if you are compromising both your health and the planet's health, but are a way of being 100% sustainable in the modern world.

Taking The Next Step

CONSIDER:

• What are your biggest challenges regarding food shopping and sustainability?
• From the information you have just read, what would be one enjoyable step/action that you can take to shop more sustainably?
• What would support you in this action?

For instance, perhaps you want to write down the shopping guidelines presented in this chapter and carry them in your wallet or print out the Creative Green Shopping Resource Guide at **creativegreen.net** for your next shopping trip. Maybe you need to stock up on bags and containers in the trunk of your car. Maybe you want to set up a week-long trial of doing without a certain product you don't support but have felt addicted to. Perhaps you want to begin simply by inventorying the foods and ingredients you use regularly and doing some investigation. ●

CHAPTER 6
MENU PLANNING
Tips from the Zen Cook

"Worry is not preparation."

—Cheri Huber

"If you do what you've always done, you'll get what you've always gotten."

—Tony Robbins

F ROM MY FIRST MEAL AT THE ZEN MONASTERY Peace Center, there was one distinguishing factor that struck me—that *zero food was wasted*. In a kitchen that cooks for 10–40 people, depending on the season, every menu is carefully and creatively designed to create zero food waste. After each meal the monks take time to meticulously scrape every ounce of remaining food from the serving bowls into the right-sized and dated storage containers for the cook to recycle into another meal. No amount is too small to save and reuse. It was a creative challenge to find ways to avoid waste and to value every ounce of food that came through the kitchen.

In order for one's diet to be sustainable in a busy, fast-paced, urban way of life, a little extra thought and planning need to go into creating menus and making your weekly shopping list. This section will offer tips for creating green menus that support your particular lifestyle, needs, tastes and pocketbook.

It will also offer ideas for planning creative menus that are "outside the box" and help you adopt a daily practice of zero waste: conscious use of leftovers, energy-efficient one-pot meals, making the most of your farmers market produce and using every bit of a fruit or vegetable.

One of the tenets of the sustainable kitchen is that we bring consciousness to each choice we make. The very act of planning your weekly menu—loosely or in detail—is an act of care and consciousness. At the monastery, a tremendous amount of care goes into food, from the quality and cost of the ingredients purchased, to how they are transported and stored, to how and when they fit into the menu to ensure that there is zero waste.

Giving extra thought to menu planning for the week might seem strange if you are accustomed to being more spontaneous in your food purchases and meal preparation, but it is a way to monitor your choices and to hold yourself accountable to your intentions. At the very least, weekly menu planning provides a helpful transitional tool until you've got the swing of sustainable shopping and cooking.

Here are some basic questions to include in menu planning:

- What produce is in season?
- How can I create zero food waste and treat every ounce of food as if it matters?
- What do I currently have available that needs to be used?
- What meals follow each other well in terms of utilizing leftovers appropriately?
- What are my needs in terms of time/schedule and what kinds of healthy enjoyable meals will fit my schedule this week? For instance, do I need to plan for "easy to pack and go" meals because I will be away from home at mealtimes?
- What are some enjoyable ways that I can gently introduce my family to a more sustainable diet without coming on too strongly with new food choices?
- If I like to snack, how can I maintain a supply of healthy, fresh snacks, without extra packaging, to take care of my needs?
- How can I create healthy one-pot meals and minimum-energy meals?
- How much can I actually prepare using whole foods that enable me to eliminate all additives, preservatives, processed and packaged foods from my life?
- What is a sustainable approach to desserts and sweets, given the impact of sugar in our lives?

The investment you make in planning a menu for the week, whether loosely or exactly, can yield a tremendous payoff. Clients of mine have successfully made the following changes:

A family that was concerned about the amount of waste they created each week through their reliance on instant, ready-to-serve meals was able to train themselves to minimize their food waste dramatically. They started by writing up a commitment to practice zero waste and then came up with a few delicious, easy-to-make recipes that took them beyond the world of packaged foods without compromising their schedule.

A mother of three was able to create a simple seasonal menu to train her children to be healthy vegetarians, although they originally ate meat at least twice a day.

A single working woman was able to rid her kitchen of junk food and packaged snacks by committing to an hour each Sunday and again on Wednesday, to prepare home-made snacks and sauces.

Ways to Approach Menu Planning

Planning my menu each week is a time for me to check in with myself, look at my schedule and budget, find out what's in season, see what surprises are in the garden and create a menu that addresses all of these elements together.

The most creative cooks know how to make a variety of wildly diverse recipes from a few basic, staple ingredients and a wide array of farmers market vegetables. You can create a "loose" menu by simply being aware of what is in season and maintaining ingredients for your favorite sustainable meals for that time period. On the other hand you can plan out exactly which meals will follow and precede other meals, so that you can recycle and reuse leftovers for each consecutive meal, thus making the most of how your ingredients complement one another.

Menus can also be planned by going to the farmers market first, seeing what appeals to you and then creating your menus from there. When you have a large garden, the menu pretty much creates itself; it's good practice as a sustainable gardener, however, to keep a close eye on how much harvest there might actually be and what you anticipate is ripening, so that you can make the best use of it.

How to Use Leftovers Wisely

COMMITTING TO NOT WASTING LEFTOVERS WILL INSPIRE (AND REQUIRE) you to become an innovative and original cook. The only rule of thumb is that you want to use leftovers quickly. Depending on how much of a dish you have left over, you can decide whether to freeze it for later use or refrigerate it to either reheat or use in another dish.

Since leftovers lose nutritional value each time they are reheated, I like to ensure that no more than one half of any new dish I make involves leftovers. For instance, if I'm making a casserole of leftover rice and beans, I will mix in freshly sautéed vegetables and add cheese on top. Here are some basic ideas to stimulate your creative reuse of foods:

Beans can be used in burritos, salads, omelettes, soups, wraps, or to make bean dip.

Vegetables, raw or cooked, can be used in salads, soups, spreads, stews, wraps, pasta dishes, sandwiches, nori rolls, burritos, pizza, omelettes, or casseroles.

Fruit can be used in salads, in smoothies/juice, to make soups, or to make desserts or baked goods.

Oatmeal or hot cereal can be heated again once or baked into bread or muffins.

Rice and grains can be used for salads, nori rolls, soups, stews, stir-frys, wraps, or baked into bread. You can also blend rice into cream-of-rice cereal for breakfast and serve it with toasted nuts and milk or make arroz con leche for breakfast or dessert.

Pasta can be used for salads, soups, wraps, or even baked into bread.

Rice noodles are great in nori rolls, stir-frys, soups, salads, or wraps.

Bread can be used to make mini pizzas, meatloaf, bread pudding, croutons, or can be turned into bread crumbs to serve as a topping on various dishes.

Leftover herbs can be turned into dressings, spreads and sauces, or added to just about any dish.

Leftover salad can be used in wraps, or pureed with tomato juice into a chilled vegetable drink.

Most food remains good in the refrigerator for three to five days. Please remember that leftovers should only be reheated once in order to preserve the freshness of the food. According to the FDA, between 40°–140°F (5°–60°C) bacteria multiply rapidly, so food should not linger in that temperature range. Leftovers should not remain at room temperature, but should instead be placed in the refrigerator, freezer, or oven to cook. Foods should not be left out for more than two hours (one hour if the air temperature is above 90°F).

Recycling the "Regulars"

If there are foods you buy (or harvest) each week that serve as "regulars" in your diet, you can develop an easy plan for using them when there are leftovers. At the monastery, for instance, there were three food-recycling tasks that were built into weekly menus no matter what:

Applesauce

As apples were always available at our snack table (both store-bought and from our own tree), the cook regularly checked the apple collection for softening apples and knew when it was time to make applesauce, prepared simply with just apples, cinnamon and lemon juice. The applesauce could then be served with our homemade granola and yogurt, or enjoyed warm on freshly baked bread. There are few things better than homemade applesauce on soft warm bread!

Oatmeal and Hot Cereal

Since oatmeal or another hot cereal was a staple every morning, the protocol was to reheat leftovers from the previous day for breakfast and then to set aside any additional leftover cereal for bread baking. We would use it to prepare fresh oatmeal-spelt bread with chunks of walnuts or whole-wheat bread with pecans and amaranth.

Croutons/Bread Crumbs

Because we were always baking fresh bread at the monastery, the cook carefully monitored bread leftovers and found secondary uses for everything from mini pizzas to bread pudding. The primary use, however, would be to chop the bread up into bite-size chunks, drizzle the chunks with olive oil and a savory herb blend and then bake them into croutons. As a last resort, leftover bread could be blended up to use as bread crumbs, a special topping for everything from scalloped potatoes to casseroles.

Some cooks I know have set "leftover days/meals" as part of their weekly menu scheduling and they simply cook extra for those days. For instance, at Green Gulch Farm in Muir Beach, California, the cook plans on a big leftovers night every Sunday, in addition to at least two other leftover meals per week, and then uses leftover salads and spreads for Bag Lunch day every Friday.

At the end of the week during meditation retreat, a meal the locals called "gruel" was served, which translates to a creative casserole made of leftovers. Gruel was often a rice, bean, vegetable and tofu dish sprinkled with melted cheese and I found myself surprised by how much I enjoyed "gruel" every time. Green Gulch Farm uses this guideline to help create less food waste, while providing three meals per day for 100–200 people each week. Imagine how we could reduce food waste on a large scale if more kitchens adopted this commitment to the creative use of leftovers!

How Does an Urban Cook Adopt These New Practices?

MY OWN COOKING INTENTIONS EACH WEEK BEGIN WITH FOLLOWING the basic guidelines that I presented in Chapter Four. I live an active lifestyle in the context of a busy urban environment. While the time I can devote to cooking is limited on weekdays, it is a peaceful, pleasurable and rejuvenating part of each day.

My diet is based on eating organic, local, seasonal foods and on what my body's needs are, what tastes good to me and what I can afford. I also choose to avoid processed foods, additives, and sugar. I focus on how to make the least expensive, easiest, greenest, most nutritious and enjoyable meals I can. I LOVE to cook and consider it a meditation. The effort and time I put into cooking supports my well-being and aligns me with my values every day.

I take time every Sunday to visit the local farmers market and then spend an hour or two preparing foods for the week. I might prepare some veggies by washing and chopping them so that they are ready to cook with or to snack on. I usually make a large pot of soup (hot in the colder months and chilled in summertime), a dressing or spread and an array of my favorite ingredients for salads, sandwiches, stir-frys or wraps.

For instance, I might toast or soak nuts and seeds, hard-boil some eggs, roast some root vegetables in the fall, prepare a homemade salad dressing, or make a large cucumber salad in the summertime. I also store my newly harvested or purchased fresh herbs in a glass of water so that they stay fresh and I am grateful for the addition of fresh basil, thyme, or mint in my menu every day of the week. I might also prepare some sprouts and chop/ freeze some fruit for smoothies.

By preparing the basics—soups, spreads, dressings and ingredients for salad and more elaborate cooking—I am fully prepared for simple, quick, and delicious meals every day. I can easily whip up a simple soup, a stir-fry, or a wrap any day of the week. I'm prepared to toss a fresh salad every day for lunch, which might include veggies, fruit, nuts and seeds and protein, with my favorite salad dressing drizzled on top. I can make nori rolls in five minutes using rice as a base, veggies and whatever leftovers I have that day and also prepare a beautiful meal for unexpected guests. The one to two hours of time I take on Sunday for food preparation after shopping sets me up for healthy (and sometimes seemingly decadent) eating all week long. I sometimes repeat the process later in the week.

There is an intention behind everything I cook. I know that if I make a batch of rice, it will serve three or four purposes: served fresh initially with beans or a stir-fry, and then tossed into a salad, added to miso-vegetable soup, or rolled into nori rolls. With this system, I have an amazing array of meals for the week and it takes me little time and little money to do it.

This process may sound complex, but it is actually quite simple. Think of cooking as an art form, like painting. If we approach cooking in this manner, we want to have a variety of ingredients available, just as an artist has different color pigments, to use creatively in the moment. In this case, the art is sustainable cooking and the colors we choose include produce that's in season, ingredients that complement what needs to be used, recipes that are human-friendly and not too time-consuming, etc.

There are certain basic ingredients it helps to always have on hand, such as garlic, ginger, onions, lemon, healthy oils, nuts, and a variety of fresh herbs. You might think of these as "primary colors." From these primary colors you can create a whole range of tastes. I'm always aware of food recycling possibilities and even when I go out to eat and order a meal, I'll often have a creative inspiration for recycling the leftovers.

All you need to do is begin practicing some of the key components I have described above and then experiment with menu planning and design. Let your senses guide you in the creation of meals that bring taste, color, smells and textures together in ways that delight and nourish you.

....

The Toxic Barrel

ANY TIME WE ARE TALKING ABOUT FOOD AND HEALTH, IT IS IMPORtant to consider the notion of the **toxic barrel**. Living 100% toxin-free in this day and age would be a challenge. Even living on a secluded property in the country, there might be contamination such as upstream residue of pesticides, or bees carrying pesticides into your garden, or air pollution carried over from a faraway city.

The "toxic barrel effect" is a metaphor in which you imagine a barrel filling slowly with water. In this metaphor, the barrel is your body and the water is the toxins that enter your system day by day from various sources of exposure. One doesn't know when the barrel will fill completely and spill over. This is the same with the body. We have resilient bodies and we seem to do fine and handle it, until one day our body has too many toxins and begins to fail us.

"**Body burden**" is a process in which substances build up faster in the body than the body can eliminate. This is also known as "chemical load" or "bioaccumulation." In my experience, most people are not aware of the toxins they ingest with their food because they are hidden in fats, sugars, MSG and other additives that are literally overloading our food supply. We are doing ourselves and our loved ones an important service when we bring awareness to this and take action by eating organically, eating simply and making more of our own food.

Here are a few tips I have found helpful for sustainable cooking:

Learn to Make Quick and Easy Gourmet Soups

I typically make a pot of soup every week. Soups can be one of the most economical, nutritious, easy, energy-efficient and delicious meals in the world; they are also a really easy meal for utilizing leftovers. While you can experiment and explore different recipes, there are three kinds of simple soups that never fail:

Basic vegetable soup:

Prepare a soup base of minced sautéed onions and garlic, to which you can add grated ginger and/or any combination of spices that suit your taste. Sauté this base lightly in water or healthy oil. It makes for a flavorful no-fail soup base. Once you've created your base, you can simply add vegetables (fresh and leftover) and enough water or stock to cover the vegetables. You might also add lentils or beans (sorted and soaked). Bring the ingredients to a boil, cover the pot loosely, turn the flame down to simmer and let the soup cook for 20 minutes at least. You can add fresh herbs if you wish at the end and sea salt or pepper to taste, cover again and turn the flame OFF for the last 10 minutes, so that the soup can cook on its own. You might also add miso, tamari, lemon, or one of your homemade sauces for added flavor. If you add beans you will want the soup to cook longer, depending on the kind of bean. You can also add fish or chicken to the pot. I have made a hundred tasty variations from this vegetable soup base.

Creamy vegetable soup:

If you have a good blender or Vita-Mix, you can make a delicious creamy soup in 10 minutes. Simply sauté some onions and garlic (optional ginger), add the vegetable of your choice to the pot (carrots, broccoli, cabbage, squash, whatever you choose) and cook for eight minutes covered or until just soft. Add a spoonful of miso, a handful of nuts (almonds or cashews are my favorites) and blend until smooth and creamy. I have dazzled many a potluck in my community with a rich creamy soup that took 10 minutes to make and cost barely anything. Cream of carrot, cream of broccoli, cream of squash, cream of whatever is in season! My favorite version is to use one head of cabbage, a handful of almonds or cashews and fresh dill. It is one of the least expensive meals to prepare, yet delicious and seemingly decadent when served with a thick slice of healthy bread on a cold day. You can add milk or your favorite non-dairy milk if you would like to. The nuts add enough protein so that this soup can serve as a meal in itself. Preparing a garnish of chopped dill, chopped basil, or shredded nori seaweed adds the final touch.

Miso soup:

After sautéing your base (onions/garlic/ginger), add the fresh garden vegetables and/or sea vegetables of your choice, always starting with root vegetables and heartier vegetables so that they can cook longer. Then add tofu or another protein, if you choose, and add any leftover vegetables you may have. Stir in the miso just at the end (being sure not to bring it to a boil, which kills the miso). Served with rice and perhaps topped with gomasio (ground sesame seeds and sea salt), lemon juice, or another topping of your choice, this is a simple satisfying meal.

In the warmer seasons, you can easily prepare chilled soups, ranging from gazpacho or creamy cucumber soup to summer fruit soup or vichyssoise.

Quick Homemade Dressings, Dips and Sauces (with fresh ingredients and no additives or packaging)

MOST PEOPLE I KNOW NEED QUICK AND EASY-TO-MAKE RECIPES FOR the majority of their meals, at least during the work week, and then make time for more leisurely meals on the weekend. Here are some ideas for how to throw together great meals that are fast, fun and easy. Again, my recommendation is to spend a little time on Sunday (or whatever day of the week you have more time to devote to cooking) making these dips and spreads to be used in varying ways during the rest of the week.

If you make the effort, you will discover the pleasure of having homemade salad dressings and sauces on hand that are made from whole organic ingredients and herbs you grow or buy at the local farmers market. It is also a wonderful way to cut down on the packaging that comes into your home and on the toxins that come into your diet. Making your own dips and dressings will not only turn your menu into that of a gourmet restaurant, it will also save you money spent on packaged dips and dressings made with additives, preservatives, sugar, excessive salt and processed ingredients.

Following are a few of my favorites: Middle Eastern Cilantro Dip, Green Goddess Dip, Miso-Pesto Spread, Lemon-Tahini Dressing, and Olive-Tahini Spread. These can be made in minutes and used as spreads on toast or served on sandwiches, salads, rice and noodle dishes, nori rolls, wraps and sometimes as a soup or stew base. The point is that these are versatile foods and this is another easy way to set your kitchen up to make easy-to-prepare foods in little time during the week. Homemade sauces can enhance your whole diet while saving time and money. Spreads are a great way to use farmers market produce for so much more than you do now.

Dressings, Dips And Sauces:

Middle Eastern Cilantro Dip:

2 bunches cilantro
1/2 cup olive oil
2 tbs water
1–2 cloves minced garlic
1 tbs plus 1 tsp cumin
½ tsp sea salt or 2 tsp Bragg's amino acids (the consistency changes slightly
   with the extra liquid)
1 tbs plus 1 tsp lemon juice

Blend all ingredients together until perfectly smooth and creamy. Add salt or lemon to taste.

This spread is strong and spicy, and it can be spread onto bread, crackers, or pita, used as a base for soups, stews, and rice dishes, or spread onto lavash rolls, or sandwiches.

Green Goddess Dip/Dressing:

14 oz. organic tofu (typically 1 package)
1 avocado
½ bunch kale or 1–2 cups leftover kale or other greens
2 tbs lemon juice
1 tbs plus 1 tsp Bragg's amino acids or tamari
½–1 cup roughly chopped fresh basil
1 small clove garlic, minced
1 tbs light miso

Cut the tofu in half and set it aside. Roughly chop the kale and steam it, stems and all, saving the liquid for stock. In a blender, blend ½ tofu, kale, lemon juice, basil, garlic, Bragg's, miso, and ½ the avocado. Pour the mixture into a bowl, dice the remaining avocado, and stir it into the spread. Then crumble the remaining tofu with your hands and mix it into the dip, to create a creamy but textured spread. Add sea salt and lemon to taste.

This spread is great for sandwiches, salads, as a dip for crackers or vegetables, or to spread on wraps. It can even be mixed with rice or quinoa for a quick meal. Serves 6.

Miso Pesto:

1 cup fresh basil leaves, packed
½ cup olive oil
1 tbs light miso
2 cloves garlic
¼ cup plus 1 tbs almonds

Combine all ingredients in a food processor or blender and blend until almost smooth. Add sea salt to taste.

This pesto can be used as a spread, served with pasta, pizza, or on a wrap, or added to soups, stews, and other hot dishes for a delicious taste.

Lemon Tahini Dressing:

½ cup tahini
2 tbs olive oil
The juice of 2 lemons
2 cloves minced garlic
½ cup water
1 tsp apple cider vinegar
1 tsp agave syrup
2 tsp tamari

Pepper to taste

This is one of my favorite salad dressings and it can also be used as a dip or a spread on sandwiches and wraps.

Olive Tahini Spread:

1 cup packed Kalamata olives, pitted
1 tbs plus 2 tsp lemon juice
1 tbs Bragg's
1 tbs water
Optional: salt or agave nectar to taste

Blend all ingredients together until smooth using a blender or food processor.

With these spreads, I can prepare a stir-fry or curry one day (for instance, adding cilantro dip or miso pesto to the base), make sandwiches and salad the next day, use the leftovers for a soba noodle salad the next day, and wrap the soba noodle salad into nori rolls for yet another meal, to dip in my homemade sauce. Wraps and nori rolls are one of my favorite ways to make a delicious meal out of leftovers. Here are a couple of ideas for how to make use of leftovers in wraps and rolls.

Nori Rolls

Nori rolls are a great way to turn leftovers into a colorful nutritious meal. One of the great things about nori rolls is that you can fill them with anything that suits your fancy. You might like traditional rice and vegetable rolls or you might like avocado and red pepper rolls with roasted cashews, and if you are an omnivore, wild-caught salmon. You can fill them with just about anything! Here is a basic recipe and some ideas to get you started.

> 2 sheets of nori
> Organic miso
> 1/2–3/4 cup cooked (leftover) rice. In my experience you can use any kind of rice and warm rice works best. You can also use leftover noodles.
> Colorful leftover vegetables cut into long thin strips if possible, such as: carrots (raw or cooked), cucumber, broccoli, beets, peppers, scallions, baked squash, sprouts, avocado, burdock, daikon, snap peas, etc. You can also add chopped steamed greens into the mix.
> Flavorful amendments include: roasted chopped nuts, sunflower seeds, fresh seasonal herbs such as basil, cilantro, mint, dried coconut, gomasio, almond butter, or a leftover spread of your choice.
> Optional: the protein of your choice, such as, if you are vegetarian, tofu, tempeh, or seitan. If you are an omnivore, scrambled or hard-boiled eggs, salmon or the sustainable fish of your choice.

Lay the nori on a flat surface horizontally. Using a butter knife, spread a little bit of miso or other spread along the far edge. Then begin spreading a thin layer of rice about 1/8–1/4 inch thick evenly covering 3/4 of the sheet of nori, leaving 1–2 inches clear at the far edge where the miso is. Then add the protein, vegetables, and amendments of your choice, laying all ingredients horizontally along the edge closest to you. Lastly, start at the edge closest to you and delicately but firmly roll the wrap into itself. It can take a few times to master the art of rolling so that the wrap stays together well. Once the roll is made, you can use a sharp serrated knife to cut it into 5 or 6 pieces per roll, dipping the knife into water in between each cut.

Arrange on a plate and serve with the dip of your choice, for instance tamari, tamari/lemon, tamari/rice vinegar, or a homemade salad dressing.

Makes 2 meal servings or a plate of hors d'oeuvres.

Lavash Leftovers Wrap

Making a lavash wrap with leftovers is an almost identical process to making nori rolls, though the end result is a different dish completely. This recipe can be modified with alternatives to lavash bread for people who are sensitive to wheat and gluten. Lavash wraps can be made to be Mediterranean, Latin, Asian, or any other influence you desire. Here is one recipe that I like, especially in the summer.

> 2 pieces lavash bread (you can also use tortillas or homemade chapati)
> Creamy spread (such as one of the homemade spreads above) or hummus, cream cheese, or tofu spread for instance
> Leftover lentils or beans
> Any of the following vegetables of your choice: tomatoes, cucumber, scallions, caramelized onions, bell peppers, avocado, or sprouts
> Any of the following amendments: chopped nuts, olives, or feta cheese
> Chopped seasonal herbs such as cilantro, basil, mint or dill

Using a butter knife, spread the spread (or multiple spreads) 1/8 inch thick on the lavash bread and scatter the lentils, vegetables, and amendments generously over the spread, leaving 1–2 inches at the far edge clear. Roll the wrap carefully into itself with your fingers. You can either use a serrated knife to cut the wrap into pieces for serving or you can eat it in one piece.

How to Use Organic, Locally-Grown Produce for More Meals than You Can Imagine

ORGANIC, LOCAL AND SEASONAL PRODUCE SERVES AS THE BASE FOR every meal I create. We get so many vital nutrients from the plant world! Most people are looking for ways to incorporate more diverse vegetables and fruits into their diets, but feel limited in terms of ways they can prepare produce for a variety of meals. If you join a CSA, you are likely to receive some vegetables you are not even familiar with, and you will want to find new and creative ways to prepare produce.

Here are some tips and creative ideas for using produce and diversifying your meals:

- Collect a wide array of colorful salad veggies to have on hand each week. Consider preparing: roasted peppers, caramelized onions, roasted root vegetables, grated beets and carrots, steamed asparagus, baked squash, fresh sprouts, and pickled vegetables, depending on the season.
- Are "salad greens" the only vegetables we can use to make salad? Why not rotate with kale, chard and other raw greens (that are more nutrient-rich than lettuce) for a more diverse experience?
- For breakfast, why not serve your eggs with a generous side of steamed or sautéed greens or use them in an omelette? Consider cooking greens as a side dish for lunch and dinner as well.
- If you make a pot of creamy vegetable soup on Sunday, consider serving it for breakfast with a side of toast and almond butter. I know eating soup for breakfast may sound strange, but try it. You might be surprised by how nice it is to have a bowl of soothing, creamy, vegetable soup to start your day.
- Can we use raw greens creatively? For example, I like to use collard or chard leaves to make healthy wraps, filled with a green goddess dip, grated veggies and toasted sesame seeds or rice, hummus and beans.
- Why not experiment with making vegetable paté or creating your own spreads, by blending up raw vegetables, nuts, seeds and herbs in creative ways?
- When they are in season, you can use zucchini or summer squash for everything from soups to spreads to smoothies, because they are so easy to grow and they serve as such a wonderful base and thickener in cooking.
- Consider making your own kim chi or sauerkraut to add a delicious source of probiotics to your diet.

Smoothies

Smoothies are another way to pack healthy nutrient-rich produce into a delicious snack or meal. I like to have a smoothie once a day and I love coming up with different combinations based on the season. I sometimes include a couple leaves of raw kale, but this is optional. It's easy to grow kale year-round where I live and wonderful for your health! Here are a few ideas to get you started:

- apple juice, yogurt, almond butter, and the fruit of your choice
- coconut water, fresh seasonal berries, hemp protein powder, and almond butter (add a scoop of yogurt if you eat dairy)
- apple juice, kale, cinnamon, avocado, agave and hemp powder
- apple juice, zucchini, kale, lemon and berries (with a healthy sweetener and hemp powder if desired)
- coconut water, ground cacao, almond butter and stevia sweetener (for a dessert smoothie)
- orange juice, banana, and protein powder

I know these combinations might sound odd, but they are actually delicious and knowing how many nutrients are going into my body when I consume these smoothies makes me feel great. Depending on the season I might add ice or fruit I have frozen in advance. Depending on the season and the type of smoothie I am making, I sometimes add lettuce and even cucumbers. Smoothies are a great way to use these vegetables.

The Palette/Menu of Interconnection

At the monastery where I trained, planning the weekly menu was a kind of dance. It required one to pay attention to what was available in the garden (what could be harvested and what had to be harvested—for instance, lettuce beginning to bolt), the weather, the number of people on the property to be fed at the time, the amount of hands available to help with each meal, the economics of each meal, the nutritional balance of each meal and of course paying attention to the taste and display of the meal. It was therefore an exercise in interconnection rather than simply a question of "what do I want to eat today?" or "what's fast and cheap to prepare?"

Most of us non-monk types may think we do not have these same factors to consider, nor do most of us cook three meals a day or have a set schedule for meals; however, each of us has a web of interconnection in our own home, property, and community to dance with. Some basics are:

- Always pay attention to the amount of food needed to avoid creating waste.
- Take a moment after each meal to carefully store the leftovers in either the freezer or the fridge.
- Take a few minutes each day to consider a creative use for the leftovers.
- When reheating leftovers, cook just the amount that is needed, as leftovers lose their vitamin content with each reheat. Remember the guideline to put something over heat no more than two times. You can add leftovers in small amounts as an accent to whatever is supplying the primary nutrition of the meal.
- Have fun with leftovers… See what kind of super creative wrap, pizza, or casserole you can make with leftovers.

Here are some examples of weekly menus that incorporate the recycling principle into simple meals. You might begin by picking one week to take on this challenge and explore how to apply this concept to your own tastes and preferences.

Sunday—Spend Approximately 2 Hours Preparing Food for the Week
- Granola (10 minutes to prep, 45 minutes to bake)
- Roasted vegetables (13 minutes to prep, 1 hour to bake)
- Pesto-Miso spread (5 minutes to make)
- Garbanzo beans for salads (soaked the night before, 5 minutes to prep, 1 hour to cook)
- Hard-boiled eggs (no prep time, 7–10 minutes to cook) and/or the protein of your choice, such as baked tempeh, organic turkey, or wild-caught salmon (cooking time varies)

- Toasted nuts and seeds (3 minutes)
- Simple soup, such as Creamy Broccoli (10 minutes to cook)
- Pot of rice (30 minutes to cook)

BREAKFAST: farmers market fruit, toast and almond butter

LUNCH: roasted vegetables, rice, toasted nuts and seeds

DINNER: Creamy Broccoli soup made earlier in the day, bread, Pesto-Miso spread

Monday

BREAKFAST: homemade granola, yogurt, toasted nuts

LUNCH (to pack): big salad with garbanzo beans, hard-boiled eggs, roasted veggies and nuts/seeds

DINNER: rice, Cream of Brocooli soup, and Pesto-Miso spread (all made Sunday)

Tuesday

BREAKFAST: farmers market fruit, homemade granola

LUNCH: big salad with seasonal vegetables, garbanzo beans, the protein of your choice, and Pesto-Miso spread

DINNER: simple bruschetta (wholesome bread baked with Pesto-Miso spread, cheese and finely chopped roasted veggies), Cream of Broccoli soup

Wednesday

BREAKFAST: scrambled eggs, greens (make extra greens and save liquid from greens)

LUNCH: sandwiches made with the protein of your choice, spread and cheese; farmers market fruit

DINNER: use all leftovers from Sunday to make nori rolls (rice, leftover spread, roasted veggies, and greens from breakfast), simple miso soup (make enough soup for 2 meals)

Thursday

BREAKFAST: farmers market fruit, granola

LUNCH: smoothie with seasonal fruit and protein powder, big salad with seasonal vegetables and toasted nuts

DINNER: one-pot meal (and make extra) of rice and lentils (25 minutes to make), steamed veggies

Friday

BREAKFAST: farmers market fruit, granola, yogurt

LUNCH: big salad and leftover miso soup

DINNER: leftover rice and lentils

Saturday—Use It All Up Day

BREAKFAST: omelette with eggs, seasonal vegetables, and cheese toast

LUNCH: leftovers wrap: chapati/tortilla, lentils and rice, spread, chopped tomatoes and avocados if in season, caramelized onions and grated vegetables

DINNER: simple pasta or GO-OUT NIGHT

Healthy Easy Snacks to Have On Hand
(Some of these can be prepared on Sunday)

- Hard-boiled eggs
- Smoothies, with farmers market fruit and protein powder
- Easy greens soup
- Nuts and seeds
- Trail mix
- Nori rolls
- Healthy crackers and cheese
- Raw chocolate protein balls
- Raw collard wraps
- Fresh fruit
- Vegetables and dip
- Rice cakes and nut butter

An Even Simpler Weekly Menu

Sunday

Prepare a one-pot meal, wash greens for smoothies, chop veggies for snacks and easy cooking, make one dip/spread/dressing, soak or toast nuts/seeds and prepare at least one easy
protein to have on hand for salads and sandwiches (such as baked tempeh, hard-boiled
eggs, or organic chicken)

BREAKFAST: smoothie with greens

LUNCH: one-pot meal

DINNER: salad with protein and spread, bread or rice, nuts/seeds

Monday

BREAKFAST: smoothie, oatmeal

LUNCH: one-pot meal, side of greens

DINNER: salad with the protein of your choice, homemade spread, bread or rice,
nuts/seeds

Tuesday

BREAKFAST: smoothie with greens

LUNCH: one-pot meal

DINNER: salad with the protein of your choice, homemade spread, bread or rice,
nuts/seeds, simple soup (make extra for 4 meals)

Wednesday

BREAKFAST: smoothie with greens

LUNCH: simple soup, sandwich with spread and cheese, fruit (or wrap with one-
pot meal and cheese, etc.)

DINNER: casserole with one-pot meal and melted cheese

Thursday

BREAKFAST: smoothie, oatmeal

LUNCH: sandwich, fruit

DINNER: pasta with protein, salad, baked pears

Friday

BREAKFAST: smoothie with greens

LUNCH: pasta salad, the protein of your choice, tossed salad

DINNER: salad with baked pears, walnuts, cheese, leftover soup

Saturday

BREAKFAST: omelette with vegetables

LUNCH: baked potatoes with grated cheese, homemade spread, and a salad

DINNER: pasta salad casserole with sauteed vegetables added in, and topped with melted cheese, and the protein of your choice.

To Consider:

Think about the amount of food that gets "tossed" in your own life, over the period of a month. What if you committed, for one month, to creating zero waste in your kitchen and see what kind of creativity this inspires in you?

Self-Reliance Is Fun and Doesn't Have to Take a Lot of Time:

Things You Can Make Yourself

If you are a real foodie, you can take it a step further and learn to prepare certain foods yourself that you have traditionally purchased ready-made. Consider a good friend of mine who uses her large organic garden as the base of her diet and makes her own bread, crackers, granola, garden-based dressings and spreads each week.

She only has to buy beans, eggs, nuts, rice, soy milk, almond butter and staples such as olive oil and butter. Another friend, although she lives in a city, grows most of her own vegetables, gets honey from a neighbor who keeps bees and sprouts her own sprouts.

Self-reliance does not have to take a lot of time. There are a number of hands-on practices you can adopt in your kitchen to improve the quality of your life, your palette and your overall sustainability.

Why Make Your Own? Rethinking our Dependency on Processed Foods

Like the simple cleaning solutions that I will propose you make yourself from wholesome ingredients (Chapter Seven), there are easy recipes for healthy basic foods that you can grow or make from scratch. This will help you to overcome the belief that your life requires lots of extra stuff: packaged stuff, stuff with additives, stuff that costs money and more stuff.

I invite you to experience the satisfaction and fulfillment of making a home-cooked meal, or perhaps preparing for yourself some food item that you have always bought in the store. Making your own food, like gardening, gives one a real appreciation for nature and food like nothing else can.

Years ago in San Francisco, a housemate discovered the abundance of olive trees growing down the street in Dolores Park. We were in a big "do-it-yourself" phase in our community house, and my housemate decided to learn to cure her own olives. We gathered fresh olives from the park (leaving plenty for everyone else who would choose to harvest), soaked them in water, and set aside two closed bins in our pantry for olive curing. Olive curing is a slow process over time and the result is one of the most delicious and sensual foods on the planet (in my opinion). My housemate fell in love with the process so thoroughly that she soon moved north to olive tree country and set out to cure olives with the pros.

Some of the foods you can grow or make on your own, and have a great time in the process, are:

- Growing your own herbs, sprouts and mushrooms
- Making your own bread, granola, no-bake sprouted crackers, tortillas
- Making your own soy milk, yogurt
- Making your own sun tea
- Raising bees/harvesting honey
- Curing your own olives
- Drying your own fruit
- Fermenting foods, such as making kim chi, sauerkraut, or kombucha
- Making gomasio (sesame seed salt) and other homemade condiments

Visit the Resource List in the back of this book for more information or pick up a copy of *The Urban Homestead*. Check out *The Monastery Cookbook* for the world's best granola recipe and bread-baking instructions, as well as pages of my all-time favorite vegetarian recipes. Try gathering together some of your friends and neighbors and find out if anyone wants to try making and trading any of the above do-it-yourself edibles. Perhaps one neighbor has an avocado tree and regularly makes guacamole, or another neighbor makes tortillas and yet another might grow sprouts. Community food-sharing is a great way to save money while eating well (and building community!)

But I Don't Have Time To Cook, Let Alone Plan Menus!

Yes and that is why this book has been written. This is the frame of mind that we are working with. How can we accept this and work with it, rather than let it limit us? This morning, for instance, I was supposed to wake up early, meditate and then write for three hours before 10 a.m.

The alarm didn't go off, however, and I slept in for over an hour (it's a Saturday, after all). When I finally woke up, I plopped down onto the meditation cushion, knowing that meditating in the morning is non-negotiable for me. I then started writing, noticed it was time for a breakfast break and then I heard a voice say, "You don't need to prepare food. You've got plenty of energy. Just keep writing."

Really? I felt a little suspicious, but I kept writing. Then I stopped. I know my body and I was aware that taking some time to make myself good quality food would be a wise decision. I know that I am well worth the time it takes and that if I don't prepare something to sustain me during the day, I will feel the impact later. I therefore took off half an hour from my writing to prepare a simple delicious breakfast and lunch. I took care of myself and then continued on with my writing, feeling nourished and energized.

Consider that a sustainable kitchen requires more participation in the cycle of our food than we are used to. It also requires compassionate self-discipline. Perhaps it's time to trade in some of the time we might spend watching TV, surfing the Internet, or checking Facebook to do something that will bring you even greater fulfillment.

Perhaps you can only find a couple of extra hours in your week for food preparation, but those hours are worth it. That may be all it takes to make a significant change in your life and begin to revolutionize your relationship with food. Perhaps you have already made such a change and noticed the benefits. Investing time in cooking and menu planning will only improve your health and overall well-being.

About What We Eat and What We Are Feeding

"I don't eat junk food and I don't think junk thoughts."
—Peace Pilgrim

THE FOOD I MAKE MYSELF IS AN ACT OF CARE AND IT TAKES CARE OF me on many levels. I love that I live in a city, but am nevertheless able to eat a diet based on organic local whole foods, avoid additives and processed foods entirely and eat a delicious balanced affordable diet. In the past, I have followed certain diets and disciplines that were supposed to be healthy, but instead were detrimental to my health and well-being. What I have learned through experience is that food isn't necessarily about "shoulds" and "prescriptions" because what may be appropriate for one person's body type, lifestyle and nutritional needs may not be appropriate for another's. It is about consciousness and ultimately learning to care for and pay attention to our bodies and at a more subtle level.

I am not here to preach any diet prescription. I am not a doctor nor am I an expert on diet. I am, however, someone who values peace, sustainability and health and who enjoys the interconnection I experience through sustainable cooking and eating. I have been, at various times in my life, a macrobiotic, a meat-eater, a devout vegetarian, a vegan, a gluten-free dieter, and I have experimented with raw foods. I have also struggled with food sensitivities at times in my life and I have healed health challenges through diet as well.

In my experience, food is just like everything else in our lives. The underlying beliefs with which we approach our lives are reflected in our relationship with food. For example, consider the messages we might be giving ourselves with the following:

"Life is about hard work and scarcity."
"There is not enough love to go around."
"If I do not drive myself to perfection, then I'll be a failure."
"I must take care of everyone else's needs first."
"No matter how hard I try, I'm just not good enough."

These are some examples of personal beliefs that might be reflected in our food choices. Are you aware of any underlying beliefs that might direct your relationship with food?

It is not ultimately possible, in my experience, to eat sustainably unless we have a kind relationship with ourselves and can be present for our relationship with food. There is a lot of unconsciousness around food in our culture and there is a lot of well-being to be tapped into by bringing awareness to this aspect of our lives. When I am centered and feeling peaceful and in my body, I naturally choose what nourishes my body, mind and soul. When I am rushed or stressed or my attention is involved elsewhere, I might make a food choice that actually affects my health negatively in some way. Have you had this experience?

I have learned that getting centered and letting my centered self choose the meal takes the best care of me. It is always helpful to pause and check in with ourselves before a meal, to tune in for a minute and notice how we are feeling. If I'm having a particularly stressful day, I like to use mealtime as an opportunity to pause and come back to a centered, peaceful place.

I've learned a couple of things in my life and one of them is that preaching my diet to someone else just isn't in good taste; however, I think it is important for me to at least present the following information so that others can choose what they want for their lives. In that spirit, here are some things to consider in approaching meals:

Don't put junk into your system—ever. Given the "toxic barrel" effect, why would you want to do this?

The healthier your diet is, the more you are healthy all around. A healthy diet is a golden investment in your long-term health.

There is some very useful information out there about diet, but it is best absorbed when each person learns *by experience* what actually makes a difference for his or her own body. Learn to trust your own experience over what you read.

Don't worry about what you eat… just be conscious about what you eat.

It's a disservice to ourselves to think we need to control ourselves into having a healthy body. If we take care of our bodies and practice living in the present, we will do more for ourselves than if we worry ourselves into the "perfect" diet. The point is if we get out of the way and let ourselves find our natural rhythm with eating, our bodies will thrive in a state of health and balance.

Everything in moderation, even moderation.

If you want your kids to eat healthy, why have any junk food around? Why not model the alternative?

We can only fully experience the pleasure and sensuality of a meal if we take the time to enjoy it and stay present.

If you get off track with a meal or with an entire day of unhealthy eating, simply drop any self-judgment and get back on track with the next meal.

CONSIDER:
- **What food wisdom have you developed on your path?**
- **Do you follow this wisdom?**

Sustainable Sweets: Having a Choice

BEYOND MY PERSONAL BIAS ABOUT SUGAR THAT HAD ME ONCE RAGING to a relative about what we should and should not be feeding my niece (OK, it was a not-so-centered day), sugar is a very important topic for us to address. The average American consumes two to three pounds of sugar each week, which is not surprising considering that highly refined sugars in the forms of dextrose (corn sugar), sucrose (table sugar) and high-fructose corn syrup are added into so many of our staple foods. These foods include bread, breakfast cereal, peanut butter, mayonnaise, spaghetti sauce, ketchup, canned foods, beverages, and microwave meals.

Most doctors/medical experts agree that sugar contributes to the following health problems (just to list some of them):

- Suppressed immune system
- Hyperactivity, anxiety, depression, concentration difficulties and crankiness in children
- Kidney damage
- Increased risk of coronary heart disease
- Interference with absorption of calcium and magnesium
- Tooth decay
- Acidic stomach

- Increase total cholesterol
- Weight gain and obesity
- Increased risk of Crohn's disease and ulcerative colitis
- Diabetes

It is unfortunate that one of our culture's biggest "treats" has such harsh consequences for us. Isn't it strange that one of the ways we celebrate has such a negative impact on our bodies? As a cook, I have learned how to prepare healthy and delicious sweets that take care of the people I am feeding and make their bodies feel good or even better than before they consumed it.

This is a much better experience than eating a sweet that can have harsh consequences on your health. I find our culture's relationship to sugar indicative of strange beliefs that we hold about pleasure and punishment. Nature is rich with healthy sweets and a kitchen aligned with nature utilizes alternatives to sugar, including fruit and fruit-based sweeteners, **agave** and natural sweeteners such as **brown rice syrup**, molasses, **stevia** and **xylitol**.

I encourage people to make informed choices about the role of sugar in their lives and perhaps to consider how to redefine their definition of pleasure derived through sweets. I acknowledge that we all have different perspectives about dessert and I share my perspective, taking into account that we have varying degrees of sensitivity to foods and varying tastes.

Some of us have no problem at all consuming a piece of sugary, white-processed-flour, chocolate cake. I am so food-sensitive, however, that I need to watch my intake of any form of sugar because of the way it makes me feel afterwards.

Today, as I write, I am looking around me at the food offered in the deli section of the café where I sit. The selection of sweets is all based on white sugar, heavy butter and white flour. The alternative that is offered at this deli is not much better: a Nutrasweet-sweetened frozen yogurt with zero fat, lots of chemicals and zero taste as far as I can tell. What is that all about? Why not learn to make healthy sweets and have a relationship with sweet treats that is nourishing to our souls and not depleting to our bodies and spirit?

Over the years in which I have asked myself these questions, I have found some delightful alternatives. I am known to arrive at a potluck with an unforgettable chocolaty dessert that shocks people once they learn the ingredients. I have also been known to surprise people with raw chocolate balls that are (honestly) the best treats ever, yet are actually a protein-packed food made with wholesome ingredients that vary according to the season.

Here are some ideas for SUSTAINABLE SWEETS. Some of these recipes are below. Others are easy to access online or in the cookbooks on the Resource List:

Summer

Vegan chocolate mousse pie served with fresh strawberries

Summer fruit soup

Raw chocolate balls—Summer version made with blueberries

Homemade fruit sorbet

Fall

Creamy Coconut Bliss served with fresh blueberries (Coconut Bliss is a natural agave-sweetened coconut-based ice cream available in health food stores. Please see the Resource List for more information.)

Pumpkin pudding

Raw chocolate balls—Fall version made with dates

Winter

Baked apples/pears

Almond agave clusters

Spring

Fresh fruit, served alone or with raw chocolate fondue

Raw chocolate balls—Spring version made with apricots

Here are a few delicious dessert recipes that offer varying alternatives to conventional sugar.

Homemade Fruit Sorbet

This is a delicious easy-to-make dessert that can be adapted to the seasons. Try it with: apricots, plums, berries, bananas, melon, mango, citrus fruit, and more, in whatever combinations appeal to your palate.

4 cups of fruit in bite-sized pieces

1 juiced lemon or lime (or a mix of both)

¼ cup agave syrup

First, freeze the fruit. Then blend it using a food processor or Vita-Mix until very finely chopped. Next add in all of the ingredients and blend it together until smooth and creamy. Serve immediately or store in the freezer, allowing 15 minutes for thawing before serving.

Serves 6.

Raw Chocolate Balls

These delicious chocolate treats are protein-packed and can be served as dessert or a healthy snack.

- ½ cup almonds, blended
- ½ cup dried blueberries, blended (can substitute with a local dried or fresh in season fruit)
- 4 tbs hemp powder
- ¾ cup plus 4 tbs plus cacao
- 4 tbs plus coconut oil
- 2 tbs plus agave
- 1/2 cup dried coconut
- 2 tbs almond butter
- Optional: coconut to roll the finished chocolate balls in

First, use a food processor or Vita-Mix to blend the almonds, cacao (if it is not already blended) and coconut. Set these ingredients aside in a bowl. Blend the dried fruit. Mix the dried fruit into the bowl and add all of the wet ingredients. Stir the mixture with a spoon and then knead the mixture with your hands until everything is evenly mixed and the dough is moist enough to stick together. If needed, you can add additional agave or coconut oil for consistency. Roll into 1 1/2–2 inch balls.

Please note that this chocolate ball recipe can be varied according to what is in season. For instance, in December I might add dates to the blueberry mix, or substitute them altogether, while in July I might add ripe strawberries. Makes 9 chocolate balls.

Vegan Chocolate Pudding Pie

Every community I have lived in has their version of a tofu chocolate pie. This is a version my sister perfected and it is truly decadent!

> 3 boxes of Mori-Nu silken tofu (12.3 ounces each) or approximately 37 ounces of silken tofu
> ¾ cup sweetener—maple syrup or agave (or a blend of the two)
> 1/8–1/4 cup apple juice
> 2 tsp vanilla
> 1 ¾ cup chocolate chips or barley malt chips

In a blender, mix the tofu, sweetener, apple juice, and vanilla until creamy and smooth. Melt the chocolate chips in a double boiler. Pour the melted chocolate into the mixture and blend again until creamy and smooth. Pour the mixture into a pie crust and let it chill and set in the refrigerator for at least four hours or even overnight. For a quicker dessert, you can skip the pie crust altogether and serve alone as pudding. Unless you have a large blender or Vita-Mix, you may have to blend the ingredients in batches.

Recipe makes 2 pies. (You can also halve the recipe to make one pie.)

Summer Fruit Soup

This recipe is adapted from *The Monastery Cookbook* (see Resource List) and can be served as a dessert or as part of the main meal, depending on your style.

> 3 c. orange juice
> 3 c. plain yogurt
> 4 c. fresh berries or chopped summer fruit of any kind, or a mixture of both
> 1 tbs lemon juice
> 1 tbs agave nectar
> A pinch of cinnamon and nutmeg

In a large bowl, whisk together the orange juice and yogurt. Add remaining ingredients and serve chilled. Serves 4–6.

Baked Apples:

4 large firm apples
¼ cup agave nectar
1 tbs lemon juice
1 tsp cinnamon
¼ tsp ground nutmeg
1 c. apple cider or ½ c. water
Optional: ¼ c. raisins
¼ c. finely chopped, toasted walnuts, pecans, or almonds

Preheat the oven to 350 degrees. Core the apples whole. Sprinkle with lemon juice and place the apples in a glass baking dish. Mix the agave, spices, and optional ingredients together. Fill the apples with this mixture. Pour the apple cider into the bottom of the dish and cover it with a lid. Bake for 25 minutes.

This dessert can be served warm or at room temperature, and can be served alone or with yogurt or ice cream. This dessert can also be made easy in a solar oven.

Reflections on My Sunday Ritual

Planning my weekly shopping list is an act of self-care. I look at my schedule, consider my goals and intentions for the week and align my menu to support those intentions. For instance, if I have a week with a big project or deadline, I like to eat really simply and limit cooking as much as possible while making sure I receive good nourishment.

When I have a little more time for cooking, I like to create more elaborate meals and put extra attention into activities such as seeking out unusual in-season produce, gathering fresh herbs for garnishes, perhaps planning a solar-cooked meal and making other special additions to my menu. In the heat of summertime I like to keep extra hydration around and I will make sure to collect herbs for a gigantic batch of iced sun tea. If I have a week of more day trips and meetings than usual, I prepare additional healthy snacks and travel foods to have on hand.

Preparing for the week ahead in this way makes me feel taken care of every day.

Creating the time for this organization and planning ahead really helps to keep me in alignment with my commitment to personal and planetary sustainability. In that planning, I am able to address everything from what kind of food I'm eating, to how much I am spending and how much waste my food intake creates. I find that without some form of planning ahead, I'm much more likely to run into situations where I cut corners, make compromises and veer away from my intentions.

On some Sundays, I will have a special date with a friend or my mom to go to the farmers market together and then afterwards spend a couple of hours cooking together for the week. The time we spend cooking and doing dishes together is time we get to visit and catch up. I then pack my food into labeled jars and know that for Monday morning, my fridge and freezer are filled with what I need to feel strong, centered and well-nourished throughout the week. ●

Chapter 7
SETTING UP A SUSTAINABLE KITCHEN:
Tips from a Hippie Grandmother

"The fewer items you have, the less time it will take to manage them."

—Anonymous

ONE OF THE FIRST ECO-KITCHENS I EVER STEPPED into belonged to my friend's hippie grandmother, who lived on a small homestead in the woods in Oregon. Her kitchen smelled of fresh rosemary, dried sage and freshly baked bread. The walls were natural wood and the window looked out upon an orchard, a garden with chickens, a pet goat and—to help "close the cycle"—a sizzling hot compost pile.

The pantry was lined with glass jars, while more upside-down jars with cheesecloth sprouted herbs by the window and a dehydrator sat by the back door. The kitchen felt cozy, warm, simple and uncomplicated. Dried herbs hung from the rafters and there were bowls of soaking beans on the counter. She used **solar tubes** for lights and had worked out systems for water collection and energy efficiency. Everything seemed to have a purpose and her property had a fun Swiss Family Robinson feel to it that I loved at the time.

While homesteading may or may not be your style, some of the basic wisdom of her "hippie kitchen" can easily be transferred to a more urban setting.

If you are a cook, you know the difference between cooking in a kitchen that is designed for enjoyment and efficiency versus a kitchen that is messy, disorganized, or sterile. A green kitchen is set up specifically to help you live in alignment with the principles of sustainability. In order to do any project successfully, you want to begin by setting up your space to support your intention.

In a recent consultation with a client, we laughed about how many kitchen items that she never uses were cluttering her kitchen: empty vases, specialty appliances her husband bought for "fun," decorations people gave her as gifts, extra items in storage "just in case," etc.

We also found that she didn't have the practical BASICS she might want to have in a green kitchen, such as an efficient water purification system, a good place to store compost scraps and to dry plastic bags, healthy storage containers and a solid, well-organized recycling system. This made her efforts to be green a lot more energy-draining than they needed to be, as she hunted down places to dry bags and lost fresh veggies in the back of her fridge and could never find the right containers when it was time for a shopping trip.

This section will help you to discern what you might want in your sustainable kitchen and what you might NOT want. Let's review the guiding principles for a sustainable kitchen.

Guiding Principles

- Conscious consumption of resources
- Conscious disposal of resources: zero waste
- Awareness of our energy use and carbon footprint
- Commitment to a safe, non-toxic world
- Responsibility for sustainable food security both locally and globally
- Financial sustainability
- Connection with a sense of place and community through food
- Mindfulness
- Efficiency and ease in design
- Giving back/generosity

At the Zen monastery where I trained, the kitchen was the heart of the community. We took care of the kitchen and the kitchen took care of us. There was mindfulness in how the meals were prepared and mindfulness in how they were cleaned up. The entire community participated in cleaning up every meal and no food was wasted. There was a sense of being cared for and a spirit of kindness pervaded every aspect of the kitchen. It was a model for harmonious living. Everyone who participated in meals with us was touched at a deep level by the attention and care that went into every aspect of the meal. I think most people recognized it pretty quickly as a model for how every aspect of life could be experienced peacefully.

A Peaceful Kitchen

CONSIDER:

Think about how your kitchen is set up already. How do you feel when you enter it? Consider the ways your kitchen takes care of you and the ways it does not. Imagine yourself entering a space that feels warm, relaxed, calming, beautiful, peaceful, nourishing, nurturing and loving. Your kitchen is an integral part of your home and family life. It nourishes the soul and provides sustenance to all who enter it. Consider what items you might want to add or take away from your kitchen to help create the atmosphere you want. Are there any organizational changes that would improve the design of your kitchen?

The Role of the Kitchen In Our Lives

In the distant past, our kitchens were called "common rooms." They were a mix of a kitchen/living room where numerous activities took place. The central focus was the large hearth, as it was the only source of heat and light and here women cooked or sewed, children played and small gatherings took place. Our kitchens have changed dramatically over the years and there has been a gradual movement since World War II that has led to the disintegration of the family dinner, a steady decrease in the number of Americans who actually cook, and a drop in food quality and nutritional value.

Despite these changes, the kitchen is still the hearth of most homes, and whatever tone we set in our kitchens is reflected in our lives. The kitchen sustains us through all of the different seasons of our lives (the celebrations, the day-to-day, the challenging times) and says a lot about our attitude toward ourselves and the world.

The shift that has taken place over time has been accompanied by increasing cultural ignorance about our food production system and how it relates to sustainability and global food security. Many people today eat the majority of their meals on the go and have little connection to the source of their food or control over how sustainable their meals are. Rather than our food serving to connect us to nature, our food often appears as packaged, processed, machine-made "stuff." Our food doesn't come from plastic or from machines, however—our food comes from nature.

By following the guidelines laid out in this book, anyone can incorporate the principles for a sustainable kitchen into their own kitchen—whether you live in a city, suburb and even when you are on the road. By changing the tone of our kitchens to being sustainable (eco-friendly and human friendly) in every way, we will experience increased health and well-being and simply feel better about the world we live in at the end of the day. We will also be, specifically, cutting down on fossil fuel use, pollution, trash, topsoil loss and a host of other environmental problems and threats to global food security.

You may want to go the whole way and do a green makeover of your diet, kitchen and cooking habits, or you may not be ready for that yet. Wherever you are, this book is written to support you in actualizing change rather than just thinking about it. There are many shades of green and in each decision you make, you will see the deep green choice and the light green choice and choices in between. All you need to do is to make the greenest choice you can make in each situation you address and appreciate yourself for every conscious choice you make.

Areas Every Natural Kitchen Needs to Address

YOU MAY ALREADY HAVE IMPLEMENTED SOME OF THESE IDEAS INTO your kitchen or they may be entirely new to you. Because most of us were not brought up with these guidelines in our kitchens, I will introduce you to the basic areas that need to be set up and addressed in a green kitchen:

- A water purification system
- A water recycling system
- Energy-efficient appliances
- An energy-efficient cooking system
- Safe food storage containers and cooking supplies
- A green eco-friendly pantry
- A water-wise dishwashing system
- Space for food preparation
- A radical recycling/creative reuse center
- A non-toxic cleaning section
- A green shopping section

- A green coffee/tea station
- A sustainable packaging station
- An herb parlor (fresh herbs, dried herbs, perhaps even drying herbs)
- A space for organizing information

How to Address Specific Areas In the Kitchen

Water Purification Systems

Both water purification and conservation are *primary* considerations for the green kitchen. I wish I had an easy answer (for us all) regarding water, but all I can do is to provide the information you need to make your own choices about a truly complex challenge that we face. I have provided information about water purification products and more extensive reading and website recommendations in the Resource List but will provide some basic guidelines here.

While the water quality varies in different cities and municipalities, we generally need a water filtration system to treat for lead, bacteria, chlorine, fluoride and industrial pollutants of all kinds. Think of water as a very friendly substance. It travels to you, most likely, from far away, and whatever water touches along the way it brings with it. It comes into contact with a lot of things... antibiotics, pesticides, pharmaceuticals, fluoride....By the time it reaches you, in the words of a colleague, it is like a "chemical soup."

I run into misconceptions all the time about water. The most common misconceptions are:

- Tap water is fine.
- Plastic bottles are fine. I've been using them for years.
- I use a Brita pitcher... that's enough, right?
- I get my water delivered... what's wrong with that?

The public has finally been alerted to the health dangers of drinking water from plastic containers (which I discuss later in this book) and, due to environmental factors, we know that using fossil fuels to produce and transport plastic is not a direction we can sustain. Until there are water purification plants set up in every municipality that are equipped to supply healthy and unpolluted water, I feel that it is up to every individual or household to ensure the quality of your water. Consider investing in clean water an investment in your long-term health and in how you feel every day of your life.

I recommend first educating yourself about your region's water quality (this information is available online, as noted in the Resource List) and making SURE you have a clean water source for both drinking and cooking purposes. Based on research I have done, here are the steps I have come up with:

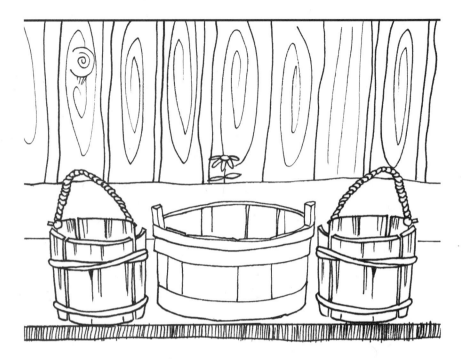

• Never drink plain tap water.
• Get test reports about the water in your area from the water utility company (for free) or a private lab. In addition, you can buy a TDS tester (which tests for total dissolved solids) for $25.
• Purchase a water filter to attach to your tap directly and base your choice on the particular conditions of your water as stated in the report. Different filters take out different pollutants.

The type of purifier you choose will depend on what pollutants you need to take out and what you can afford. For instance, basic carbon filters (typically all the filters available at places like Lowe's and Home Depot) take out chlorine and a few other basics, but not chloramine. As chloramine is as toxic as chlorine, if your water contains it, you need a different kind of filter altogether. (One I recommend is Culligan.) Few filters remove much of the fluoride from our water, and fluoride comes to us in a much more potent form than it used to. (Go Beyond Organic is a good choice for this.) If you do opt for a carbon filter, consider choosing one with a biodegradable filter.

Though pricey, one of the most thorough purifiers available is a four-stage **reverse osmosis** system (which includes a sediment filter, carbon block, reverse osmosis system, and post carbon block. See Oxygen Ozone on the Resource List). If you do use reverse osmosis, consider that it can waste water in the process of purification (another challenge) so you would need to find a company that can recycle any water wasted, for instance, to feed plants.

Debra Lynn Dadd, author of *Home Safe Home*, recommends that we take a further step. She points out that for truly healthy water, it needs to be both purified of toxins and alkalized or "reenlivened," ideally with a medical-grade alkalizer. While pollutants can be removed from water, the result is often denatured water, with a deadened quality compared to natural water. Some reverse osmosis systems address this issue as a final step.

Debra recalled an experience of drinking water from a natural spring at Mt. Shasta, California, and realizing that she was tasting real water for the first time. She reminds us that our drinking water should mimic "the real thing" as much as possible.

I wish we could all afford this more expensive system to purify our water, but there are other quality filters that can be connected to your tap). To get a basic sense of affordable options on the market and to compare cost-effectiveness, you can visit **waterfiltercomparisons.net**. If you cannot afford a water filter, another healthy option, though less convenient, is to support your local water store, where you can ask to view their test results and fill a jug for only 25 cents.

A water filtration system is non-negotiable in a sustainable kitchen. There are a lot of unknowns about the exact amount of toxins in our water, and how much humans can handle. In the words of Colin Ingram, author of *The Drinking Water Book*, "You can reduce your overall health risk by reducing your overall toxic load." Rather than accept so-called "safe" levels of pollution, it is best to reduce as many pollutants in your water as you can by making conscious choices.

We must also consider the impact of our water choice on the environment. For instance, why would we waste more fossil fuel to make and ship plastic bottles for our most basic human needs?

If you are in a position where you have to buy bottled water, follow these guidelines (although there are some conflicting views on this issue):

1. Purchase the label that says "spring water."
2. If not available, choose "purified water" or "distilled water."
3. Avoid the label that says "drinking water." There are no accepted regulations in place to differentiate this water from regular tap water.

Water Recycling Systems

I recommend learning to separate household water into three categories:

1. Fresh purified water for drinking and cooking
2. Primary water for washing dishes, cleaning, or watering plants, but not ingesting (for example, water from the tap and water that you collect in a bucket while it is heating)
3. Secondary water from washing dishes, for cleaning and watering plants (for instance, water you have washed dishes in using biodegradable soap can be used a second time for watering outdoor plants and trees)

None of your kitchen water ever needs to go directly down the drain.

For basic water conservation, I highly recommend a low-flow faucet (which can reduce water flow up to 50%). If you attach an add-on flow restrictor, you can reduce the rate of water flow through the faucets by 50–75%. Aerators make the flow seem greater by adding air bubbles to the water and this can reduce water usage by 50–75%.

Water Conservation Tips

- Use only what you need!
- Find uses for secondary water.*
- Practice collecting water that runs while you are waiting for water to get hot. Consider that in our homes, water faucets account for 12 percent of our water use. Have a bucket in the kitchen for collecting this water to feed plants and animals, or to use for cooking or cleaning.
- Stop leaks. A dripping faucet at the rate of one drop per second uses seven gallons per day; a steady drip uses 20 gallons per day or 5,000 gallons a month.
- Do not run water continuously for dishwashing and rinsing. Wash dishes by hand, as instructed later in this chapter and ideally use tubs or a Hughie Sink (a water collector set inside the sink, which you'll read more about later in this chapter).
- Reuse the same cup or dish whenever possible to avoid unnecessary washing. Consider giving each member of your household a labeled cup/mug that he or she uses regularly during the day to avoid creating excess dishes to wash.
- To wash produce, fill a bowl of water to monitor the amount used, rather than letting the tap run.
- Use a brush rather than the force of water to remove food from dirty plates.
- Vegetables should be steamed, baked, or stir-fried, but never submerged in water that you would dump out afterwards. Use any leftover cooking water for soups, stock, sauces and so on.
- Always run the dishwasher when it's full and use the correct cycle.
- Post a water conservation reminder by your faucet!

*Please refer to the Non-toxic Cleaning section for information on soaps that are safe for secondary water.

Energy-efficient Appliances

Our kitchens use 20–25 percent of our household energy, according to the American Association for an Energy Efficient Economy. Kitchen appliances are not all created equal. In terms of conventional appliances, refrigerators use more energy than any other appliance, followed by dishwashers. Refrigerators use up to 11% of household energy and older models can use up to 14% of your total household electricity use. This makes refrigerators one of the biggest contributors to your kitchen's carbon footprint.

Consider that until the late nineteenth century, we didn't use refrigerators. People took responsibility for their own immediate use and storage of food through processes including fermentation, dehydration and ice production or ice delivery. The first refrigerator was invented in 1876 by Carl von Linde. By 1937, more than 2 million Americans had refrigerators; by 1980, 80% of Americans did; and, by 1995, 99.5% of Americans had them.

Here are some tips for lessening the carbon footprint of your refrigerator:

• **Check the door seal.** Simply place a piece of paper so it sticks out when you close the refrigerator door. If you can't pull the paper out, the seals are good. If you can, you are losing cold air and need to have this fixed.
• **Don't leave fridge doors open,** even momentarily to pour a glass of milk. It takes energy to cool warm air that gets in.
• **Do not over-fill your fridge.** Over-filling slows down circulation.
• **Clean the coils at the back at least once per year.** Make sure there is good air circulation between the back of your fridge and the wall.
• **Keep the fridge away from heat.** Keep it away from vents and other appliances like the dishwasher or stove.
• **Store only cold items in your fridge.** Put cold items back in quickly and never store hot foods inside. Always let food cool first.
• **Clean the fridge out regularly.** This keeps it organized and provides good air circulation.
• **Keep the temperature between 35-38°F (1.7-3.3°C).** You can check the temperature by putting a thermometer into a glass of water set up on the middle shelves.
• **Defrost in the refrigerator.** Defrosting frozen foods in the fridge actually helps to maintain coolness.
• **Keep the freezer full.** A full freezer functions better than a partially filled one. Use containers filled with water to fill extra space.
• **Defrost your freezer regularly, at least once per year.** If there is more than 1/4 inch of frost, the motor will start to strain itself.

- **Keep your freezer at 0 degrees.** Do not place hot foods inside. Let them cool down first.
- **Invest in an Energy Star refrigerator, if possible.** Energy Star refrigerators are required to be 20% more efficient than any other products. Many cities have programs which will help pay for a portion of the more energy-efficient replacement refrigerator.
- **Get rid of old models.** Buy better energy performers that meet governmental standards and regulations. They are better insulated, have more efficient compressors and have better door seals, which all contribute to the improvement of energy efficiency.

Dishwashers are another appliance to watch out for. They have a high-powered heat element that adds to their carbon footprint. Some tips to lessen the carbon footprint of your dishwasher are:

- **Don't prewash dishes with running water.** Simply scrape dishes or set them to soak in the sink or a tub of water first.
- **Wash dishes when the machine is full.** This saves water and is more efficient.
- **Turn down the temperature of the water a bit.** Check to see if you have this option.
- **Air-dry your dishes** by opening the door on the last cycle.
- **Empty the filter or food trap regularly.**
- **Don't use the "temperature boost" or "dry" feature.**
- **Look for Energy Star labels when shopping for a dishwasher.** These indicate water and energy savings.

Beware of the hidden cost of electricity. Consider that for every kilowatt of power we use for electricity in our homes, another three kilowatts of fossil fuels are burned at a power plant to generate that electricity. In other words, electrical power is the most expensive form of power we use. Think of the fossil fuels used to create the electricity as primary energy, and the electricity at your home as secondary energy. We are doing ourselves and the environment a service whenever we cut down on our use of electricity or secondary energy.

Pay attention to your energy use in the kitchen and honor the energy you use by practicing conservation. Turn off lights when you are not using them, unplug appliances that draw energy from simply being plugged in, operate appliances during **non-peak hours** and see how many ways you can find to lessen your footprint in this area.

Appliances and Items that Are Useful to Have

In the cooking section, I will share how it could be helpful to have the following supplies and appliances on hand and will go into more detail regarding their use:

- Bamboo steamer
- Crockpot or "slow cooker"
- Toaster oven
- Solar cooker
- A reliable blender that you use consciously (or a hand-crank or bicycle-powered blender)
- Low-wattage appliances

* I recommend that you have a reliable blender in a green kitchen to help you use your produce in ever-creative ways and to help you with do-it-yourself practices that require blending. Though a blender or Vita-Mix use energy, they are generally used for such short time periods that they are not major energy drains in a kitchen, but you need to use them consciously. If you are able to, I recommend purchasing a hand-crank blender or the stationary-bike blender, which require you to generate your own power.

Items That Don't Belong in a Green Kitchen

Items you may want to consider removing in order to transition to a more conscious kitchen (which we will discuss further in the book) are:

- Microwave
- Plastic food storage containers
- Unhealthy pots and utensils
- Unnecessary energy-drawing appliances

A Green Pantry

A NATURAL KITCHEN IS COMMITTED TO WHOLE AND UNPROCESSED foods purchased in bulk as much as possible. We are moving beyond the age of a pantry full of packaged rice, pasta, cereals, crackers, snacks, junk food, individually-wrapped foods and disposable straws. Instead, how about a system of well-organized bulk foods stored in glass jars?

In terms of its production, glass is the safest food storage material for both humans and the environment, and glass jars are a widely available, free, reusable material. In your pantry, you can store the following in glass jars: rice, oats, grains, nuts, seeds, beans, lentils, pasta, cereals, dried fruit and specialty items such as dried mushrooms, sun-dried tomatoes and sea vegetables, such as nori, hijiki and kelp. You can also store all of your flours, sugars, protein powders, etc. in glass jars.

Be sure to set things up efficiently in your pantry, arranging the items you use regularly in the front and center, with newest items in back (for instance newly purchased cans of tomatoes) and older items in front, so that you use them first. You might have a section for baking, a section for fruit, and a section for supplements that you take. The point is to arrange your pantry in the way that is the most human-friendly and efficient.

An Efficient and Water-wise Dishwashing System

Unless you have a very energy/water-efficient dishwasher, hand washing is the more eco-friendly choice for the green kitchen. Some of us were taught to wash dishes by turning on the tap and letting it run the entire time we are cleaning dishes and utensils, but this is NOT the idea we are going for here. Depending on how many people share your kitchen and how many meals are cooked, you can come up with your own system to save water and energy. Here are some ideas:

The system we used at the monastery was "mindful hand washing." This system required three tubs in the sink: prewash, wash and rinse. (You can set the first tub outside of your sink, followed by two tubs in your sink and a dish rack or drying space.) In the morning, the tubs were filled (or at the first wash) and then water was reused and recycled throughout the day. So...the first tub can have a squirt of Shaklee Basic G or other non-toxic bleach alternative (see the Resource List for more on this). The second tub would have soapy water. The third tub would be rinse water. As the first tub became dirty, it would be dumped (for instance outside to water plants). Then the soapy water would get moved to the first tub and receive a squirt of Basic G. The rinse water would become soapy water and a new tub of clean rinse water would be filled and this process would go on throughout the day. What works about this system is that it requires continual recycling and paying attention to saving water. If you rarely cook three full meals a day, this method is easily adaptable to your main meal in the evening or to a few breakfast dishes and then more dinner dishes, enabling you to use minimal water for both.

You can also consider purchasing a Hughie Sink, a sink-shaped tub with a handle and a spigot that sits in your sink and collects dishwater very efficiently. If you do your dishes inside the Hughie Sink with soap that is greywater-appropriate (see the Non-toxic cleaning section for specifics) you can simply remove the bin afterwards, with the greywater inside of it and use the spigot at the bottom of the Hughie sink to easily water ornamentals, trees and other plants. You might also use the sink for soaking dishes or simply as a means for collecting excess water that might run as you are waiting for tap water to heat.

Another technique is one Julia Russell at L.A. Eco-Home taught me. She simply scrapes her dishes as soon as she is done with them (so nothing dries up); sprays a mix of dish soap and water onto each dish and cleans it with a sponge, and uses one tub full of rinse water to rinse each dish in after it is spray-cleaned.

If you have been in the habit of letting your water run, I recommend posting a gentle reminder in your kitchen, right above the sink, to help you remember to turn off the water when you are not using it. It can be hard to change our habits and it is important to support ourselves in every way we can to make the transition.

A Space for Mindful Food Preparation

Have you noticed that some kitchens are not actually designed with culinary tasks as the priority? Have you ever cooked in a kitchen where the act of actually preparing food felt spatially in conflict with everything else going on there? I recommend setting up a clearly designated space for food preparation and cooking that is as spacious as you have the room for.

Make whatever adjustments you need for it to be body-friendly. For instance, a block can be useful to stand on if the counter is too high for you. Or place it under your cutting board if the counter is too low. You might also consider the material that cutting boards are made of. I prefer those that are made from either bamboo or **FSC-certified** wood or recycled wood. Bamboo is not only one of the fastest-growing plants on the planet, but it also gets harvested by a trimming process instead of uprooting the whole plant in the way that trees get harvested for wood. (For more on bamboo kitchen products, visit the Resource List at the back of this book.)

I like to have my compost right next to where I am doing food preparation. One of my favorite kitchen innovations at Julia Russell's Eco-Home is a compost bin with a cutting board on top built directly into the kitchen counter. When you slide the cutting board out, there is a sliding drawer below so that you can place food scraps directly into the bin. Inventions like these make a world of difference in terms of making green cooking efficient.

A Center for Radical Recycling and Creative Reuse

The recommendations offered in Chapter Two make it simple and easy to reuse and recycle every single resource that comes into your kitchen. It requires a time investment to set this system up, but the reward is huge. It will be simple and pain-free to reuse and recycle just about EVERY MATERIAL that comes into your kitchen. A Radical Recycling Center includes:

- Recycling bins
- A composting system
- A plastic bag drying rack
- A towel rack/clothesline for drying towels (to lessen your reliance on paper products)
- Organized storage for creative reuse

Consider that one can cut down on trash output by 50% simply by composting!

A Space for Non-toxic Cleaners

In a sustainable kitchen, it is vital that we move beyond our reliance on toxic chemicals for cleaning. There is no reason why all cleaning supplies cannot be healthy, inexpensive, and equally effective. Today there are easy alternatives to chlorine bleach, ammonia and phosphates that can cut grease, scour and disinfect as well as any "unhealthy" product. There are many green cleaning supplies currently available in stores, even in chain supermarkets these days, but they are not all created equal. (See the Resource List for more information about cleaning products.)

It's important to review the full list of ingredients, the type of company producing the product, the geographical location of the company in relation to where you live and the type of container in which the cleaning product is packaged. If you buy your cleaning supplies, I recommend choosing companies that use the simplest ingredients and package their product in bulk concentrate that you can dilute and use in a small reusable spray bottle.

Every green cook I know finds the cleaning solution that works best for them. For instance, Julia Russell has for years relied on one of these two simple cleaning mixtures in a spray bottle for ALL basic kitchen cleaning: either Shaklee's Basic H, 3 T mixed with one pint of water, OR Ecover, 4 T to 1 pint of water. If you would like to create your own healthy and non-toxic cleaning products out of the most basic ingredients, the following is a basic "how to" list:

Scourer

Use baking soda and water or half baking soda and half salt; scrub and rinse well. For chrome and stainless steel, dip a soft cloth into ordinary white flour and rub object until it shines.

Non-toxic Cleaning Products

- baking soda
- borax (note that this should not be applied in greywater to plants)
- lemon juice
- table salt
- white vinegar
- phosphate-free soap
- flour
- microfiber cloths and water to polish windows and mirrors

Degreaser

1/2 cup (125 ml) pure soap (I recommend Dr. Bronner's Castile soap)
1/4 cup (60 ml) lemon juice
3 cups (750 ml) hot water

Drain Cleaner

Pour 1/4 cup (60 ml) baking soda and 1/4 cup (60 ml) salt down drain. Then add 1/2 cup (125 ml) vinegar; cover the drain with a stopper and wait 15 minutes. Flush it with boiling water.

Or pour 1 cup (250 ml) salt down drain, followed by boiling water.

Disinfectant

1 tsp (5 ml) borax
2 Tbsp (30 ml) vinegar
1/4 cup (60 ml) pure soap
2 cups (500 ml) hot water

Oven Cleaner

Apply a paste of baking soda and water; leave it to soak for at least two hours or let it sit overnight. Remove with soapy cloth or apply straight vinegar. Then wipe it with wet cloth, rinsing frequently in warm water.

Dish Soap

If you are using greywater from your kitchen to water trees and ornamental plants, it is important to know that phosphates, salt and borax should all be used very sparingly on plants. And NONE should be used on edible garden plants. Follow the guidelines below to choose the appropriate soap for greywater. These specifications are offered by Brad Lancaster, a Northern Arizona permaculture designer and author:

Always read ingredients of the soaps you use, rather than trust labels.

Always use phosphate-free soap. (If you apply phosphates to plants, then you are not gardening organically.)

In areas with alkaline soils (which is most of the Western U.S.) it is best to avoid salt, sodium of any kind, and boron because they will make the soil more alkaline. Liquid soaps generally have less salt than powdered or bar soaps.

Three generally safe choices are Oasis, Bio-Pac, and Dr. Bronner's liquid soaps, but some of Dr. Bronner's and Bio-Pac's liquid soaps contain sodium, so it is necessary to read the ingredients.

If ingredients are not listed, it is best to assume that the soap is not safe.

Greywater can be applied to fruit trees where the food does not touch the water, but never use dark grey sink water on vegetable gardens.

For more information, please read the greywater chapter of Brad's second book, *Rainwater Harvesting for Drylands and Beyond, Volume 2*, or visit his website at **harvestingrainwater.com**.

A note about chlorine bleach:

NEVER USE BLEACH IN YOUR KITCHEN OR HOME AT ANY TIME. Skin absorption of chlorine is now on the EPA's Top 10 Carcinogen Watch List. In addition, according to the U.S. Council of Environmental Quality, people who drink chlorinated water have a 93% higher risk of cancer than those who do not.

Some alternatives to chlorine bleach are:

• Oxygen bleach, a non-toxic hydrogen peroxide-based bleach (which can be used for kitchen cleaning or to whiten your laundry)
• Basic G (a germicide and alternative to bleach made by Shaklee)
• GSE (grapefruit seed extract) by Nutribiotic, which is a milder but effective germicide

Other cleaning tips:

Save second-hand water collected in a bucket for cleaning purposes.

Buy biodegradable sponges. To keep them clean and free of odor, place them in a bowl, boil hot water, and pour it over them once a day or as needed.

If you buy new rags or kitchen towels, consider that conventionally grown cotton is one of the most pesticide-heavy crops there is and choose organic cotton, hemp, or bamboo towels instead, if possible.

You can make your own scrub sponge by rolling a couple of old socks up and encasing them in the netting from storebought lemons, garlic, and other produce.

Save money by diluting things such as store-bought hand soap with water.

Clean as you go! This approach cuts down on bigger messes and actually lessens the amount of soap you use.

A Space for Organizing Information

It can help things run more smoothly to have basic information in your kitchen posted, such as cooking times for grains and beans, a chart of seasonal foods, measurement conversions for recipes, a place for tracking produce expected from your garden, the weekly list of produce to expect from your CSA (Community Supported Agriculture) organization, money spent, a recycling chart and your weekly menu plan.

A Towel-Drying System/Clothesline

I RECOMMEND CUTTING DOWN ON OUR USE OF PAPER TOWELS AND napkins from our kitchens as much as possible and using cloth instead. It has been estimated that paper napkins produce up to 15 times more solid waste than their cloth counterparts. You can use biodegradable sponges, cloth napkins made from hemp or organic cotton and microfiber cloths for cleaning. Old T-shirts that would otherwise be thrown out are great for cleaning.

If you do choose to use paper towels or have a specific need for them—for instance to season your cast iron pots with oil—always buy unbleached paper towels. These can be used as a source of carbon for your compost rather than being thrown away.

Every green kitchen should have a good old-fashioned clothesline outside or a retractable indoor clothesline. (See the Resource List at the back of this book for a list of clotheslines I recommend.)

A Personal Note About the Satisfaction of Using Clotheslines...

Living in Southern California, I can practically hang my towels and clothing to dry 365 days of the year. If you set up your clothesline either under an awning or indoors (see the Resource List in the back for ideas on this), you can use your clothesline every day of the year. I enjoy hanging my kitchen towels or clothing up to dry. It is a simple pause in my day for mindfulness and taking a minute to care for every towel or every piece of clothing I wash. My clothes are always in good shape and I believe last longer when cared for this way. I no longer like to "throw my clothes" in a dryer, when I can instead enjoy the ritual of mindfully taking care of each item.

Plastic Bag Drying Rack

THE PURPOSE OF A PLASTIC BAG DRYING RACK IS TO ACKNOWLEDGE that plastic bags (even in our attempts to avoid them) do come through our kitchens from time to time and can be a valuable resource to reuse. Why not wash them (or simply shake them out if they only stored dry goods), dry them with a cloth and hang them dry to reuse appropriately (ideally not for food storage) over and over and over?

I can promise you, though it sounds simple, you are unlikely to follow this system without an appropriate bag-drying rack. They can come in many shapes and sizes and you can also construct your own. For the record, you never want to wash plastic bags in the dishwashing machine due to leaching of plastic.

The best reuses I know of for the plastic bags that do come into your life are:
• Picking up your dog feces (as an alternative to using the biodegradable bags on the Resource List)
• For trips, packing shoes or a wet bathing suit
• For young children and infants, packing a damp washcloth for wiping sticky hands and faces or to stash soiled diapers
• Freezer storage for items that are hard to store other ways
• Storing water bottles or containers of liquid when packing for air travel

Green Shopping Station: Making Shopping Trip Preparation Easy

A GREEN SHOPPING TRIP REQUIRES US TO BRING ALONG A FEW THINGS with us, rather than just relying on the checker to supply disposable bags. I recommend having an area of your kitchen that is designated storage for shopping bags, bulk buying bags and produce bags, or extra plastic bags and twist ties, empty containers for bulk foods and containers for any prepared foods you buy. This directs creative reuse for shopping trips to the right place and helps you, in no time, be perfectly prepared to shop in a more conscious way. I also recommend storing extra cloth bags in your vehicle for unexpected shopping trips.

Green Coffee/Tea Station

More than 50 percent of Americans drink coffee every day. Conventionally grown coffee is one of the most pesticide-intensive crops in the world. Of the 330 million cups consumed each day, as of 2008, **fair trade** coffee (where coffee growers get a fair price for their labors) made up just over 1/% of the entire coffee market, despite the fact that it is the most traded of all fair trade goods. Now consider this breathtaking statistic: The $3 many Americans spend every day for a latte at Starbucks is equivalent to the daily wage of a Central American coffee picker. Considering the implications of conventional coffee production—from the environmental to the socio-economic—in keeping with the principle of conscious consumption of resources, it is vital to purchase organic fair trade coffee. This simple action could have a positive and long-reaching impact (and ripple effect) over time.

If you are a coffee drinker, consider taking these simple steps:
• Invest in fair trade organic coffee!
• Set up an eco-friendly water purification system.
• Create a system for composting the coffee grounds.
• Invest in a French press coffee maker (which is more energy-efficient than conventional coffee makers).

Why not find a way to align our most esteemed beverage with our values, from its production to its disposal?

Coffee Filters
• Those made with paper whitened by chlorine can contain trace amounts of the highly toxic synthetic chemical dioxin. Studies have shown that half the dioxin in paper filters actually leaches into freshly brewed coffee. Good alternatives to white paper filters are:
• Unbleached filters, which can be composted
• Cloth filters, made of unbleached cotton muslin, which can be reused daily for up to two years. They simply get rinsed thoroughly with plain hot water after each use.
• Gold-plated filters, which last many years, are easy to clean, and usually cost from $15–25
• French press coffee makers, which have their own simple filtering mechanism

Tea Bag Alternatives
If you are a tea drinker, I recommend investing in bulk teas and setting up a tea station and a place for tea bags to sit and wait for reuse, if you use tea bags. Most tea bags can be used at least twice. Ounce for ounce, loose tea often costs less than half as much as bagged tea. It is also usually of much higher quality than the "tea dust" they put in many tea bags. Another reason to opt for loose tea is that tea bags made from paper whitened with chlorine can also contain traces of dioxin, which can leach into your drink. You can use metal strainers and tea infusers to easily brew loose tea. Reusable tea bags can also be handmade from cloth. It is possible to find organic (and even locally grown) bulk tea and fair trade tea in minimal packaging. You can also learn how to make sun tea in Chapter Eight. For more information on conscious coffee and tea consumption, visit the Resource List.

Sustainable Packaging Station

A sustainable packaging station makes it easy to find what you need for packing snacks, lunches and other to-go meals, while honoring your commitment to zero waste and using eco-friendly, non-toxic materials in your kitchen. For your sustainable packaging station, I would have on hand:

- Cloth lunch bags
- Reusable lunch bags
- Eco-friendly food-storage containers such as stainless steel or glass
- Parchment paper
- String
- Recycled aluminum foil (if needed)
- Soy wax paper (if needed)

For more detailed information about these items, refer to Chapter Nine and the Resource List.

Herb Parlor

Fresh Herbs
Fresh herbs are a vital part of a green kitchen, as we move away from being over-dependent on salt and processed foods and move toward cooking that savors the variety of nature's palette. Fresh herbs like parsley, cilantro, basil and thyme can last up to two weeks if stored properly. Wash the herbs and set them on a towel to dry. Place them in a cup of water, cover loosely with a cloth bag or parchment paper, and set them on top of your refrigerator or in another cool, dry place, changing the water every couple of days.

Dried Herbs
You can easily store dried herbs (that you buy in bulk or dry yourself) to ensure a long shelf life in the following types of containers or reusable containers:

- opaque glass
- clear glass
- glass canning jars
- metal
- recycled bottles
- ceramic
- wood

Taking the Next Step

Right now, review the list of ideas for creating a green kitchen and note the area(s) where you feel you are already making a positive difference. Then, look over the list again and see what area(s) would make the biggest difference for you to address today. I recommend that you PICK ONE PLACE TO BEGIN. Pick an aspect of your kitchen that you feel confident about organizing completely from beginning to end, while beginning to make changes in other areas as your schedule and creativity allow. If there is one aspect of a green kitchen for you to begin with, what would it be? What ONE STEP would bring you the most gratification and make the most difference in your kitchen? What can you do TODAY as part of that step? You can refer to the workbook in the back of this book to support you in the process.

Common Sense Design Tips for a Green Kitchen

IT'S BEST NOT TO USE CARPET IN THE KITCHEN, JUST SMALL AREA RUGS, as carpet will get damp and attract mold. If you have any mold in your kitchen (or home, for that matter), it is important to get it tested.

Since you often stand for periods of time in the kitchen, consider a **cork** mat or cork flooring. Cork is both body-friendly and eco-friendly in that it is a highly renewable resource.

Windows should be open to let fresh air in and to allow moisture generated from cooking out.

A good range hood, appropriately sized for the kitchen, will eliminate mold problems as well as reducing the amount of smoke you are exposed to while cooking.

Kitchen cabinets and other built-in items should be free of synthetic (urea) formaldehyde. Formaldehyde is a common household air pollutant and its effects range from allergic reaction to cancer... not something you want in your kitchen or elsewhere in your home for that matter.

Large **EMR** (electromagnetic radiation)-generating appliances, such as refrigerators, should be placed away from where people spend large amounts of time. EMR can be cancer-causing with heavy exposure.

A water filtration system must be installed for your kitchen tap. This is vital if you live in a major city.

Healthy non-toxic pots, pans and food storage containers and materials must be utilized.

Renovating Your Kitchen: For Those of You Starting from Scratch

Some of you might have the wonderful opportunity to completely redo your kitchen green. Others of you can take these things into consideration where and when you can. First, remember that eco-friendly building materials have never been so widely accessible. There are beautiful and stylish kitchen building products available that are made of recycled bottles, recycled plastic, natural resin, bamboo, agricultural by-products that would otherwise get thrown away, and so many more eco-friendly options.

Green building products can be more expensive, but prices vary and hopefully will become more affordable over time. Always choose non-toxic materials and finishes and always avoid **VOC paints** (conventional paints that contains volatile organic compounds). VOC paints release low-level toxins into the air for years after their application and release high levels of carbon into the atmosphere. Good ventilation, natural lighting and surfaces that are easy to clean without the use of harsh chemicals are steps in the right direction. Find out more about these materials in the Resource List.

At the writing of this book, new green kitchen models and products are being manufactured and are becoming more available to the average consumer.

The Renovation Checklist

Avoid particle board cabinet units that contain urea-formaldehyde (usually finished in plastic laminate), which is classified by the European Union as a likely human carcinogen. Choose solid wood or metal cabinets or recycled solid wood units. Cabinets made without urea formaldehyde are now also widely available.

Choose energy-efficient appliances with an Energy Star label.

Choose a solid countertop, such as stainless steel or solid wood. Some healthier types of countertops are made with recycled aluminum, sustainably mined, made-in-the-USA quartz, recycled paper, and concrete. Wood needs to be properly sealed and is only a good choice for less moist climates. Some laminate countertops release chemicals. Tile is not ideal because the grout holds bacteria, while granite often contains radon and also is over-harvested.

Avoid vinyl flooring, which can emit chemical fumes. Rather, choose stone, tile, natural linoleum such as Marmoleum, or reclaimed wood from used building material depots. Cork and bamboo flooring are good alternatives to endangered wood species such as teak and mahogany.

Use eco-friendly paints that are low- or zero-VOC, now easily found in paint stores, or a natural wall covering such as American Clay.

Supplement natural light from your windows by using light colors on the ceiling and walls. Consider installing solar tubes for light and using energy-efficient LED light bulbs or light strips where you need light bulbs.

Check with contractors and installers that the sealants, glues and finishes they're using are certified for indoor air quality (Greenguard, for example).

Talk to plumbers about hot water access—a small tankless heater under the kitchen sink can provide all the hot water you need within 30 seconds, wasting less than a half cup of water. ●

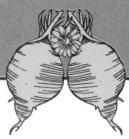

CHAPTER 8
COOKING TO CONSERVE ENERGY

"We must not, in trying to think about how we can make a big difference, ignore the small daily differences we can make which, over time, add up to big differences that we often cannot foresee."

—Marian Wright Edelman

As a kid, my family took a lot of camping trips. As our campfire would die out at the end of a starry night and before we climbed into our tents, zipped up our sleeping bags, and went to sleep, we would first take a bunch of whole potatoes, wrap them in tinfoil and place them in the hot coals to cook slowly and deliciously overnight.

When it was time for breakfast and to start our campfire again, we would take out those perfectly warm, soft cooked potatoes with a delicate crust, seasoned with a tad of woodfire sage, and add them into our breakfast omelettes, or just break them open and eat them whole.

Those slow-baked potatoes were always a looked-forward-to treat and required no extra energy other than the heat from the quieting fire. While most of us do not make campfires in our own backyard, the idea of finding creative and energy-efficient ways to cook in our own kitchens can bring the same degree of satisfaction and delight. Energy-efficient cooking is one of the delights of a kitchen aligned with nature.

For those of you who are tired of our culture's over-dependence on fossil fuels and who want to make as minimal a carbon footprint every day of your life as possible, cooking is an area which requires only simple steps to dramatically reduce the energy expended. Cooking is not the biggest energy drain in our kitchens—it's only a small part of the 20–25% of household energy that gets used by the kitchen.

As mentioned in Chapter Seven, large appliances such as your refrigerator and washing machine suck up most kitchen energy. However, cooking is an area where most of us don't know the basics about staying green. When I am preparing a meal, I consciously ask myself: How can I cook to conserve energy? You can easily save energy when cooking with your conventional stove and you can also design systems to save even more energy utilizing appropriate technology such as solar cooking, haybox/retained cooking, or integrating DIY permaculture techniques I will describe in this chapter.

I find it incredibly satisfying to learn how to do MORE with less. Whether this means baking my potatoes in the aftermath of a campfire or cooking by the free rays of the sun, or whether this means preparing the most tasty meal I can imagine just by massaging the leaves of raw kale I harvest from my garden with a bit of olive oil and sprinkling it with garlic and sea salt, SIMPLICITY is SATISFYING.

The first order of business is to have a clear understanding of the everyday ways we can avoid wasting energy in cooking conventionally. Here is some age-old grandmother wisdom to include in your awareness as you cook:

Common Sense Ways to Avoid Wasting Energy in Cooking

Stovetop Cooking

Turn gas as low as possible.

Oversized pans waste energy, so match your pan to burner size; a six-inch diameter pan on an eight-inch burner wastes almost 50% of the energy produced by the burner.

Use flat-bottomed cookware that rests evenly on the burner surface. This cooks faster.

Cook with the lid on whenever possible and make sure that lids fit tightly. Cooking without the lid uses three times more energy! Remember this when heating water, boiling eggs, preparing oatmeal, etc.

Once boiling, turn the flame down just enough to maintain it. Turn the burner off at least three minutes before it's time. Your food will still cook at the same temperature and save energy.

For oatmeal, hot cereal, rice and other grains, boil, simmer and turn off the burner earlier than you think…In other words, boil rice with the lid on for 10 minutes, then let the pot sit for 10 minutes. Oatmeal can simply be brought to a boil and then allowed to slow cook with the heat off.

Use steamers on top of pans, so veggies and rice are all cooking on one burner.

Defrost frozen foods in the refrigerator to reduce cooking time.

Keep cooking appliances clean.

If you are cooking on a gas stove, check from time to time to make sure that the flame is well-shaped and blue. If the flame is yellow it's a sign of energy inefficiency.

Consider using a **Kill-A-Watt** to learn about the energy requirements for each of your household appliances so that you can make informed decisions. A Kill-A-Watt is a device that enables you to measure the energy use of each appliance.

Oven Cooking/Baking

Don't bake with the oven door open.

Make sure the oven door seal is tight.

Turn the oven off just before food is done. Let the food cook for 10 minutes while on OFF. The heat will remain the same.

Preheating an oven is reserved for baking breads and pastries. Otherwise, it is not necessary. If you need to preheat, don't preheat longer than necessary; 10 minutes should be enough. There is never a need to preheat when broiling.

Use the oven as full as possible but not overloaded.

Use the right size utensil for the quantity cooked: flat, shallow casseroles cook faster than deep ones and should be covered when possible.

Glass or ceramic baking dishes allow you to lower the baking temperature by 25 degrees, since these materials retain heat better than others.

Don't keep checking the progress by opening the door. An oven with a window and lit interior eliminates the need, as do reliable recipes.

Keep the oven clean, especially the heat-transfer surfaces.

Lining the oven with foil can reduce indoor air pollution by keeping the interior clean. Check the operation manual first to be sure to not interfere with the oven's operation.

Clean self-cleaning ovens right after use to take advantage of residual heat. Always scrape off what you can first in order to hasten the process.

Don't use the oven to heat the house. This is not only inefficient, it can be dangerous.

Thawing Foods

Thaw frozen foods in the refrigerator first, rather than in the oven, in order to reduce cooking time.

What Kind of Cooking Appliances are Most Energy-Efficient?

The do-it-yourself renewable energy cooking techniques offered later in this chapter are by far the most sustainable choices because they do not involve fossil fuels, but as we transition collectively to a lifestyle that is no longer fossil-fuel dependent, there is a middle way to be found. Here are some basics to consider:

Gas stoves actually come out as the better choice over electric stoves when it comes to overall sustainability. Yes, electricity is 45% more efficient than gas and, according to the American Gas Association, you get 34% more heat for your dollar out of electricity at the burner; however, when hidden costs such as the power needed to generate electricity and power lost through transmission are figured in, electricity does not do so well for long-term sustainability.

Microwaves

Our culture is addicted to microwave ovens, but I am not an advocate for the microwave as part of a green kitchen. Though they generally take less cooking time, create less heat in the summer and are energy-efficient in some ways, I feel that microwaves are not a good choice for long-term sustainability when we consider the following:

Food safety

Radiological health and how little we know about microwave safety

The amount of packaging and wraps used in microwave cooking

Quality of cooking

The "quick and unconscious" attitude of mind that a microwave cultivates

Microwaves have only been sold to the public since the 1960s. Today, more than 90% of American households own a microwave. Yet studies over the past 30 years remain very controversial about the overall safety of microwaves. I find microwaves to be one of those technologies that we have dove into as a culture in our quest for convenience, without being knowledgeable about the long-term effects. As David Goldbeck, writer of *The Smart Kitchen*, says, "We are in the process of microwaving away 50,000 years of glorious culinary history in order to satisfy a dubious quest for convenience."

Microwaves do not necessarily use less energy than conventional cooking does, either. Generally, microwave ovens consume as much or more energy than electric stove tops do, but less than electric ovens. Microwaves also do not do well compared with the pressure cooker. Prepared microwave foods are also HIGHLY energy-intensive to manufacture. And studies have shown that the increase in plastic food packaging (that goes to the dump) due to microwave use has been tremendous.

What's more, microwaves are known to result in nutrient loss in foods. Considering each of these factors, if sustainability is our goal, does it not make sense to curb our use of the microwave? In my opinion, microwaves encourage a cultural attitude of "no need to pay attention" and "it's OK to trade in health for convenience." Is it really worth trading in health, food quality and sustainability for the convenience of heating your meal as fast as you can?

Finding the Middle Way

If you feel the need to use a microwave, are you willing to find a middle way that is appropriate to your life and cut down on the amount of meals you use it for? For instance, perhaps you can plan ahead so you no longer use it for defrosting, or perhaps you would like to use it only twice a week instead of every day, or even use it only for emergencies? What makes the most sense for you?

Special Products to Assist with Energy-efficient Cooking in the Green Kitchen

There are a few special products that you may want to invest in for your green kitchen:

As mentioned in Chapter Seven, pressure cookers can save 50–75% energy, as they utilize steam to cook.

The toaster oven is very energy-efficient, as it only requires heating a small space, so it is ideal for cooking for one or two or for reheating leftovers.

Stacked bamboo steamers are helpful for one-pot cooking.

Convection ovens draw less power than an oven. A small fan circulates heat better and can reduce the temperature by 50 degrees and shorten baking time.

Specialty low-wattage appliances, such as the Press Express handheld food processor (300 watts) or the Magic Bullet, a little blender with a small container area and thus low-wattage, are intelligent alternatives to conventional appliances.

Hand-crank blenders are a fabulous alternative to electric blenders (and can also be taken on camping trips). In general, blenders and food processors do make a carbon footprint because they have motors; however, they are typically used so briefly that they are not a huge energy drain. Simply be very mindful of your use of these appliances or purchase a hand-crank blender if you want to go fully green.

Pedal Power

One of the most fun inventions for a green kitchen is the bicycle-powered blender. It takes only 60–90 seconds of pedaling a bike to make a smoothie on a stationary bike blender. A bicycle-powered blender not only allows you to generate your own power but also makes less impact in the aspect of production, as most components are recycled and there are no electrical parts involved. For instance, Fender Blender (**bikeblender.com**) uses recycled HDPE plastic for 75% of the plastic required for a bike blender, and a percentage of their metal also comes from a recycled source. While bike blenders take up space and may not be something that every kitchen can handle, you can always buy a Fender Blender Universal model, which mounts on the rear rack of a bicycle you already have, and you can remove the blender on weekends. For more information on where to buy a bike blender or how to make your own (though this is quite a commitment) visit the Resource List.

Creative Alternative Cooking Techniques That Can Cut Down on Energy Use (and Cost) by 20–100%!

For one year of my life, I used a solar oven for 90% of my cooking. I find solar cooking to be incredibly fun, efficient and cost-effective. I built my solar oven with wood, glass and foil—and a friend and I used it to prepare our meals every day in good weather. I would wake up, prepare my lunch (or dinner), set it in the solar oven and then go about my activities for the morning (or for the entire day). I would come back for lunch (or dinner) and my meal would be warm and ready for me to eat. On a clear morning, the temperature inside a solar oven can reach 200°F and will stay 300–350° midday.

Imagine how relaxing it would be to be able to prepare your dinner in the morning, set it in the oven before going to work, and return home to a perfectly cooked meal waiting for you. There are some foods that get cooked very quickly in a solar oven. For instance, I have baked cookies in 20 minutes on a hot day in a solar oven, while something like a soup or stew will take hours longer. Is this technology applicable to city life? Absolutely…. My opinion is that most people simply have yet to experience the effectiveness (and delight) of solar cooking and have a hard time believing that the sun alone can cook our meals (from soup to baked chicken to lasagna), heat and purify our water and also bake cookies.

In the United States, we currently use less than 1% of the possible energy we could get from the sun. Solar energy is the oldest, simplest, cleanest and least expensive technology, yet it remains the least utilized. In Los Angeles, where I run Creative Green Sustainability Consulting, we average 329 days of sunshine per year. My hope is that solar cooking here will catch on and that all families will have a solar oven in the backyard or even on a balcony or porch (perhaps instead of or alongside their barbeque).

At the end of this chapter, I will offer solar cooking recipes and you can visit the Resource List to find out how to make your own solar oven. If you wish to buy a solar oven, you can do so through The Solar Living Institute or Solar Cookers International. Models of solar ovens vary from a foldable cardboard "camping cooker" to a solar wall oven that stands in your backyard.

Amanda Bramble, founder of Ampersand Sustainable Learning Center in New Mexico, says, "The solar wall oven has made me fall in love with solar cooking, partly because it's so user-friendly, you don't have to put it away, it's just always available to cook. I like how it cooks food slowly and I can leave for the day and there's no fire hazard—it won't burn your food, heat up your house, or waste your money."

When asked what her favorite foods to cook in her solar oven are, she says, "Sweet potatoes are great, one of the easiest and yummiest things to cook and they are good both 'cooked enough' and almost overcooked… sweet and gooey. I don't like to spend a lot of time cooking, so I go for the one-pot meal: Make a casserole with potatoes, vegetables, throw some eggs and cheese in there and there's dinner." Soups are also a great choice for a solar oven: One simple recipe is to cut up potatoes into one-inch cubes, add an array of other vegetables such as onions, chard, carrots, and kale, and put them in a dark pot. Cover the vegetables with water, stir in bouillon and spices, and place it in the solar oven. This soup takes just a few minutes to prepare and is truly satisfying.

Other simple ways to use the sun's energy for cooking are:

Sun Tea

Sun tea is delicious and only takes a minute of your time. You can set a batch of tea out in the morning or afternoon and return a few hours later (or that evening) to find it perfectly steeped. All you need is a large glass jar. Fill it with purified water and fresh or dried herbs of your choice (tea bags also work if you don't have access to herbs). Cover it and set it out in the sun. When the tea is prepared, I like to add a squeeze of lemon and perhaps agave for sweetener and serve it over ice. If you make a large batch, you can store the jars in your refrigerator and have sun tea to access all week long.

Solar Sundrying

You can solar-dry any fruits or veggies that are ripe and still good to eat, but nothing on the verge of spoiling, of course. You can set up a collapsible solar food dryer for use in any hot, dry place that can be well-ventilated. This can be set up in a garage, metal shed, empty greenhouse, or even the back seat of a car, van, or bus!

Putting it All Together: Creative Systems for Energy Efficiency

At Ampersand Sustainable Learning Center, cooking rotates between a solar oven, a rocket stove (to be explained) and conventional cooking utilized with adjustments for energy conservation. Amanda Bramble lets the weather and her taste buds dictate her choice. On a sunny day she'll go solar and if cloud cover comes and the meal still needs cooking, she just wraps a turkey bag and blanket around the pot and it keeps on cooking.

For things she can't cook solar, such as pan-frying or stir-frying, she uses her rocket stove. This is a do-it-yourself stove that uses fuel such as small twigs and branches and yields high combustion efficiency by directing the heat onto a very small area. Rocket Stoves are easy to make yourself (Visit **off-grid.net/2009/05/04/rocket-stove-video/**) or you can purchase a factory-made rocket stove through Aprovecho Institute in Oregon (**rocketstove.org/**).

Some cooking tips from Amanda: On a rocket stove, "it's easy to burn things, so you want foods that can get a little crispy... It's helpful to have one person cooking and one person to tend the fire... and it's especially fun to cook popcorn!" From time to time, Amanda will use her gas stove for cooking and to reduce the use of propane, she wraps a metal sleeve (i.e. a piece of bendable metal flashing) around the pot with a ¼-inch space around the pot, which directs the flame right up that space; it superheats the pot and cooks faster. Her kitchen is designed to make it easy to cook while saving fuel no matter what the weather is.

Haybox Cooking

This cooking method, also known as **retained heat cooking**, is another simple and effective technology to include in your cooking patterns. Haybox cooking was invented back in the day when grocers sold bulk items in large tins. Farm wives would take the empty tins, line them with hay and then, after preparing a stew or soup and bringing it to cooking temperature, they would set it in the hay-lined tin and let it remain slow-cooking until the farm workers were ready for it at lunch. The point is to utilize long, slow, retained-heat cooking to produce a delicious and nutritious meal using minimal energy. Retained-heat cooking uses 20–80% less energy than normal stovetop cooking. Five pots of beans with a haybox uses the same amount of fuel as one pot of beans without a haybox. If you are not the do-it-yourself type, you can also invest in a crockpot, which is the modern version of haybox cooking. Again, you can prepare your meal and leave it in a crockpot for 8–10 hours to slowly cook.

The Cob Oven

One of my favorite eco-homes, designed by a couple of teachers in Oregon, has a beautiful earthen oven built into the side of the kitchen. It is an energy-efficient way to bake bread, pies, pizzas and anything else you might bake in a conventional oven, and it simultaneously heats the home. The couple has creatively designed a wood storage closet into the same wall, with a door on both sides of it, to make collecting wood for the kitchen easy!

Cob is a mixture of earth, sand and straw... yes, mud from your very own land can be used to build your home and make your oven. A cob oven uses sticks and logs (large logs are not necessary) to build a fire, which eventually gets capped with a clay cover (with a drain pipe for the smoke) so that the oven retains heat for long periods of time. It is a simple and beautiful technique for baking that any urban greenie can build in his or her own backyard.

Blackberry Cob Pie—As Close to the Earth As You Can Get

I once stayed with friends at an intentional community on the Northern California coast, where we were living as close to the earth as you can get, sleeping under the stars and bathing in a stream on the property. One of the meals we cooked there I will never forget. We woke up in the morning to go for a swim in the ocean and to collect wild seaweed for both the kitchen and garden (seaweed is almost as good as farmyard manure for plants and can be used for composting and mulching). Then we took a hike through the forested parts of the property to gather sweet, wild blackberries. Later that day we got to work washing the berries and preparing them into blackberry pie with braided crusts, baked them in our cob oven, and then turned our ocean vegetables into a delicious stir-fry with garden produce, cooked over a campfire. When our meal was complete, we packed it into a basket and trekked it to the beach to watch the sunset and feast on our meal, created entirely by food growing in and around the property where we lived.

While this vision may seem far-fetched for a city dweller, the addition of a cob oven in your backyard can be a naturally extravagant treat for the epicurean in you. (And it is entirely possible to collect wild edibles in cities; this is known as the art of "wild crafting.")

Other Examples of What Is Possible

If our point is to cut down on our energy use and carbon impact in the kitchen, we can discover or invent new solutions by using the concept (once again) of creating a closed cycle. Are there creative ways that you can see to apply this concept to energy conservation in your kitchen or on your property?

Here are some fun examples that you may want to read more about:

Vegawatt

This generator powers entire restaurants with their own waste vegetable oil! For more information, visit **vegawatt.com**.

Gaviotas

is an intentional community in Columbia; the drinking/cooking water pump is powered by a seesaw and merry-go-round on the children's playground. For more information, visit **friendsofgaviotas.org**.

Arcosanti

is designed to utilize the heat generated from an extensive food-growing greenhouse system to provide heat for the entire community. For more information, visit **arcosanti.org**.

Anything is possible when we work *with* nature. Imagine a future where we no longer use fossil fuels to ship our food, but rely on local organic food systems; where we ride our bikes to the market to buy bulk goods and then blend our morning smoothies while using the stationary bicycle. Imagine cooking your meals with the sun's rays in warm weather and powering your car with your waste vegetable oil.

Here are some recipes to get you started cooking in a solar oven or in a crockpot.

Solar Cooking Recipes

Sun-browned Brownies

1/2 cup vegetable oil
1/3 cup maple syrup, agave nectar, or a blend of both
1/2 cup soy yogurt
1 1/2 cups whole wheat flour
1/2 cup carob powder of cocoa
1/2 cup nuts

Mix wet ingredients togetherwith a wire whisk. Then add dry ingredients and lightly stir with a wooden spoon. Pour into a well-oiled 8"x8" baking pan. (Since the brownies themselves are a dark color, it's fine to bake them in a glass pan rather than a dark pan.) Bake these brownies for one hour (if you want them quickly and the sun is very bright) or allow them to bake all day.

Serves 6–8 or fewer.

Sun Lasagna

1/2 lb (8 noodles) spinach or whole wheat lasagna noodles
4 cups crushed tomatoes
1 tbs dried basil or 2 tbs fresh basil
1 tbs dried oregano or 2 tbs fresh oregano
3 cups Swiss chard or other fresh greens, chopped
1/4 cup grated soy cheese (Monterey Jack type)
1 lb. tofu mashed
1/2 tsp nutmeg
1 tbs Bragg Liquid Aminos
1/4 lb. mozzarella-type soy cheese, shredded

Tomatoes and herbs are mixed together in a cast iron pot; chopped greens are added and the ingredients are cooked briefly and removed from the pot when limp. Mash the tofu separately and grated Jack-style soy cheese. Then layer one-third of the tomato mixture, alternating with noodles, repeating the layers two more times and top with shredded mozzarella-style soy cheese. Cover tightly and sun-bake half a day or until done.

Note: Lasagna noodles (and other pasta) may not hold up well in this process. The result is still delicious. Enjoy it for what it is, but don't expect it to be like the oven-baked variety. Serves 4–6.

Golden Glow Soup

4 cups cooked* winter squash, peeled and cut into small chunks (carrots or pumpkin also work well)
4 cups of soy milk, rice milk, oat milk, or almond milk
1 tsp each: ground dry mustard, turmeric, ground ginger, cumin
1/2 tsp cinnamon
Dash of cayenne pepper (optional)
1 cup vegetable stock or water
1 tbs honey or agave nectar

Pour 1 cup soy milk into a blender and add 1 cup squash; blend until smooth. Repeat the process with the remaining squash and milk. Then combine all ingredients in a dark pot, cover and simmer all day in the sun.

Serve hot to 6–8, depending on if it is the main meal or an addition.

*To cook squash: If the sun's energy allows, on the day before making this soup, cut the squash into pieces, set in a deep baking dish, cover and steam (no water is needed) all day long, or until soft. If it's a cloudy day, cut the squash in half, remove all of the seeds and place it face down in a baking pan. Bake at 350°F until soft when you touch it, approximately 1 hour (more or less depending on size of squash). You can also bake it whole, which takes approximately twice as long.

Crockpot Recipes

Vegetarian Crockpot Chili

1 onion
2 small zucchini
1 small garlic clove
8 oz. mushrooms
1 large can crushed tomatoes
1 can each: red kidneys, garbanzo beans, white kidneys, black beans (If you
    use dried beans, you must soak and cook them first.)
2 1/2 cups prepared brown rice (Rice soaks up the extra moisture that
    comes from crockpot cooking.)
1/8 tsp powdered red pepper
1 tsp cumin
2 tsp oregano (or substitute your favorite chili seasonings)

Chop all of the vegetables and lay them on bottom of the crockpot. Add the
tomatoes, beans, rice and seasonings. Do not mix everything together. Turn the
crockpot to low and allow it to cook 6–8 hours. At the very end, stir everything
together well and add salt and pepper to taste.

Vegetable Paella (Crockpot)
Adapted from *The Best Slow Cooker Cookbook Ever*

10 ounces packaged frozen chopped spinach, thawed but not drained
2 cups converted white rice
4 cups homemade vegetable stock
1 green bell pepper, chopped
3/4 cup chopped roasted red peppers
1 large onion, chopped
2 garlic cloves, minced
1/2 tsp saffron threads (or turmeric)
1/2 tsp cumin
1/8 tsp cayenne pepper (or to taste)
1/2 tsp salt
1/4 tsp freshly ground pepper
13 3/4 ounces canned quartered artichoke hearts, rinsed and well drained
16 ounces packaged frozen mixed vegetables, thawed

1. In a 3 1/2- or 4-quart electric slow cooker, combine the spinach (undrained), rice, stock, roasted peppers, onion, bell pepper, garlic, saffron, cumin, cayenne, salt and pepper.
2. Cover and cook on low heat for about 4 hours, or until the rice is just tender but the grains are still separate; watch closely toward the end of the cooking time.
3. Stir in the artichokes and the thawed vegetables. Increase the heat to the high setting and cook, uncovered, for just 10 minutes longer. Serve immediately.

Serves 6 to 8.

Further Ways to Reduce Your Carbon Footprint In the Kitchen

- Use cloth bags when shopping to avoid plastic.
- Avoid products with excessive packaging.
- Keep the use of plastics, paper, napkins, etc. to a bare minimum.
- Recycle faithfully. Compost faithfully.
- Use water in the kitchen sparingly and use cold to start, as it requires energy every time you turn on the hot water.
- Turn off lights and appliances when not in use.

*If you need to use a bag for your trash, use eco-friendly biodegradable bags instead of plastic bags. While the ability of these bags to biodegrade in landfills is poor, due to poor air circulation, my opinion is that they are still a much better choice than plastic, if they are made from GMO-free corn. Both the way they are produced and their impact once discarded is much more earth-friendly than plastic.

Taking the Next Step

What is one step that you can take to be more energy-efficient in your cooking? What would support you in taking this action? ●

CHAPTER 9
SAFE COOKING POTS AND FOOD STORAGE CONTAINERS

"He who does not mind his belly will hardly mind anything else."

—Samuel Johnson

THE MONASTERY KITCHEN IS THE HOME OF MY ALL-time favorite cooking pots: a sturdy, heavy, well-crafted set of dark cast iron pots and pans. Every evening on retreat, the largest of the cast iron pots would be used for serving a delicious batch of colorful soup that warmed the body and the soul. The pot would hold cream of cauliflower soup with a garnish of peas and herbs one day, colorful minestrone another day, and my all-time favorite, creamy winter-squash miso soup at another meal.

At the end of every meal, during cleanup, the senior monks would attend to cleaning and treating the cast iron pot. This special job was left for the senior monks, because such a pot required extra care. The heavy pot would get carefully washed and scrubbed, rinsed well, and still dripping, carried over to the stove (quite a muscle builder this pot was) to be treated with heat and oil. A monk would gently add just enough canola oil to the pot and use a teeny tiny piece of unbleached paper towel (so as not to create waste) to massage the oil into the contours of the pot evenly as it quietly "cured" over a small flame.

This massage often felt like a way of thanking the pot or giving back to it for doing its blessed job as the container of such nourishing soup. At the exact moment when smoke began to rise from the pot, it meant that the curing was done. The stove was turned off and the pot was left to cool, before being used for another satisfying meal the following night.

In a natural and sustainable kitchen, we bring the same attitude of mind and appreciation for the pots and vessels that we use and, in doing so, we also pay as much attention to the types of pots and vessels we use that we pay to the quality of food that we eat or the water we use to cook with.

Safe Cooking Vessels

COOKING POTS AND PANS VARY DRAMATICALLY IN TERMS OF SAFETY and sustainability and this is an area every green cook should pay attention to. We have become accustomed to cooking in Teflon and other sprayed cookware that exude chemical toxins into our food and indoor air, storing our foods in plastic containers and Ziplocs that get thrown away, and never giving a thought about or creating a standard for how restaurants are cooking or storing our food. If you care about your health and the health of your family, then this is an area to bring awareness and discernment to. It is not difficult to follow healthy cooking guidelines and keep your food from harming you! But it requires vigilance, as there are so many toxins in the world of cookware and food storage.

In my research, I try to find information from independent, nonprofit research groups beyond the Food and Drug Administration (FDA), because the FDA has been wrong in the case of toxic chemicals before (and face it, the FDA is backed by billion-dollar firms). There have been far too many cases where the FDA has deemed something safe that we find out down the road is a major health hazard.

As a sustainability coach, I consider the following materials to be safe to use for cooking:

- **Cast iron**—It conducts heat evenly and is perfectly safe to cook in.
- **Stainless steel cookware**—This is made from a combination of iron and other metals. It is a durable product that is safe to use. Most stainless steel cookware is made with copper or aluminum bottoms and I would opt for pure stainless steel if you can. In addition, the inside of some stainless steel cookware is labeled 18/10, which means 18% chromium and 10% nickel. If you are allergic to the metal nickel, you can try 18/8 or 18/0.
- **Glass**—It is non-porous and does not react with food.

- Eco-friendly ceramic cookware—There is a wide array of ceramic cookware available today. One of my favorite brands is Emile Henry, a French company that also includes energy efficiency in some of their designs.

I encourage people to use the following materials with care:

- **Pottery** may contain lead in the glaze that can come into contact with and enter the food stored in it. Pottery made in the U.S. has to meet safety requirements, but it is best not to prepare food in pottery made from Mexico or Latin America because of potential lead levels. Please do not ignore labels; if it says *Not for food use,* don't use it!
- **Anodized aluminum** is generally considered safe, as manufacturers claim that a final stage in the anodization process seals the aluminum, thus preventing any leaching into food; however, I use aluminum with caution due to the links between aluminum and both brain degeneration and bone loss, among other health issues.
- **Copper** is typically lined with tin or stainless steel. The Food and Drug Administration cautions against using unlined copper for general cooking because the metal is relatively easily dissolved by some foods with which it comes in contact.
- **Iron and steel** cookware is sometimes manufactured with enamel coating. Enamel-coated cookware is safe to use, is stain- and scratch-resistant and does not absorb odors, Back in the 1970s, toxic cadmium was an issue in the pigments of imported enamel cookware, but after an FDA ban, manufacturers stopped using pigments with cadmium.

I encourage people to NOT use the following materials for cooking:

- **Aluminum** (including limiting the use of aluminum foil as much as you can). While the impact of aluminum has been controversial, aluminum toxicity has been proven to result in brain deterioration, bone loss, speech problems, anemia, lowered liver function, digestive problems and impaired kidney functions. I wouldn't want aluminum in my own kitchen!
- **Teflon** or other non-stick pans have a coating, which can chip off over time and come into contact with food. While there is some controversy over the health effects of this, the FDA has said that these particles pose no health hazard. In addition a non-stick pan can give off fumes when heated at high temperatures and pollute our indoor air, as well as causing pollution when being manufactured. Studies have linked the primary chemical to cancer and organ damage in animal tests, and tests suggest that it is already present in the blood of "virtually every American." The EPA says DuPont has agreed to eliminate new emissions by 2010.

The Apache Bean Pot

Living in an eco-collective in San Francisco, our kitchen had a collection of handmade micaceous clay pots crafted in New Mexico by an Apache medicine man named Felipe Ortega. These pots were stunningly beautiful and simple in design. Holding one felt like the soft smooth earth in your hands.

The Apache have an ancient tradition of making pottery with micaceous earth and the particular pots we had were known as Apache Bean Pots, perfect for cooking rice and beans. Felipe claims that these earthen pots are the fastest cookers in the West. This was, indeed, my experience of them and beyond their efficiency, no vessel is more appropriate for holding a wholesome organic meal than a handmade clay pot. (For more information, visit **felipeortega.com**)

Traditional cultures around the world demonstrate a wide array of natural means for cooking, but Westerners have become accustomed to the metal pot, pan, and stove. Let us open our minds to traditional approaches to cooking and exploring new options for cooking healthfully and sustainably, in response to the resources available and regional qualities of the place in which we live.

Food Wrapping and Packaging

Food wrapping and packaging invites yet another element of investigation into the safety of our kitchens. Remember, in aligning our kitchen with nature, we are choosing "Commitment to a Safe Non-toxic World" (Sustainable Kitchen Principle Number Four).

In Western culture, habits for food storage and packaging regularly compromise this principle, as we have become addicted to the likes of Tupperware, Ziploc bags and aluminum foil. Not only do we choose to package our food in unhealthy and toxic containers, but the manufacturing of these products also causes pollution and we create unprecedented waste by throwing away a great deal of disposal packaging.

In my experience, addressing this area requires true commitment and tenacity, unless we are to settle for doing things "the way everyone else does." We can learn to make wiser choices in the materials we use and care for those materials appropriately, for instance by washing and reusing wax paper or tinfoil when we do use it. As you bring these habits into your own kitchen, keep in mind that doing so will not only be beneficial to your health and the health of the planet, but it will help seal the shift in habits that we NEED to make culturally.

> *"If not us, who? If not now, when?"*
> —Chief Seattle

Here are some guidelines for bringing consciousness to our food wrapping and packaging choices.

The following materials are good choices:

- Glass
- Stainless steel
- Unbleached parchment paper
- Untreated soy wax paper
- Silicone baking sheets—Silicone is made from common sand, the same stuff glass is made of, and it is safe to use for baking and cooking. A silicone baking sheet is a sheet of silicone that can be reused over and over again.

Do not use the following materials for food storage:

- **Plastic containers**
- **Aluminum foil**
- **Bleached parchment paper**
- **Aluminum foil**—Do not use aluminum foil to cook food in or wrap food with. If you need foil for loosely covering a baking pan, use foil from recycled aluminum and use it sparingly. When I make roasted root veggies or roasted sunchokes, this is what I use, but I gave up using it for daily cooking long ago, after becoming more aware of the dangers of aluminum.
- **Saran Wrap**—My favorite alternative is parchment paper. I like to just wrap sandwiches in a clean cotton towel or use a glass container, but if you need to wrap a sandwich, you can use parchment paper. Place the sandwich in the middle of a square of paper, fold it up and tie a string around it.

The following materials can be used with these considerations:

- **Wax paper**—Wax paper is coated with paraffin, a petrochemical wax. Wax paper bags can be useful for big events, but are not the ideal. A good alternative is Lehman's All Natural Wax Paper, which is made with 100% soybean wax.
- **Tape**—Most tape is made of plastic, so I like to have reusable cotton string on hand instead.

For more information and a complete list of green food storage options, please visit Debra Lynn Dadd's site "Debra's List" at **debraslist.com** (search on "food storage"). Debra Lynn Dadd is a world-class expert on how to create a toxin-free home and I rely on her site for expert information regularly.

Freezer Storage

There are alternatives to plastic that work for freezer storage, such as Pyrex glass and Natural Value's Freezer Slider Bags, which are made of recycled material and are free of Bisphenol A and phthalates. You can also find a middle way by reusing recycled plastic bags or plastic containers at times, particularly for non-liquid frozen foods. A good rule of thumb is to only choose plastic reusables for storing solids, not liquids.

Glass can break when frozen, so if you intend to freeze something long-term in glass, make sure the glass is tempered or specifically labeled "freezer-safe." In general, freezer bags and wraps need to be thick enough to keep moisture in and freezer odors out.

Here are some basic tips for eco-friendly freezing:

• **Freeze in small portions:** The faster food freezes, the fresher it will taste once thawed. As a general rule, remember that if you freeze large portions in large containers, food takes longer to freeze.
• **Squeeze out excess air:** Where there's air, there will be freezer burn. Get as much air as possible out of bags and if you put food in a container, make sure that the food fills the entire container. However, when freezing liquids, you actually need to leave an inch or so at the top of the container, as liquid expands when it freezes. Soups and stews can keep well in the freezer for up to three months in this way.
• **Stash strategically:** Allow hot foods to cool down before freezing them. Then, when placing an item in the freezer, leave plenty of space around the container so cold air can circulate around it. This allows the item to freeze faster and thus taste fresher once it's thawed. Once it's fully frozen, you can stack it in another part of the freezer.

Here are some ideas for freezing the following items:

• **Berries and other small "squishable" items such as cooked pasta:** Spread on a baking sheet and freeze until solid. Then transfer them into an eco-friendly storage container. This method will prevent them from clumping together as they freeze.
• **Bread and bagels:** Slice bread and halve bagels before freezing them so you can easily remove the number of servings you need once they are frozen. Also, place bagel halves into the freezer bag back-to-back so they're less likely to stick together.
• **Pancakes and waffles:** Let them cool, separate them with wax soy wax paper to prevent sticking and then place in a storage container. ●

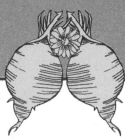

CHAPTER 10
HOW TO GROW FOOD IN YOUR OWN BACKYARD

"One of the most important resources that a garden makes available for use, is the gardener's own body. A garden gives the body the dignity of working in its own support. It is a way of rejoining the human race."

—Wendell Berry

A S A GARDENER, OVER THE YEARS I'VE HAD THE unique opportunity to learn about biodynamic farming, bio-intensive farming, permaculture design, and I have even experimented with what is called "lasagna gardening." There are so many wise approaches to gardening out there and you can learn a lot from various techniques—but what interests me the most is what we can draw from all of these techniques. What is the core of sustainable gardening? I've learned that there are a few basic principles that apply to all these techniques, which I will outline in this chapter.

Gardening is about "getting down to earth." It requires your time, care, observation, and the willingness to learn about the relationships within the garden. While this chapter will ground you in a basic knowledge of sustainable gardening, you can only develop your learning through experience, rather than expecting to learn how to interact with nature through studying a book. As a gardener, engage yourself fully and be prepared for the unknown, the unexpected, the puzzling, and the miraculous.

These are some of the things I love about gardening that a textbook can't teach you: Doing hard work builds my muscles but it is not so hard that I can't do it myself; getting dirty, especially getting my hands dirty; using my bare hands to de-clump soil that I am preparing or to loosen the delicate roots of a plant I am putting into the ground—touching the soil connects me intrinsically to the sacred earth; learning to see insects not as "bugs" I might normally disregard but as tiny incredible creatures who share my garden with me and with whom I am invited to observe and develop a unique relationship; and lastly, letting my garden keep me honest, because I have to show up for it no matter what and it will give instant feedback if I don't.

There are truly few things as satisfying as learning to grow your own food. Nothing is better than going outside and watching a bean you planted burst through the soil and begin spiraling its way up to maturity, exploding into unforeseen colors and patterns, or tasting your first ripe heirloom tomato and having an experience of sweet perfection.

Gardens are full of surprises and delight and serve as useful teachers for city folk in how nature works. The organic gardening movement is spreading through American neighborhoods and backyards quickly and as a reflection of that, for the first time since the Depression, organic food is growing on the grounds of the White House this year.

As the organic gardening movement spreads, it is important that people learn how to practice sustainable organic gardening—for instance, learning to conserve water while gardening, take proper care of the soil, build good soil, and practice Integrated Pest Management (IPM). Sustainable agriculture is focused on working **with** nature by "giving back" to the soil and practicing the art of observation.

> *"Start with one bed and tend it well."*
> —Alan Chadwick

The most important and useful thing I was ever taught about gardening is to remember that, as a gardener, my job is to grow soil. Healthy plants come from growing good soil. By focusing on soil, I get something far more rewarding than just food: a long-term relationship with the plot of dirt I'm working on and a garden that will sustain itself long-term, becoming even richer and healthier over time.

As a gardener, whatever I put into the effort will come back to me. I can watch "dirt" turn into something that is unmistakably sacred: soft rich earth filled with worms and beneficial soil microorganisms. Good soil ensures higher nutrition in garden produce, better water filtration (thus less watering required), fewer pests, and less work over time. The bottom line is: healthy plants require healthy soil.

On the other hand, if my focus is on "growing the most plants and biggest plants I can, as quickly as I can," I might be prone to use pesticides and Miracle-Gro or plant inappropriately. I will simply be gardening from a misinformed premise and will miss out on the great opportunity to become intimate with the earth. Gardening is a dynamic interplay of soil, sun, water, insects, plants, and micro-organisms. A gardener's success comes from honoring this interconnection and working *with* nature. If we look at large-scale conventional agriculture, we can see how the emphasis on producing "the most, the biggest, the fastest" has wreaked havoc on the environment, soil health, and the quality and nutrition of produce.

Before You Begin

Test your soil. There is risk of toxic chemicals such as lead in urban soil. It is important to test it to find out if you can work with what you've got or if you need to build garden boxes and bring in new soil. Visit the National Sustainable Agriculture Information Service (**attra.ncat.org**) to locate soil testing in your area.

Find a sunny spot in your yard and design your garden beds. Anyone can start a thriving, life-enriching garden in an urban setting. Try not to let yourself feel bound by spatial limitations and remember that there are many ways to design your garden. Plants can grow upward, outward and downward, and beds can be designed in any shape to produce a plethora of vegetables in a small space. This is a perfect place to practice creative reuse and find unique containers for growing your garden (for example, a tire, an old bathtub, an aged wheelbarrow). Think both horizontal and vertical.

You may only have the space to create a container herb garden, or you may have the space for a large raised-bed vegetable garden that supplies the bulk of your diet. I have helped people to start gardens in containers, in tires, on hillsides, and in a downtown industrial lot. For those of you with little space, you can start a successful container garden or vertical garden on your balcony, or join a community garden to grow your food in.

Gather your compost. If you are not already making compost, now is the time to begin. You can learn how to create compost from kitchen scraps in Chapter Three. Meanwhile, go out and buy a large bag of organic compost (or a truckload, depending on the size of the space you are working in!) to give your soil the humus it will need at the very beginning.

Set up an efficient watering system. You will need a good watering can for seeds and new seedlings and an effective hose. I recommend a hose reel to keep your garden tidy and an adjustable watering attachment to allow for a variety of settings, including a soaker and mister setting. I prefer hand-watering to irrigation (or along with irrigation) if your garden is small enough to manage, so that you can pay better attention to how much water gets used.

Learn what climate zone you are in. There is a lot of helpful information online to help you navigate being a first-time gardener. It's helpful to know what zone (growing climate) you are growing in, so you can access the right information for your needs. For instance, someone gardening in Los Angeles, Zone 10, is able to grow different crops than someone gardening in the Sierra foothills.

Begin attracting beneficial insects, if they do not already visit your garden, even before you begin planting vegetables. Read more about this further in this chapter.

....

How to Create Healthy Soil

"A frog does not drink up the pond in which he lives…"
—Native American proverb

Growing healthy soil is the ultimate goal of an organic gardener. This requires us to be in the consistent practice of giving back to the soil rather than depleting it. Soil is a mix of mineral, water, air, and organic matter. Creating balanced soil creates healthy plants that attract fewer pests and require less water.

Organic matter is key to soil health and it is important to apply this to the soil regularly. It is a priority of every gardener to take kind care of the soil you are growing in by applying organic matter, practicing crop rotation, protecting the soil, and utilizing the tools I will present in this chapter. When people invite me over to assess their poor tomatoes or stunted eggplant, it almost always comes down to not taking care of the soil.

To Dig or Not to Dig? The Benefits of Double-Digging

In my gardening workshops, there is a moment some people have called the "just before getting dirty" moment where they think they would rather stay clean. They think they would rather be onlookers and just watch the group get dirty while they stand aside and watch. And then their turn comes and they are offered a shovel and they get out there and reluctantly roll up their sleeves… and then something happens. They get dirty and loosen up and have fun and relax and begin to fall in love with getting dirty. I watch this over and over again in workshops. Next they begin to fall in love with worms. The unexpected happens to us when we get out into the garden.

Conventional agriculture tends to over-till the soil (especially with the use of tractors), which causes unnecessary erosion and damages microbial life. The most effective technique I have found for working the soil in a non-invasive way is double-digging, part of the bio-intensive technique developed by John Jeavons, a leader in the sustainable agriculture movement and founder of Ecology Action (**ecologyaction.org**). At the beginning, I highly recommend digging your soil as a way to begin creating healthy, well-balanced, aerated, and nutrient-rich growing soil. While single-digging allows us to get one foot deep, double digging enables us to loosen (but not disturb) the soil 24 inches deep.

"Double-dug beds, with soil loosened to a depth of 24 inches, aerate the soil, facilitate root growth and improve water retention… (reducing water use from 67–88%!) The health and vigor of the soil are maintained through the use of compost. Close plant spacing is used to protect soil microorganisms, reduce water loss, and maximize yields." The benefits of double-digging include saving water, using less space, attracting fewer pests, and being body-friendly for the gardener.

To learn to double-dig, I recommend reading *How to Grow More Vegetables* by John Jeavons or attending a training course given by his organization, Ecology Action.

I sometimes have had to single-dig when I have been especially busy or at a time when I was dealing with physical injury and my body simply didn't have the strength for anything beyond single-digging. If you find yourself in a situation where single-digging is necessary, single-digging can be done simply by following these steps:

Water your soil well 24 hours in advance, if it is dry. Clear your soil so it is bare. Rake off any leaves or mulch covering the soil, pull out old weeds unless there are just a few, and remove any irrigation tubes that may be in place. You can simply pull it to the side without dismantling it entirely. Cover your soil in two inches at least of organic compost. Add a sprinkle of any amendments that you know your soil needs. Then simply step onto your shovel, digging it into the soil one shovel's length, turn it over and gently chop the soil if there are any bulky sections. Do this in rows for an entire bed. At the end take time to de-clump the soil with your hands and then rake it out into a nice smooth bed.

Double-digging is a more involved process, but it is 100% worth the investment of your time and energy. I cannot emphasize enough the beauty and quality of soil that can be created by double-digging; however single-digging is perfectly sufficient if the amount of physical labor you can do is limited.

Your Toolbox as an Organic Gardener:

Please consider the following basic tools for soil and plant care as you plan/design your garden.

Crop rotation

Plan your garden with the principles of crop rotation in mind. Simply stated, there are great benefits to not planting the same thing twice on a plot of land. I like to wait three years to plant the same thing. If I've got tomatoes in plot A in the summer of 2009, then I can wait three years before planting it again. There are likely to be tomato horn worm larvae in the soil and planning ahead can help you to avoid future infestations. In addition, plants have different impacts on the soil they are grown in. A tomato is a heavy feeder, so it leaches a lot of nutrients from the soil. A bean is a heavy giver, so it gives a lot of nitrogen back to the soil. A carrot is a light feeder, so it takes just a light amount of nutrients from the soil.

The basic guideline for crop rotation is:
Heavy feeder (fruit or leaf crop)
Heavy giver (legume)
Light feeder (root crop)

You can plant a heavy feeder, such as corn, eggplant, or chard in the summer, followed by a heavy giver, such as cover crop or snow peas in the fall, followed by a light feeder such as carrots, beets, or burdock in the wintertime. My favorite way to give nitrogen back to the soil is to sow **cover crop,** otherwise known as "green manure," once a year in each bed. Cover crop is seed sown entirely for the benefit of the soil and one of its uses is to reduce leaching following a main crop. (My favorite is a mix of seeds that may include alfalfa, vetch, and rye.) Fall or winter are my favorite seasons for cover crop... just after a hard-working productive summer season when it is time for the garden soil (and the gardener) to rest.

What to Plant Where: Companion Planting and Polycultural Gardens

JUST LIKE HUMANS, THERE ARE PLANTS THAT LIKE AND BENEFIT ONE another and plants that do not. There are plants that have favorite "companions" in whose presence they thrive, while also having "antagonists" that they don't do so well around. I've planted beets with pole beans with little growth, and have watched the very same plants thrive enthusiastically when moved next to a row of onions.

I've found it very helpful to have a basic knowledge of companions and antagonists when planning my garden. For example, basil does well with tomatoes, peppers, and marigolds. If you plant a bed of tomatoes, basil, and marigolds, you've got a nice mix of salad veggies with edible flowers that attract beneficial insects. Carrots like bush beans, lettuce, tomatoes, onions, radishes, peas, and sage. They don't like dill.

If you plant a bed of carrots, beans, and tomatoes, you've got a nice mix of heavy feeders, heavy givers, and light feeders. You've got plants growing up out of the soil and down into the soil, so you're making good use of space. The pole beans can also be trained up a trellis in the middle of the bed, or can grow up the tomatoes. Melons, for instance, like corn, nasturtium, and radishes. You could grow a bed of melon with nasturtiums on the edges to attract beneficial insects and have radishes in between the plants, which are lower growing and can help mulch the soil, since melons grow further apart but spread out a lot. What I'm encouraging is planting **polycultural** beds. For a complete list of companions and antagonists, you can visit **companionplanting.net**.

A classic example of companion planting is the Three Sisters. In this Native American agricultural technique, one plants corn, squash, and pole beans together in the same bed. The corn grows upwards, the beans climb their way up the corn stalks, and the squash grows lower to the ground and mulches the soil, protecting the soil for the benefit of all of the crops. These three crops are perfect companions and a wise use of space. The Three Sisters are a fun combination to plant in your own backyard if you live in a sunny climate.

How Much To Plant

BE CAREFUL HOW MUCH YOU PLANT. AS A GARDENER AND COMMU-nity cook, I have routinely run into a time each summer when I have more "fill-in-the blank" than I can handle. I've learned to get extremely creative with cucumbers, summer squash, cherry tomatoes, eggplant, and other eager summer crops. Once, caught up in a wave of over-enthusiasm about the idea of using a deep-rooting crop to help aerate the soil of a long garden bed at the Monastery, I decided to plant rows and rows of burdock. In the fall, it all ripened at the same time, and as the rainy season was coming and could rot the roots, we had to harvest and eat it all in a short period of time. I love burdock and all extremely unusual foods and roots, and appreciate the medicinal qualities of burdock tea, but for the community, it was a little overwhelming to suddenly have this strange-looking root show up in everything from stir-frys to salads to tea to main dishes. When planning your garden, learn to really look ahead from the chef's perspective (in addition to using the cycle of crop rotation) and think about exactly how much you might want of a certain vegetable before you put it in the ground.

Integrated Pest Management

The only RULES I have in gardening are the following:

THERE IS NEVER ANY NEED TO USE PESTICIDES, HERBICIDES, OR FUNGICIDES FOR ANY REASON.

THERE IS A KIND SOLUTION TO EVERY ECOLOGICAL PROBLEM. ALWAYS CHOOSE THE SOLUTION TO A PEST PROBLEM THAT CAUSES THE LEAST AMOUNT OF HARM.

All of the solutions to our gardening "problems" exist in nature and often the solution begins by changing our interpretation of a problem. Addressing pests without chemicals requires time, attention, and commitment. At first it may seem like more time than you are used to spending in your garden, but if you are serious about gardening pesticide-free, you will find the time spent a worthy endeavor. Here are the primary steps of integrated pest management:

• Plan ahead.
• Practice keen daily observation.
• Find natural solutions to address pest imbalances and infestations that occur, based on your observation.

Planning Ahead

Planning ahead is the most important aspect of Integrated Pest Management. If you can avoid attracting pests to your garden to begin with, your life will be easier and your garden more abundant. The number one encouragement I would give to new gardeners is to attract as many beneficial insects to your garden as possible. I cannot emphasize enough the importance of this. Some ways to do this are:

• Plant fragrant, tubular flowers in a variety of sizes to provide plenty of nectar for the bees and beneficial insects you want to attract.
• Provide habitats for your beneficial insects to thrive in, for instance, evergreens or hedges provide them with cover.
• Keep the ground well mulched to provide additional cover and hold in moisture.
• Hang a hummingbird feeder in a tree by your garden.

Another aspect of planning ahead involves placing plant protection barriers to protect seedlings and deter pests that may come. Examples of this include:

• Installing chicken wire fencing beneath garden beds if your yard is susceptible to gophers
• Making plant protection collars from old cereal boxes or yogurt containers and setting them up around young and vulnerable transplants.
• Setting up traps for pests that may come. For example, if you know you live in earwig territory, you can place crumpled-up newspaper inside a plastic container or plastic gardening pot, place it upside down on a stake in the garden beds and it will attract any earwigs that come. You can check it daily, empty it, and relocate them to someplace outside the garden.

The Art of Observation

Practicing keen observation enables you to catch any pest problems that may arise early. Make it a practice to go out every day and spend a few minutes simply observing your plants. Think of them as your children and check under their leaves, notice their skin tone, pay attention to their body posture. These check-ins are a time for you to learn how to read your plants and let them communicate with you.

If you catch pests early on, you will save yourself much time and energy taking care of them. I've had aphid infestations that I've caught at the beginning and then it's only taken two weeks of devoted soap spray treatment to get rid of them. On the other hand, caught one week later, I've had infestations take treatments twice a day for over a month until they're gone.

To give a grosser example, the difference between picking just a few squash beetles off your pumpkin leaves is definitely preferable to spending one hour every day picking off more than you've ever seen in a childhood horror movie and dumping them in water.... The choice is yours. Take your pick. Speaking from personal experience, I'd opt for just a few squash beetles any day!

Preparation also involves planting correctly. I like to put collars around the seedlings I transplant and put pest deterrents around the specific plants that a pest is likely to be attracted to.

Natural Solutions and Homemade Remedies

If you find pests, immediately investigate to find out what kind of pest you are working with and what its life cycle and habits can tell you about your action plan. The next step is knowing what kind of natural pesticide mixtures to blend for the pests that show up. These solutions can be made up in your kitchen out of inexpensive everyday supplies and can successfully repel a wide range of insects.

Soapy water sprays can be used for aphids and spider mites. When using any of these sprays, it helps to wet both sides of the leaves and to repeat after a rain or as often as necessary. Flour and salt can also be used to repel pests, as a dust to suffocate or dehydrate various kinds of caterpillars. Cutworm attacks can also be discouraged by sprinkling wood ashes around the base of plants.

Here are some natural pest deterrents that have worked for me:

Homemade Soap Sprays

Soap is a deterrent to soft-bodied insects such as aphids. It disrupts insects' cell membranes and it kills pests by dehydration. To make a soap spray, simply dissolve 3 tablespoons of liquid soap (not detergent) into a gallon of water, fill a spray bottle and apply this solution to your plants.

Homemade Garlic Spray:

1 bulb garlic
1 quart water
1 medium onion
1 tablespoon cayenne pepper
1 tablespoon liquid dish soap

Run the garlic through a garlic press. Mince onion and mix garlic and onion into the water. Add the remaining ingredients except for the soap. Let this mixture steep for an hour. Add soap and your spray is ready to use. It can be refrigerated for up to one week and the garlic and onion can just stay in the mixture.

Herbal Insect Repellent:

If you have access to the leaves from tansy, lavender, and sage, each of these plants has strong insect-repelling qualities. You will need an ounce of leaves from each plant. Place the herbs in a 1-quart jar. Fill the jar with boiling water and let it steep until the water cools. Or make an infusion by steeping the herbs outside in the sun as you would make sun tea. Drain off the liquid and set this solution aside. Then dissolve 1 teaspoon of soap in 2 cups of water. Add 1/8 cup of the herbal solution and mix well. Use a spray bottle to coat the entire plant with this repellent.

Hot and Spicy Spray:

You can also combine hot peppers and garlic with a soapy solution. In a blender, puree 2 hot peppers and 2 cloves of garlic. Add 3 cups of water and 2 tablespoons of biodegradable soap. Then strain the mixture and fill a spray bottle with the solution.

Lastly, never take your pests personally or your garden too seriously. I've had new gardeners call me in trauma because pests had attacked their vegetables and they had thought they were doing "such a good job."

As the gardener, let us never believe that we are in control. Nature has its own agenda and, usually, nature has much better plans than ours. If something gets attacked, consider that you might just be able to share some of your harvest with a family of critters, or even plant a small portion of your garden for them. I've had success deterring ants (which can actually be quite pesky in a garden) from my crops by actually digging a hole in the soil and putting a large amount of food scraps there for them to eat up instead of being attracted to my beds.

One of the most creative gardeners I know once planted a circle of sunflowers on the outside of his whole garden so that the neighboring squirrels would go for them and let the rest of the garden be. And it worked! To sum up Integrated Pest Management, plan ahead, practice observation, and apply natural solutions. Always work *with* nature and not against her and you will get the best results. And never take pests personally!

Permaculture Garden Design

PERMACULTURE DESIGN IS AN APPROACH TO DESIGNING HUMAN HABI-tats and agricultural system in harmony with nature. Permaculture design offers a set of principles—similar to the principles for the sustainable kitchen presented in this book—serving as guideposts that give humans a way to work with nature in designing sustainable systems. Here are a few examples of how permaculture principles can be easily applied to the food garden.

One of my favorite elements of permaculture design in gardening includes the concept of **stacking functions**. These allow us to make the most use of space and discover effective ways for an element in the garden to serve many purposes at once. An example of this would be to plant "living mulch."

While people typically choose things like straw, leaves, and wood chips for mulch, planting a living mulch such as chamomile serves two purposes: 1) It protects soil from erosion and maintains moisture (the goal of mulching a bed). 2) It provides an edible herb to make tea out of. Another example of a stacking function is planting daikon root in a bed that needs soil aeration. The daikon is a delicious vegetable to eat. It is a root that can be planted for crop rotation but it is also doing a service for your soil due to how deep it roots.

Permaculture design encourages creative reuse of every resource on hand, and a garden is a perfect place to invent and discover creative uses for things you might not have imagined being useful. Read Chapter Three for some ideas on how to cultivate a relationship of creative reuse between the kitchen and the garden. You might also consider setting up reuse systems for water by using secondary water (greywater or rainwater) to feed your garden. I know a couple that watered their large front yard garden for an entire summer with rainwater they had collected during the year.

Permaculture also emphasizes human sustainability and reminds us to make our gardens user-friendly. I find that people often leave this important element out of garden design and create systems that take extra work (such as an inefficient hand-watering systems or beds that are uncomfortable to work in). One example of incorporating human sustainability into your vegetable garden is the idea of **keyhole gardening**. These are often round or horseshoe-shaped gardens planted near the home that allow easy access to plants that are used on a regular basis, such as salad vegetables and herbs.

Remember human sustainability as you design your garden. Why not plant your vegetables as close as possible to your kitchen to make for easy harvesting? Why not set the compost right outside the kitchen door? What about planting perennials (plants that do not need to be reseeded each year) rather than annuals? Consider the wisdom of growing a collard or kale tree that gives tons of nutrient-rich leaves throughout the year without you having to till the soil or replant kale each year.

Watering Wisely

IT IS EVERY GARDENER'S RESPONSIBILITY TO SET UP WATER-WISE SYS-tems. I don't recommend relying on an irrigation system without carefully monitoring it. While it can be useful to set up an irrigation system to assist you, water-wise gardening comes down to the art of observation. As a rule, never water your crops in the full sun or even in the middle of the day. Watering should be done in the morning and/or the evening, when the least amount of evaporation will occur and the plant is in no danger of sunburn.

Rather an exact rule of "how often should I water?" become used to watching and testing the soil (with your finger, or with a shovel: sticking your shovel in the soil and seeing if the bottom of the shovel is moist when you remove it from the soil.) Seeds just planted need to be allowed to moisten and let the soil get dry before wetting it again. New seeds may need to be watered once a day or twice a day or even three times a day, depending on the seed, the season, and the climate. Young seedlings like big puddles around them that will encourage deep roots to grow.

Consider that if you are just lightly watering the top surface of the soil you are simply encouraging weeds, but not encouraging healthy root systems. Most people water too often with not enough water. More mature plants may get watered three times or even once a week, depending on the weather. Again, if you deep water, it is not necessary to do this too often.

The Summertime Watering Ritual

In the heat of summertime, toward the end of an active day, when the sun is just beginning to settle down and shine its rays more gently before setting, is the ideal time to go out and water the garden. I like to take my time, giving concentrated and focused attention to each plant, luxuriating in the garden as I water each plant. I watch the thirsty plants perk up as their thirst is quenched and feel my own body relax as the warm sun touches my skin. I get to notice how each plant has grown, glimpse evidence of budding fruit, and see how each plant has benefited from my care and attention, or note where a plant may need some attention, and watch the earth soak up the water as if saying "thank you." It often feels as if the garden is an extension of my own body and the watering ritual is a time of purely "giving back."

Tips for Watering Appropriately

If you water lightly just the surface of the soil, you will encourage weeds to grow and you will not be watering the roots of the plants well.

Be mindful of runoff when you are watering.

The ideal times to water are in the morning before the sun is high or in the early evening. Plants can get sunburned if they are wet under the sun and, in addition, this is simply a way to avoid evaporation.

Watering frequency will change due to the season and maturity of your plants.

Occasionally it is helpful to water from above the plant to clean both sides of the leaves.

Sowing Seeds and Transplants

I RECOMMEND EITHER STARTING YOUR OWN TRANSPLANTS OR FINDing a reliable source of locally grown, organic seedlings. These days, you can often find a good source at the farmers market. You can buy organic seedlings or start your own transplants. If you have a large garden and want to maintain a steady food supply, consider planting every three weeks to continue succession planting as plants mature. That way all of one crop is not ready to harvest at the same time.

How to Sow Seeds

I like to sow seeds in the morning and transplant in the afternoon. Sowing seeds is easy. Most seed packets have printed on them all the information you need to sow them successfully. As a basic rule, sow a seed as deep as the seed is long. The most important thing is how you water the seeds you sow. You don't want to flood the soil or pound it so that you disrupt the soil. You do want to regularly and often spray the soil lightly with a mister. With the exception of hearty plants such as corn and beans, which can grow through straw mulch, wait to apply mulch until after seedlings are a few inches tall.

How to Transplant

Before transplanting, always water the plants you are going to transplant to support them in their transition. It is best to transplant in the afternoon or early evening rather than in the morning. When transplanting, it is important to handle the seedlings as carefully and as little as possible. When taking them out of a pot, you should attempt to hold them by the soil around the roots. Turn the pot upside down and carefully take hold of the soil and roots. If the plant needs to be touched then hold it by the tips of the leaves. If they were grown in flats, use a hand fork to lift a section from the flat and go from there, pulling one plant at a time. Try to keep as much soil around the root as possible.

It is important to note that if this is done on a hot, dry, or windy day you should place the section on a wet towel covering three of its sides. The optimal time to transplant is the early evening. The seedling can overcome transplanting shock best when climatic conditions are most moderate. If it seems that the plants roots are grown too tightly together, you can carefully spread the roots in all different directions.

When planting, follow these basic steps:

• Be sure to place the seedling in a large enough hole to bury the plant up to its first set of true leaves.
• Press the soil firmly around the seedling, but not too tightly.
• Add a handful of compost around the base of each plant.
• Then water the plant to help settle the soil around the roots, to eliminate excess air spaces and to provide an adequate amount of water for growth.

Newly transplanted crops require extra care and attention. Monitor them numerous times a day for the first few days to see how they are adapting to their new soil and make sure that they are well mulched.

How to Grow Cooking Herbs and Salad Veggies in Containers

IF YOU DO NOT HAVE A BACKYARD, YOU CAN CREATE A BEAUTIFUL THRIVING oasis on a balcony or patio with just a handful of pots or planters. Here are some easy herbs and salad veggies to grow in containers.

Basil
• Companion Crop: tomatoes
• Antagonist Crop: rue
• Lighting Requirements: prefers full sun

Chives
• Companion Crop: carrots
• Lighting Requirements: can be grown in shady area during the summer months. Needs at least four hours of direct sunlight to grow, seven hours are preferable and 11 hours are even better.

Lemongrass

- Lighting Requirements: prefers full sun
- Weed barrier plant, good on edges of garden

Lettuce

- Companion Crops: carrots, radishes, strawberries, cucumbers
- Lighting Requirements: can be grown in shady area during the summer months. Needs at least four hours of direct sunlight to grow, seven hours are preferable and 11 hours are even better.

Mint

- Companion Crops: cabbage, tomatoes
- Lighting Requirements: prefers full sun

Parsley

- Companion Crops: tomatoes, asparagus
- Lighting Requirements: can be grown in shady area during the summer months. Needs at least four hours of direct sunlight to grow, seven hours are preferable and 11 hours are even better.

Rosemary

- Companion Crops: cabbage, beans, carrots, sage
- Lighting Requirements: prefers full sun

Sage

- Companion Crops: rosemary, cabbage, carrots
- Antagonist Crops: cucumbers
- Lighting Requirements: prefers full sun

Tarragon

- Companion Crops: good throughout the garden
- Lighting Requirements: can be grown in shady area during the summer months. Needs at least four hours of direct sunlight to grow, seven hours are preferable and 11 hours are even better.

Thyme

- Companion Crops: good throughout the garden
- Lighting Requirements: prefers full sun

Tomatoes

- Companion Crops: chives, onions, parsley, asparagus, marigolds, nasturtiums, carrots
- Antagonist Crops: kohlrabi, potatoes, fennel, cabbage
- Lighting Requirements: prefers full sun

Seed Sowing

Herb seeds have long germination periods of 22–28 days. Seeds should be planted as deep as the thin vertical dimension of each seed, or as the seed packet tells you. Here is a list of spacing needs for common cooking herb seeds:

Seed	Spacing
Sweet Basil	6 inches
Chives	5 inches
Lemongrass	24 inches
Spearmint	15 inches (mint spreads underground— keep it contained or plant it where it can keep going.)
Parsley	5 inches
Rosemary	18–24 inches
Sage	18 inches
Tarragon	12–18 inches
Thyme	6 inches

Leaf Mold

The bottom 1/3 layer of your container should be lined with a leaf mold or compost. Leaf mold is simply partially decayed leaves. It will add additional nutrients to the plants.

To make leaf mold, fill a large garbage bag with leaves collected in your yard and moisten them lightly with water. You can reuse a plastic garbage bag for this. Seal the bag closed and cut a few slits in it for air flow. Let this bag sit for six months to a year, checking it every couple of months for moisture, and adding water if the leaves are too dry.

Key Points for the Organic Gardener

In organic gardening, always remember the following ways to work with nature and be the helpful observer:

Plan your garden with the principles of crop rotation in mind: heavy feeder, heavy giver, light feeder.

Design your garden for the most efficient use of space, to grow intensively and to grow plants that like each other.

Practice integrated pest management and begin by planting lots of plants to attract beneficial insects.

Water wisely and rely on the art of observation.

Honor your soil. Never step on bare soil and never leave soil uncovered.

Save some of your seeds and participate in a global seed-saving revolution.

Sow seeds in the morning and transplant seedlings in the afternoon or early evening. ●

CHAPTER 11
EATING ON THE GO, PACKING A LUNCH, AND DINING OUT

"Humans are the only species on the planet that don't live by zero-waste principles. Zero waste is a call to action that aims to bring an end to the current 'take, make, and waste' mentality of human society."

—Michael Jessen

ZERO WASTE ON THE ROAD

O H, THE IRONY. AS I SIT DOWN AT MY FAVORITE café to write this chapter on "Eating on the Go," where the cashier knows me and always gives me a ceramic "for here" cup for my tea, there is a new cashier today and I forget to ask. Ugh… the flow of my day feels disrupted by the fact that I suddenly have a plastic cup in my possession… a plastic cup in my karma. I don't "do" plastic!

I let go and accept the fact that in that one moment, by not paying attention, I ended up supporting the plastic industry. I thank life for a reminder that these things happen when I'm not "present" and attentive, and I come up with a creative plan for how I will make the most use of the plastic cup that is now in my possession. First, I can reuse it for storing food—berries from the farmers market this afternoon, granola or salad-to-go tomorrow.... Yes, it is the perfect size for a travel container and it has a lid!

I may be an extreme example, but remaining conscious of my trash output when I am out and about allows me to avoid plastics and to create minimal trash each week. I simply feel a lot better about my world knowing that I'm doing my share to not contribute to the disease of trash and pollution.

When I first moved back to Los Angeles after living as a monk, my sister had to remind me to tone it down from time to time, because I was so focused initially on the concept of zero waste that it often surprised the people around me. Rather than watch my companions at a restaurant leave uneaten food on their plates, I would choose not to order from the menu and instead offer to take the leftovers for myself. (I didn't care much for social etiquette.) As I adjusted slowly to the world outside the monastery, I found a middle way to practice zero waste that involves being prepared, practicing the three R's (Reduce, Reuse and Recycle) and not behaving too strangely in public.

While there are some cities that have intelligent systems for the citywide reduction of waste (think of Portland, Seattle, San Francisco, or other cities you may have visited in New Zealand, Germany, Austria, Denmark), most cities still do not.

It can be tremendously frustrating to spend a day out and not see recycling bins on sidewalks, at the park, or even at cafés and small markets. (I've even been in health food markets that do not recycle.) While we can say that this is outrageous and unacceptable, it is a reality in many places. Until there are more comprehensive municipal systems set in place to support zero waste on a city level, it is up to the consumer to learn to deal responsibly with waste.

It takes vigilance to practice a zero-waste lifestyle living in a city, or even to cut down on the amount of waste, but it is easy to do once you get the swing of it, and I find it a lot of fun. It is a sort of game I play every day. The purpose of this chapter is to invite you to play the game and bring consciousness to your eating habits on the road. The primary steps we will discuss include:

- Carrying an urban eco-kit
- Carrying your own water vessel, at the very least
- Supporting the refillables industry
- Saying no to plastic
- Cooking at home more
- Packing a waste-free lunch
- Supporting the conscious restaurant that offers eco-friendly packaging alternatives over "any old joint"

What Is an Urban Eco-Kit?

IF YOU ARE READY TO GO THE WHOLE NINE YARDS, INVEST IN AN URBAN eco-kit and free yourself from the world of disposables once and for all.

Carry with you in your purse or backpack:

• A safe food storage container—ideally glass or stainless steel, like SIGG or To Go Ware. This container can be used to carry your urban eco-kit ingredients.
• A cloth napkin—made of organic cotton or hemp.
• Eating utensils—options include metal utensils, a bamboo set, chopsticks, or sporks (made by Bambu)
• A reusable stirrer—this can simply be a disposable stirrer you use again and again.
• A shopping bag—I like Chico bags for this purpose because they can so easily fit into your food storage container.
• A vessel for liquids (cup/mug/water bottle)

In your car, you may want to have a small box that contains another urban eco-kit along with these additional items:

• Shopping bags
• Eco-bags (for produce or bulk foods)
• A couple of food storage containers

If you equip yourself with these things, you will simply be prepared for zero waste wherever you go. You will be relieved, life will be simpler, and you will leave a lesser trail of waste behind you each day. If you find yourself on an unexpected errand, you will have reusable bags for it. If you need to pick up some prepared foods or bulk food somewhere, you will be ready for it.

If you are thirsty and need some purified water, you will have it with you. You won't ever have those moments of "Darn, I meant to remember shopping bags," or "I didn't expect to have to run an errand," or "Here I am at Starbucks; too bad I don't have my own cup." I easily carry my urban eco-kit in a backpack and can also fit it into my day bag/purse.

If you take these ideas into the workplace, they can be contagious and can help develop an improved level of green awareness among your colleagues. Instead of the daily run to Starbucks for a cardboard carrier of coffee-filled paper cups, with a little preparation, everyone can have their own labeled and reusable travel mug instead. Rather than stacking a pile of Styrofoam cups by the coffeemaker, people can use and reuse their own mug or there can be ceramic mugs available, with a washing system to be followed by everyone that uses one.

What Is the Best Drinking Vessel to Use?

I DRINK A LOT OF WATER AND PERSONALLY LIKE TO HAVE A GOOD COL-lection of water bottles, primarily reusable glass bottles that I collect, for instance from kombucha or fruit juice jugs. I also like to have a good stainless steel bottle for travel or long hiking trips, when an even sturdier bottle might be useful. I like to keep glass bottles of water in my fridge for use anytime.

Here are some examples of safe and unsafe drinking vessels:

Safe drinking vessels
- Glass (reuse thick-walled bottles such as Perrier or kombucha)
- High-grade quality stainless steel (i.e. Kleen Kanteen)
- SIGG EcoCare (their line is made with water-based liners). Note that if you ever notice that the liner is damaged over time, it is time to recycle your bottle.
- High-grade, new eco-plastics (that do not contain Bisphenol A or phthalates)

Avoid
- PET (polyethylene terephthalate) plastic bottles
- Cheap metal bottles, especially aluminum bottles other than SIGG. The plastic liner is likely to leach and then eventually peel off and give you aluminum toxicity. In my opinion you are better off using a polycarbonate Nalgene bottle than a cheap aluminum bottle.

Other considerations

People always ask me how to discern the benefits of stainless steel versus aluminum. The bottom line is: Always choose stainless steel. SIGG bottles are an interesting invention because they are actually aluminum coated in a polymer, which is a form of plastic, but as their coating is water-based and non-toxic, it does not leach residues. It is still a plastic liner, but it is not considered a danger.

Also, be aware of toxic plastic bottle lids and metal lids that become rusty and then leach as they age. As a rule, ALWAYS WASH OUT ANY NEW BOTTLE A FEW TIMES to wash off toxic residues from the manufacturing process.

Refilling beverage bottles

In many European and South American countries, as well as in Canada, the practice of refilling beverage bottles is alive and well, but in the United States we have headed in the opposite direction. In the 1950s, most of the beer and soda bottles in this country were accepted by stores to be returned to the manufacturer to be used 10–30 times. Coke bottles averaged 50 refillings. Since the 1960s, the use of glass bottles has steadily declined and single-use aluminum and lightweight glass bottles have become the norm. By 1991, less than 9% of beer and soft drinks in the United States were sold in refillables.

Consider these facts about refillables:

Refillable glass bottles are the most energy-efficient single-serving container available. One glass bottle, refilled an average of 10 times, requires about 75% less energy to manufacture than aluminum cans or new glass bottles made from recycled glass.

Refillables reduce solid waste. GE Plastics, which manufactures refillable milk jugs and bottles, estimates that if all the schools in New York City switched from paper cartons to refillable plastic milk containers, the city could save at least $500,000 per year in trash removal costs.

In addition, refillables also create jobs, because bottling plants that wash and refill require more labor than those that use one-way containers.

Lastly, refillables saves money! Twelve months after switching to refillables, the Rainier Brewing Company of Seattle, Washington and Blitz-Weinhard in Portland, Oregon, reported having saved enough energy to serve 3,441 homes for a year.

Say No to Plastics

It may just be me, but I think there is something bizarre about paying attention to the types of foods we eat and then storing the food in unhealthy plastic containers. I also think it misses the point to buy health-conscious food products (ranging from raw desserts to organic herbs) stored in plastic. For a long time, we were not aware of the health and environmental impact of plastics. We are no longer ignorant. We now know that they leach toxins into our food and into the environment.

Yet knowing this, many people who are concerned with consuming healthy food still resist addressing the issue in their own kitchens, or they feel that they don't want to spend the extra money it might take to convert to glass containers (not realizing that this change doesn't have to actually cost much!).

Other people simply continue purchasing and storing food in plastic containers because "this is the way I've always done it and I see no problem with continuing." Others say, "What can be that dangerous about Tupperware?" There is almost a humorous element in that question, but the fact is, most plastics are disastrous for both human and environmental health, so a better question might be, "What is so hard about letting go of Tupperware?"

In an age when my friend Ann, a 12th-grader in high school, has to learn about environmental disasters such as the island of plastic that stretches twice the size of the continental United States across the Pacific Ocean, it is clearly time for us to learn the honest impact of our reliance on plastics and to embrace new solutions.

Do we really want to have to tell our children and grandchildren that our ignoring the problem out of "convenience" destroyed their oceans? In addition to the traumatic impact of plastics on marine and wildlife, as I like to point out continually, there is another degree of irony when our food production system causes harm to another part of the web of our food production—in this case, the ocean. The process of feeding ourselves should be a source of nourishment, not a source of pollution.

Let's also review the ways that plastics impact human health negatively. I have found that in working with clients, the addiction to plastics can be a hard habit to break. Let's be clear about ALL the reasons to move away from plastics so that we have an educated base to work from.

Consider the following:

• Plastic has been proven to cause endocrine disruption, which can lead to cancer, immune system suppression, birth defects and developmental problems in children.
• DEHP plastic (diethylhexyl phthalate), which is used for food packaging and plastic wrap, has been proven to cause cancer.
• Plastic has been proven to cause direct toxicity, as in the cases of lead, cadmium, and mercury.
• Plastic #7, polycarbonate with Bisphenol A used for water bottles, has specifically been linked to causing cancers, impaired immune function, diabetes, hyperactivity, and early onset of puberty from low doses.

Face it, the use of plastics in our kitchens and for food storage completely negates all of the principles of a sustainable kitchen. It is time to get over our laziness, push past our comfort zone, and create new habits to pass down to the next generation. You will feel so much better when you see a dramatic reduction in the amount of both trash and recycling that you create each week through the use of plastics, and your new green habits will give you the peace of mind of the earth steward for which we are striving.

Contrary to popular belief, human existence is not dependent upon plastics. Plastics have only been around in the forms we know since the 1950s, though they were developed and refined beginning in the early 1900s. Cellophane was invented in 1900, PVC created in 1914 and polyethylene was invented in 1933. The first mineral water bottles in PVC were not manufactured until 1960! We've only been using plastic sandwich bags since 1957.

Since the 1950s, plastics have grown into a major industry that affects all of our lives—from providing improved packaging to giving us new textiles, to expanding the production of cars and computers. Plastic has played a key role in the emergence of supermarkets, because it has allowed us to rely less and less on fresh foods by giving us a way to maintain "freshness" in transport. Since 1976, plastic has been the most used material in the world and was voted one of the top 100 innovations of the century. Today it is typical for me to walk into a client's home and find a giant collection of stacked plastic Tupperware in their kitchen!

The good news is that if you generally buy whole foods and follow the shopping guidelines and food storage guidelines presented in this book, you won't have any plastics in your life to begin with. If you take on the task of cooking more to-go meals in your own kitchen, you will rely less on prepared, packaged foods.

Why Cook at Home More? The Road to Avoiding Food Packaging

EACH OF US NEEDS TO FIND OUR OWN EXPRESSION OF HOW TO BE AN earth steward in regard to our particular lifestyle. We all have different schedules, different financial capacities and different interests, hobbies and tastes. But the fundamental question is the same for us all: How can I align my life with "what is best for all" so that I am contributing to the solution rather than perpetuating the problem?

Choosing to cook at home more can deeply support your intention to live in alignment with the principles of sustainability, simply because when you eat out or order prepared food you don't have the same degree of control over where your food comes from or how it's cooked. Organic, prepared foods do tend to be pricey and most of the organic food you purchase for takeout or delivery comes in plastic packaging.

If, on the other hand, your lifestyle and income afford you the ability to eat daily at organic restaurants where you can feel good about all the aspects of what went into your meal, then this section may not be useful to you. There are also more companies now offering healthy takeout foods in biodegradable containers. Nevertheless, the most affordable and zero-waste way to go is to prepare your food at home.

How to Pack a Waste-free Lunch

Here are some things I recommend having on hand for packing lunch and to-go meals. My favorite source for these things is To-Go Ware, **to-goware.com**, a company that makes easy-to-carry, two-tiered lunch boxes with a handle (often with a plate or salad dressing container included), as well as compact reusable utensil sets.

- A stainless steel lunch box
- Reusable utensils
- Cloth napkin, ideally made of organic cotton or hemp

You might also consider the options of Snackballs or a Wrap 'n Mat, especially if you have kids:

Snackball

This is a small round reusable container designed to hold snacks for babies and children, but I have found it a useful product for adults as well. Snackballs are BPA-free, phthalate-free and PVC-free and are useful for carrying small snacks such as nuts, trail mix, or berries.

Wrap 'n Mat

This is a reusable product created to wrap sandwiches, which you can wash out between uses. It is literally a mat that you wrap. I'm still on the fence about this product in some ways because I tend to prefer natural materials such as hemp or organic cotton, but clients have found it a useful option, because it is so easy for parents and children and helps to cut down on trash. It is lined with PEVA, which may not be as eco-friendly in its production as a more natural material like hemp, but PEVA is a non-toxic, vinyl plastic, so it gets points for non-toxicity. (There's a good description of PEVA at **healthybuilding.net/pvc/ SortingOutVinyls.html**.) We are not avoiding plastic by using Wrap 'n Mat, but we are avoiding using a different plastic bag every day. It has a plastic layer that is next to the food, but it is one good step in the right direction.

What Does a Waste-Free Lunch Look Like?

A Typical American Lunch (Disposable)

- sandwiches sealed in plastic bags
- fruits and vegetables, chips, pretzels and other snacks sealed in more plastic bags
- prepackaged treats like chips, cookies, granola bars, cheeses, yogurts, applesauce, etc.
- disposable juice boxes, juice pouches, soda cans, water bottles and milk cartons
- plastic forks and spoons
- paper napkins
- reusable lunchboxes and disposable paper and plastic bags

A Waste-free Lunch (Reusable)

- sandwiches and other main dishes, fresh fruit, fresh vegetables and treats in a reusable lunch container
- cloth napkins
- stainless steel forks and spoons
- reusable drink containers
- reusable lunchboxes or bags

With this type of lunch, lunch food items can be bought in larger quantities. The packaging can be left at home for reuse or recycling. Waste-free lunches are not only a wise environmental choice, but they are less expensive as well.

What Does It Cost to Pack a Waste-Free Lunch?

A Disposable Lunch		A Waste-free Lunch	
1 egg salad sandwich	$1.25	1 egg salad sandwich	$1.25
1 yogurt	.85	1 serving of yogurt	.50
1 granola bar	.45	1 serving of granola	.35
1 apple	.30	1 apple	.30
1 package of carrots and dip	.65	1 serving of carrots and dip	.25
3 plastic bags	.12	water	0
1 juice pouch	.35	cloth napkin	0
1 plastic spoon	.04	stainless steel spoon	0
1 paper napkin	.01	Packaging	0
TOTAL	$4.02	TOTAL	$2.65

Disposable Lunch	Waste-free Lunch
$4.02/day	$2.65/day
$20.10/week	$13.25/week
$723.60/school year	$477.00/school year

723.60–477.00 = **$246.60 savings** per school year per person

Tips for Entertaining

When you are planning a party or event, whether it be for a small group of people or fairly large, consider enjoying the spirit of the celebration you want to manifest from the moment your planning begins, and allow yourself extra time to find ways to make the party or event sustainable.

Here are some ideas to get started:

• Do NOT use disposable plates, napkins, utensils, or cups.
• Consider instead using either washable dishes or biodegradable dishes and cloth napkins.
• Plan the menu, centerpieces, and decorations to match the season, including the use of organic materials that can be recycled.
• Have a "conscious disposal of resources" scheme built into your event planning, and this might include composting, sending food remains home with guests in biodegradable containers, or delivering leftovers to a homeless shelter.
• Use bio-bags instead of plastic trash bags for the waste that you do create.
• Use your celebration as an opportunity to share with others the benefits of a sustainable kitchen, rather than see it as an opportunity to abandon the principles of sustainability.

When Eating Out: Support Conscious Restaurants

Choose restaurants that pack leftovers and takeout in compostable and biodegradable containers.

Talk to your favorite restaurants. See if they will shift to eco-friendly takeout containers. My favorite restaurant here in L.A. ended up selling such containers!

If you are a coffee drinker, find a place near you that serves organic fair trade coffee and always bring your own mug.

Locate vegetarian restaurants at: **vegdining.com/Home.htm**

Visit Slow Foods International for a list of conscious restaurants: **slowfood.com**.

The Traveling Epicurean

When we travel, we have another opportunity to "give back" by supporting sustainable farmers and local cuisine. Some people like to find ways to eat exactly the same kind of food they can eat back home when they go on a vacation or long trip, which always makes me sorry for their missed opportunity to be a cultural epicurean and get to know a culture completely different from their own through their taste buds. In addition to eating the local food and expanding your cultural exposure, see how you can maintain the spirit of "giving back" and support the local economy and environment by making the most conscious choices you can regarding the food you eat.

Over the writing of this book, I was gifted with the opportunity to spend five weeks on a tiny mostly undeveloped island in the Caribbean. The islanders didn't have even a degree of the Western mentality of "whatever I want, when I want it" due to the level of poverty and of what was available, but there were still plenty of variations regarding sustainable food, packaging, shipping, etc.

We found the only organic farmer on the island (and really the only source of greens on the island) and called in every week to place our order of fresh organic vegetables and herbs, so the farmer would know how much to harvest for us. While we also supported some of the local restaurants and discovered tastes we had never experienced before, these vegetables and fruit harvested in our own backyard made up the bulk of our diet.

We gathered fruit every day from the trees in our tropical backyard, in the three waves in which they arrived: first mangoes, then guanabanas, followed finally by passion fruit. We got a certain amount of greens each week and whatever vegetables were available, and supplemented with new flavors of peppers and herbs we were not used to, prepared some of the most delicious, simple, healthy, beautiful meals I have ever had.

This diet was also more in tune with the Caribbean climate than some of the Western options that had reached even this island, and the experience was one of being taken care of by nature to the richest degree. As we could hardly keep up with our mango harvest (a daily routine) we would eat some, freeze some, and visit the local wild horses every few days to deliver the batch of mangoes that were bruised and gone to insects before we could get to them, thus closing the cycle and in another act of "giving back." ●

CHAPTER 12
SUSTAINABLE COOKING FOR CHILDREN
The Natural Magic of Food

"Never give children a chance of imagining that anything exists in isolation.

Make it plain from the very beginning that all living is relationship.

Show them relationships in the woods, in the fields, in the ponds and streams, in the village and in the country around it. Rub it in."

—Aldous Huxley, *Island*

W HEN I WAS A KID, I LOVED CHOCOLATE, BUT I also had the model of a father who taught me to enjoy dried fruit, carob, the simplicity of nut butter and bananas on whole wheat bread, and simple wholesome treats he made for himself. He did not preach natural foods, but he did model them, while allowing others to eat as they chose to. I attribute my passion for sustainability to his model, as he was the first environmentalist and natural cook I knew.

My dad was the cook in our family, a classic '80s "Mr. Mom." On Sundays, after we had friends over for a slumber party where he would play Monster with us or dress up as Gertrude (a favorite play-acting character), he would make a big batch of pancake batter and serve "pancake art." Using a baster, he would design and "paint" pancakes onto the grill in the shapes of the letters of our names, flowers, or our favorite animals. I even recall eating a plate of parrot and monkey pancakes one day when I was studying the rainforest in school.

These touches (and many touches that my dad brought to the kitchen) made one feel like life was full of magic. On school days, he would make my lunch and, in addition to putting a special note inside, he would draw a picture on every lunch bag (the dark ages of the brown-bag lunch) that I would look forward to.

Now, as an adult looking back, it tickles me to no end remembering this man taking such delight in creating food art for his children. We now do this for my niece, though we use cookie cutters for her pancakes, and I can say without a doubt that she looks forward to this pancake ritual every weekend and it has become part of her childhood cooking school. Food can be an opportunity for us to remember the magic and creativity in nature and to find ways to bring this ritually into our lives.

Parents face a whole set of challenges (and opportunities) around how to green their children's meals. In my time as a sustainability coach, numerous parents have approached me needing help with changing the eating and cooking habits of their families. Some typical questions are: "How can I transition my kids to a vegetarian diet when I'm not even sure how to do it healthfully for myself?" and "I depend on packaged foods for my kid's lunches—how can I address this issue successfully?"

In this chapter, I will share some of the success stories of these families, as well as offer the perspective of the most conscious nanny I know and examples from some of the communities discussed in this book. In addition to offering ways to turn children on to the natural magic of food, I will offer simple solutions for addressing the primary challenges of how to adapt the principles of sustainable eating to fit a child's active lifestyle.

The Challenge: How to Adapt the Principles of Sustainable Eating to Fit A Child's Active Lifestyle

The primary challenges for parents are:

• How to Get Children to Eat Healthy Foods (The Importance of Organics)
• How to Avoid Excess Packaging
• How to Curb Food Waste

Creative Solutions for Helping Children to Eat Healthy

Start Early

Every parent I know who has made the transition to a green diet swears by this. I recently heard about a mom with three children who moved to healthier meals after her oldest child had already grown used to a less healthy diet. Her experience has been that while her two younger children have readily taken to their new diet, it has been much, much more difficult for their older sibling.

Her three-year-old loves greens, fresh fruits of all kinds, lentils and smoothies, while her 13-year-old asks for Big Macs and pizza. She bakes bread for the family and while the younger kids love whole-grain bread, her oldest child will only eat white flour. The lesson learned from her experience (and that of many other parents) is that it can be much harder (but not impossible) to make the transition once the old-school diet has already been taught.

If you are the parent of an infant or toddler, take advantage of the opportunity to start your child early on the road to good health. The best way to do this is to make your own baby food. There are many ways to do this, including making batches at a time and freezing some of it. I offer guidelines for how to make your own baby food at the end of this chapter and books for further reading on the Resource List.

Be the Model—A Parent's Responsibility

The bottom line is if you do not want to see your children eating junk food, why have that food around at all? Do yourself the favor of modeling the healthy diet you want your kids to follow and let your enthusiasm be contagious to them. One client of mine, a mother of two, has said that the single most important thing in raising her kids on a green diet has been to expect from a very young age that her children will eat everything she and her husband eat. They will simply eat what is served for dinner, with no special catering and "mac 'n cheese" mentality.

Be Persistent (Don't Bend the Guidelines You Set)

Many mixed messages and much manipulation can occur at mealtime, even by well-intentioned parents. Parents may say one thing and then never follow through; for example, a parent may tell her children to eat the vegetables on their plates—but then give in when a child refuses. This type of mixed messaging can be disastrous, as children are much more sensitive and perceptive than we often suspect.

My suspicion is that parents can get so stressed with the details of their lives that it often seems easier to give in to their children's demands (including a refusal to eat specific foods), i.e., to take the easy route at a time when persistence and integrity is what would really make a difference for their kids. Setting clear guidelines and following them is a kindness to your children. Anytime you bend guidelines that you have set you are sending a mixed message and children pick up quickly on that (and then run with it).

Presentation Is Everything—Food Art

My mother is an artist and she regularly set up food-art projects for us growing up. She made us green eggs and ham, make-your-own-face sandwiches with shredded lettuce hair and tomato lips and, of course, homemade cookies to decorate.

Following the pancake tradition my dad began, I recently found her making orange pumpkin-shaped pancakes with a green stem for my niece for breakfast. Being conscious and creative about food presentation can really jump-start your efforts to turn your kids on to sustainable food. Some examples of how to get creative with food are to:

- Incorporate different colors into every meal
- Use cookie cutters at unexpected times, for instance with sandwiches and fruit (and pancakes!)
- Serve food-art meals for the whole family to partake in
- Serve snacks on skewers, like kabobs
- Serve celery or carrot sticks with almond butter decorated with raisins and nuts
- Serve fruit cut into pretty shapes and arranged on a platter
- Use beans to make bean art mosaics
- Bake bread with your kids. From the act of mixing the "sponge" to watching the dough rise to shaping or braiding a loaf and, ultimately, pulling a loaf of warm bread from the oven to eat with butter or jam, there are ENDLESS moments of undeniable pure magic in the bread-making process.
- Turn your children on to chia, a wholesome seed that was part of traditional Mayan and Aztec diets. In preparing chia, a bowlful of spirals is created and this can be especially fun for children to watch and mix. I like to prepare it with coconut water and serve it with chunks of fresh fruit and almonds.
- Make pizza! Face it, is pizza not the ultimate magic for children? Whether you make the crust from scratch or simply buy a storebought crust and decorate it with sauce, grated cheese, and the toppings of your choice, pizza is a favorite magic food for most kids.

Sandwich Art For Kids

As a kid I always looked forward to this meal! You can prepare these sandwiches for small children, but the ingredients can be laid out for older children to create sandwiches for themselves.

Sample Face Sandwich

Cut bread cut into large circles for base (use round cookie cutters or poached egg tins). Cut piece of flat cheese to fit bread circle. An alternative would be tuna spread evenly over the bread or other healthy lunchmeat. Add shredded lettuce or shredded carrots for hair. Small florets of cauliflower and broccoli also make good hair. Add sliced olives with dab of mayonnaise in center for eyes. A slash of pimento, tomato, or red bell pepper makes good lips, and a variety of different beans cut in half make a good nose. Condiments can also be used effectively for a more personal touch.

Sample Child Sandwiches

For a girl sandwich, bread can be cut into triangles for a dress, with a small bread circle for the face. Do the same for a boy sandwich, but cut the bread into pant legs. Create faces based on directions for a Face Sandwich. Then add carrot or celery stick arms (and legs, if bread dress is short), bean shoes, and decorate with whatever other ingredients you choose. For a peanut butter and jelly sandwich, for example, a dress could be spread with peanut butter, with jelly polka dots or stripes. For a cheese sandwich, one color cheese could become the base of a dress or pants and small strips of another cheese could be layered on as stripes. Other condiments and vegetables can also be used for decoration on cheese, chicken, fish, or meat sandwiches, including mustard and ketchup, chopped celery pieces, cucumber slices, etc.

For kids, there is no reason for cooking not to be viewed as just another creative art project. When I was in fourth grade, my friend Lesley invited me to her birthday party at a local cooking school. Our menu for the night was Tuna Potato Boats, and we got to grate cheese, chop celery, swirl herbs into sour cream, and crush potato chips, before stuffing this colorful concoction into a baked potato shell to twice bake.

I can remember how proud I was of our creation (I had learned how to cook dinner!), and the following week I went to the market with my dad to buy the ingredients and share this meal with my family. Other than the fact that my little sister threw up afterwards, I was proud of my first real meal. I made this dish many more times, though my sister NEVER took to it.

Getting Kids Involved With Mealtime

From the local farmers market to meal preparation to composting, there are a hundred ways to get your children involved with the food process in a creative way. When you are at the farmers market, let your kids explore and sample different kinds of fruits and vegetables that appeal to them and, as one successful green mom I know says, "Always buy what they choose and find a good way to cook it, even if it wasn't the zucchini, for example, that you would have chosen."

Following this simple advice will ensure that your child will be interested in eating this vegetable or fruit at home and make him or her feel empowered. Other ways to involve your children in mealtime are the following:

Setting the table.
• Cutting/peeling food for meal preparation. Pumpkin-carving knives are great for this. You can buy your child a special child's knife when he or she is old enough.

- Harvesting from your garden if you have one.
- Putting kids in charge of the compost…. Most kids get excited about compost!
- Picking one meal per week that is something you have never made before, perhaps inspired by your farmers market trip, and including the kids (and entire family) in the process of cooking and trying this new experimental food.

Imagination Salad

When I was three years old, my family moved to a new neighborhood. Since I had no friends there, in her wisdom my mom posted an ad on my behalf on the community board that said, "LITTLE GIRL NEEDS FRIEND." Ruthie's mom responded to the ad, and Ruthie and I have been close friends ever since. One of our favorite activities growing up was "imagination salad." We would take a big empty salad bowl and wander around the backyard and neighborhood picking plants and flowers to create a giant colorful imagination salad. We knew this was not an edible salad, but we liked to pretend it was and we spent hours, walking and harvesting, to create a diverse and colorful salad in the big bowl. I find it fascinating that as young girls we felt naturally inclined to gather, harvest, and engage with the plant world in this way. Neither of our families gardened at the time, but inherently we seemed to know that this was a pleasurable sensory experience.

Dinner: Creating a Space for Mindful Meals

Mealtimes can be overwhelming and hectic in families, but it's possible to make them a peaceful and enjoyable time. In talking with different families, I have learned the value of creating a transition time before eating dinner together. If you let your kids snack during the day, set a time, at least 1½ hours before dinner, when snacking stops. Remind your kids each day, just prior to that time, that "snacking will soon stop," so that they can take care of their hunger as needed. Then, before dinner, take time for everyone to wash up and assist with the ritual of dinner by either setting the table or helping to prepare the food that will be served.

A word of advice to parents: It can be helpful to take a couple of minutes (just two minutes may be all that is required) to check in with yourself so you can help to create a mealtime environment of peace and relaxation. Perhaps breathe slowly, or "center yourself" in whatever way works for you, before meeting the dynamic of your family.

Some activities families might want to do together in this spirit are:

• Taking a moment to acknowledge where all the food on your plate came from.
• Having each child bring a different offering to the table as part of setting up the space (for example, a flower from your yard or an interesting object from the world of nature).
• Lighting candles to set a more festive tone than usual. You might want to pick a night each week to eat by candlelight.
• Creating a ritual of consciously checking in with everyone at the table, just to create an environment that is welcoming for everyone, and a place to enjoy a meal and be listened to.
• Defining clear guidelines about what is expected of your children at mealtime (for example, in some families children are asked to at least try everything at the table).
• Letting your children serve themselves (an empowering act for them as they grow older), while making sure you monitor the portions they take, to avoid food waste.
• Giving children two or three clear choices to avoid a power struggle when conflict arises around food. For instance, "you can either have more salad, more soup, or neither. It is not time for dessert yet."
• If you have a garden, let your kids gather the harvest for an edible "imagination salad" for dinnertime.

Further recommendations for dealing with and avoiding conflict around mealtime:

Have everyone eat the same meal. Too many parents cater to their child's every whim and complaint. At one point in my childhood, I recall my mother having to prepare and serve something different to every child!

The families I work with who are most successful in providing healthy food to their children simply make one meal for everyone to enjoy. The attitude of mind is "this is it…

this is dinner… I'm not making 100 different options." If it's close to mealtime, when the meal is already under preparation, and your child says, "But I want pizza!" do NOT stop the meal preparation and shift gears. Tell your child that they can have pizza tomorrow night and make a note of it.

Our children need to learn that food is a precious resource, not something to be taken for granted. They must understand that they don't need to have exactly what they crave at any moment. (You will be doing them a big service for their future lives if you can teach that to them.) If your child says that he/she doesn't like anything on the table, consider NOT cooking them something different instead. It may take one or two nights of this for your child to begin to be willing to eat what is served, but in the end he/she will learn to enjoy it.

In the long run, this learning experience will demonstrate to your children more about your values and integrity than catering to their complaints would. Some parents to whom I have provided this advice voice concern and worry about their children starving or being malnourished.

The reality, however, is that we are talking about only one or two nights and the real malnourishment is feeding your child macaroni and cheese every day because that is all they say they will eat. Remember the lesson of *Bread and Jam for Francis*? (**good**reads.com/book/show/911579.Bread_and_Jam_for_Frances**)** In this classic story, Francis decided she only liked to eat bread and jam at every meal until, much to her surprise, her parents granted her wish and she learned the hard way why this is not such a good idea.

Be Patient, But Persistent

My sister-in-law Yvonne explains that until recently salad was rejected on a daily basis by her six-year-old Olivia, but that they persisted in placing a small portion on her plate every evening just for presence—although the salad was usually left untouched. One day, Yvonne forgot to put the small salad portion on the plate and Olivia said, "Mom! Where's my salad? I eat salad—I am a vegetarian!!!" The parents now proudly report that their young daughter eats a side salad almost daily without complaining and, quite the opposite of her previous refusal to eat it, now actually seems to enjoy it.

This year Olivia's gift to her dad on Valentine's Day was a bag of vegetables from the farmers market. When asked why she chose this gift, she said, "because my dad loves vegetables!"

Be patient, but persistent and trust that your child will find his or her taste for good healthy food. In addition, if your child has one experience with a vegetable and doesn't like it, never say, for instance, "Oh, you don't like broccoli." There are a million ways to prepare vegetables and it is your job to find the recipe that your child will enjoy. (For a popular children's broccoli recipe and a unique way to serve kale, read the recipes section below!)

It can help to remember that everything is a phase. One mother said, "My son just wanted to eat bread products for a month or so… only bread. Then the phase passed and he asked for seconds of salad for dinner." Do not lose sight that the phase will pass and healthy eating habits will come back. If you remain patient and keep the expectation that kids should eat what is served at a meal, they will begin to get it.

Always have something healthy available at each meal that you know your child will like, just in case (such as black beans, lentils, kasha, homemade bread), but serve the other foods that they are resisting with the expectation that they will eat some of everything that is served. If your child ends up not liking the new food(s), then at least they will eat the black beans, for example, that were also part of the menu and that are also healthy and nourishing.

Finding the Middle Way With Dessert

I know a little girl who was brought up in her earlier years with European parents who fed her dessert at every dinner, since this is the way they had grown up. By grade school, she both expected dessert at every meal and began to favor it over her dinner. Her parents felt that she was eating too many sweets, but didn't want to turn to making dessert a "reward" for eating the meal or manipulating her in any way.

They came up with a creative Middle Way: They announced that the family would have dessert every Tuesday, Thursday and Saturday night and NOT the other nights of the week. This ended the conversation of "but I want dessert!"—and the little girl still got to enjoy dessert three times a week. At the same time, the desserts are now made of healthier ingredients. This approach provided a conscious way to move the child away from her addiction to sweets without using reward or punishment in the process.

Creative Solutions for Zero Waste and On-The-Go Food

Parents should choose from the following supplies to minimize trash when packing lunches, snacks and to-go meals for kids:

- Cloth lunch and snack bags (available from Etsy)
- Metal lunchbox and food storage containers
- Stainless steel containers with lids, or Snackballs for small/liquid snacks
- Kleen Kanteen water bottle
- Children's eating utensils (I like the kids' set made by Bambu)
- Cloth napkin

With these supplies on hand, it is possible to prepare lunches and trips to the park with zero waste! Consider that, on average, a school-age child using a disposable lunch generates 67 pounds of waste per school year. That equates to 18,760 pounds of lunch waste for just one average-size elementary school.

School Lunches and Food Waste

How many parents have had a child regularly come home from school with an untouched lunch? Sometimes the child chose to play through lunch, or simply didn't bother to finish what was packed. When he or she returns home, the child is often ready for an after-school snack and the parent obliges, throwing the uneaten lunch away. One helpful strategy to prevent such food waste is to say, "Let's see what's in your lunchbox," and evaluate if any uneaten fruit or crackers can be the snack the probably now-hungry child craves.

Other ways to avoid lunch food waste are to:

• Take note of what your child's not eating so it's not repeatedly placed in her lunchbox as part of the menu.
• Ensure that your child can open his Tupperware or other container. Is the lid so tight that s/he gives up trying to open it if it's too hard?
• Pack an ice pack in the lunch and do not always opt for the conventional meal, i.e., the sandwich that will go bad if uneaten. When cooking dinner, make enough pasta or stew or rice and beans for lunchtime and pack leftovers for your child's school lunch in an eco-friendly container beside the freezer bag (which will be reused each day) to keep any food your child does not eat safe until after school.
• Pack snacks that cannot go bad, i.e. nuts, fruit or dried fruit, crackers, homemade protein bars, etc.

DIVERSITY is the Key to a Healthy Child's Vegetarian Diet

One of the dangers of switching children to a vegetarian diet is the potential for relying too much on a limited menu. A mother recently told me that the nutritionist she consulted told her she could supply a healthy vegetarian diet for her kids by focusing on soy foods, dairy and beans. Soy, however, is a dangerous food to over-consume, especially for kids. Studies have shown that too much soy can have the following affects:

• Blocks calcium and mineral absorption
• Depresses thyroid function
• Disrupts sex hormone functions
• Is linked to diabetes, leukemia and breast cancer

Please note that feeding soy to infants is particularly discouraged and has been linked to diabetes. When reviewing the histories of 95 diabetic children, it was found that twice as many of the diabetic children received soy formula in infancy compared to children in the control group.

My approach would be to create as diverse a diet as possible. Instead of just focusing on soy or dairy for protein, consider regularly rotating the following:

- Cow milk (if your child can digest it), rice milk, soy milk, oat milk, goat milk
- Soy cheese, rice cheese, almond cheese
- A variety of complete proteins (see below)

Complete proteins include the following:

Barley, beans, sesame seeds, lentils, sunflower seeds, cornmeal, dried peas, bulgur, walnuts, oats, peanuts, cashews, buckwheat, chickpeas, pumpkin seeds, soy products, rice, other nuts, rye, wheat, pasta

Combinations of food also create complete proteins:

- Peanut or almond butter on whole-wheat bread or a rice cake
- Rice and beans
- Tofu stir-fry with rice
- Whole-grain breadsticks with sesame seeds
- Trail mix with nuts, seeds and dried fruit
- Salad with chickpeas and cornbread
- Hummus

You can also add a small amount of animal protein (milk, cheese, or eggs) to any of the groups. For instance:

- Yogurt and granola
- Salad with beans and a hard-boiled egg
- Bean and cheese burrito
- Oatmeal with milk

....

The Real Opportunity
How to Incorporate Environmental Education into Daily Life

IN MY EXPERIENCE, CHILDREN ARE THE MOST ENTHUSIASTIC ENVI-
ronmentalists. Children generally LOVE the opportunity to learn how to be stewards of the earth in every way. By following the ideas offered in this chapter, you will successfully feed your children a healthy, sustainable, zero-waste diet and have your family be much more connected to the food cycle at the same time.

You will probably find out that your children LOVE healthy organic foods, look forward to trips to the farmers market and want to participating in the kitchen. Your children, in fact, may begin to challenge YOU to be even greener.

Here are some fun ways to "take it up a notch" and really incorporate environmental education into the daily life of your young earth stewards:

• Educate your children about the trash/waste from the kitchen.
• Invite them to have a plot in the garden and teach them about the food growing cycle.
• Teach them about seasonal foods and see how excited they get picking out the proper foods for each time of year.
• Involve them in the do-it-yourself food activities offered in the section on Menu Planning.
• Make sure your children are not nature-deprived. Provide every opportunity possible for your children to grow up connected to the earth on which they live.

Make these changes and you will never turn back!

I asked an Earthaven co-founder to comment on the kids growing up in such a sustainability-focused community and she said, "The kids who live here are really lucky; they are really free. They grow up not being afraid of nature and free of the nature-deficit disorder that so many city kids have."

A visiting teacher that worked with the kids at Earthaven commented that she had never worked with a group of kids more open, kinder to one another and with less prejudice. It's actually simple and easy for children to grow up that way when they are not exposed to something else. For city parents, I encourage you to look at how far you are willing to go to give your children opportunities to connect with nature on a daily basis and raise them with the principles of sustainability (starting with the food they eat)!

Creating a Week's Menu for Kids
Using Sustainable Menu-Planning Guidelines

AS I WILL DISCUSS IN THE MENU PLANNING SECTION, THE WEEKEND can be a wonderful time to make certain items that can last your family throughout the week, when life for most families tends to get busier. Allow a special time each weekend to be a food preparation party and include your children in it. Let them help plan what will be made.

Imagine living with a parent who asked you every Thursday what food should be invited to the weekend "prep party," who then mindfully guided you to create a plan that is balanced and healthy and who then took you shopping to make the party happen.

However, if you try to convince your children that they should help you make granola for the week every Saturday and you approach it as a task that you don't particularly want to do, the thrill is likely to wear off fast—for both you and your children. Remember, you are the model for your child. He or she will learn more about food and sustainability through witnessing your relationship to it than by anything you ever say on the matter.

Sunday food-prep party

Make something like granola that can last you through the week. Other options are fresh bread or a soup that can be eaten two nights in a row. Soup can be made in large batches if it's a type that freezes well. You could even pack soup for lunch if your child has a way to heat it at school or if it is a chilled soup. Then your child can be surprised by which "food party friend" you tuck in the lunch box. Remember: if your child helped you prepare it, he or she will have a relationship to it.

Here is a sample of some menus for breakfast, lunch and dinner for children that exemplify some of the principles from the Menu Planning chapter:

Breakfasts

Sunday: Scrambled eggs, fruit smoothies with almond milk, fresh bread toast with cream cheese.

Monday: Oatmeal, milk, homemade granola mixed in yogurt, a side of fresh fruit.

Tuesday: Warm eight-grain cereal, cottage cheese, fruit juice.

Wednesday: Leftover oatmeal from Monday, yogurt, a side of fresh fruit.

Thursday: Scrambled eggs over fresh bread toast, cream cheese

Friday: A cereal that your child picked out at the bulk bin, kefir, fruit.

Saturday: If you have the kind of Saturday schedule that allows for a leisurely morning, start the day with something light, like fresh orange juice and some nuts. Then, create a fun brunch with your family that can serve as the main meal of the day. Example: whole grain pancakes with fresh fruit and yogurt or kefir. If you use cookie cutters you can cook your pancakes in different shapes and your kids will love it!

Lunches—These are based on the dinner section that follows

Monday: leftover chili from Saturday night's dinner, carrot sticks, slices of cheese, apple

Tuesday: leftover pizza from Sunday night, greens, leftover acorn squash

Wednesday: celery sticks with almond butter (using leftover celery not put in Tuesday night's soup), leftover **Quorn** sandwich (Quorn is a mycoprotein vegetarian food product.)

Thursday: leftover mac and cheese, salad, adzuki beans
Friday: leftover lentils and rice, raw beet and carrot salad
Saturday: (brunch, see above)
Sunday: Leftovers (cooked together in a minestrone soup if you are heavy on leftovers that that would be suitable for)

Dinners

Monday: Baked Quorn roast (vegetarian mycoprotein), acorn squash, quinoa, Dessert: cookies that were made on the weekend together—perhaps solar-baked cookies!

Tuesday: Cream of celery soup, brown rice, egg salad, roasted vegetables

Wednesday: Freezer fare (leftovers that you have frozen and thawed overnight to allow for a mid-week minimal-cooking meal, for instance beans or chili) with fresh bread, mac and cheese, salad with homemade dressing, Dessert: pumpkin pie

Thursday: One-pot meal: Lentils and rice with beets. Save some beets out for the Friday lunch salad.

Friday: Butternut squash soup, hummus, green beans, fresh bread, Dessert: baked apples. (It's important to introduce the notion of how fruit can be a dessert, breaking the notion that white sugar must be a main ingredient for it to be a dessert.)

Saturday: Fresh tossed salad with lots of vegetables, chili with pinto beans, brown rice. Grated almond cheese for the top. (Freeze excess chili for later and save some for Monday lunch.)

Sunday: Homemade pizza, steamed greens, Dessert: Homemade raw chocolate balls—Make them with your kids or make the dough and let your kids roll the balls.

The Broccoli Recipe ALL Kids Love

Ingredients:
Broccoli cut into small pieces—use both the florets and the stalk (peeled first)
Bragg's amino acids
Yeast

Lightly sauté the broccoli in a little water and as you cook, add Bragg's amino acids, a sprinkle of nutritional yeast and an optional dab of unsalted butter.

Kale Chips—Another Children's Favorite

1 bunch kale
1 tbs olive oil
tsp sea salt or seasoned salt
Optional: garlic, nutritional yeast, paprika, Bragg's, or agave

Preheat the oven to 350 degrees. Line a cookie sheet with parchment paper. Using your hands or a knife, remove the leaves from the kale stems and set the stems aside for making stock. Tear the kale leaves into bite-size pieces. Drizzle with oil and salt and bake for about 10–15 minutes, just until the edges brown (but don't let it burn). These can also be made in a solar dehydrator.

Part of the pleasure of having a natural kitchen is the opportunity to raise your children with the principles of sustainability as part of their daily lives. This is a service to your children and to the planet. You can expose your children to the natural magic of food while at the same time providing them with essential nutrition necessary for a healthy body and optimum growth and development. Consider the fundamental importance of basing your children's diet on organically grown whole foods.

• Children are smaller and are more sensitive/vulnerable than adults to pesticides in food. Young children are also in particular stages in their development where pesticides can be detrimental.
• Pesticides have been proven to contain damaging chemicals, many of which can lead to endocrine imbalance.
• Pesticides in food can have the most long-term effect when consumed by children.
• Processed foods have been proven to be significantly lower in nutrition and higher in health-risk factors than whole, organic foods.
• The current issue of child diabetes is another reason to feed children whole, organic foods. The amount of corn syrup and sugar that go into our processed food supply are major contributors to diabetes.

Luckily, studies have shown that children who ate conventional food and then switched to a 100% organic whole-foods diet have been cleared of toxic chemicals in one week. Why not start now and commit to feeding your children the healthiest diet you can? To take this to another level, choosing foods that are sustainably grown and sustainably transported and packaged is also imperative for securing a safe future for our children on this planet. By changing your child's diet, you will be doing them a great service now and into the future.

How To Make Your Own Baby Food

For this you will need a blender or hand grinder, food cube trays (see the Resource List for eco-friendly options), and glass food storage containers, such as reused Mason jars. After washing the fresh organic produce of your choice, you can then steam, bake, or boil it in purified water, based on your child's stage of development. Then simply mash or blend the meal with a little water, and add lemon juice (if desired) for natural flavor or as a preservative. Salt or sugar do not need to be added. The food can then be strained and poured into a glass container or be utilized immediately. If you have made a large batch, pour the purée into food cube trays or ice cube trays and freeze it. The frozen cubes can later be transferred to glass containers for later use. Be sure to label the containers with content and date. These individual portions can then be defrosted for individual meals. ●

CHAPTER 13
MINDFUL EATING
Cultivating Sensitivity to Our Bodies, Ourselves, Our Planet

"One of the very nicest things about life is the way we must regularly stop whatever it is we are doing and devote our attention to eating."

—Luciano Pavarotti and William Wright

....

"Mindfulness is the aware, balanced acceptance of the present experience.
It isn't more complicated than that."

—Sylvia Boorstein

THE POINT OF SUSTAINABLE LIVING IS TO ENSURE A healthy planet for future generations, but the immediate gift and the most direct benefit is the personal transformation of each individual who chooses to live by the principles of sustainability. The process can wake us up and help us to be more present and tune into our senses and surroundings in a new way. It can add nourishment, gratitude, and a richer awareness to our lives. Many people have told me that committing to a sustainable relationship with food has brought a deep sense of interconnection to their lives.

In the words of Wendell Berry, "Eating with the fullest pleasure—pleasure, that is, that does not depend on ignorance—is perhaps the profoundest enactment of our connection with the world. In this pleasure we experience our dependence and our gratitude, for we are living in a mystery, from creatures we did not make and powers we cannot comprehend."

Sustainability from the inside out invites us to stop and unplug from what is not working about our lives and to adopt a more peaceful, present and empowered way of being. Just as growing a garden tends to trigger delight in the natural world and a sense of awe in the simple perfection of nature, living a sustainable lifestyle tends to put us more in touch with our own perfection and an appreciation for the simple moments in our lives.

We begin to need less of the "stuff" we thought we once did, spend less time going after that "stuff," and receive more satisfaction from the life we have. We begin to enjoy the simple moments more and realize that life is full of simple moments for us to enjoy. Once we figure out that we don't need all that we thought we did and that the simpler way actually nourishes us more than the old ways of doing things, life can take on a new dimension.

One simple and direct way we can experience this new dimension is through mindful eating. As referred to in the quote above, mealtime can be a chance to stop whatever we are doing throughout the day and devote our attention to eating. In the context of urban life, mealtime can be a precious and unique opportunity to step out of the business of our day and refuel, physically and spiritually.

Try This Mindfulness Experience: Simply Eating

All you need for this experience is a piece of fresh fruit and a quiet place to sit. Take a moment to get into a comfortable position and relax your body and simply notice the sensations in your body right now... without having to fix or change anything. What are you present to right now?

Now pick up the piece of fruit and hold it in your hand and as you hold the fruit, notice:

How does the fruit feel in your hand? Notice the shape, texture, temperature and color variations... Notice your hand and arm as you hold the food...

Now begin to peel or eat it in whatever way you wish... going slowly and paying attention to your body and your breathing as you eat, simply receiving the fruit in grateful acceptance.

Notice the first taste and the subtle variation of tastes as it evolves from one to the next. Notice your own mind as you eat... Is there a desire to rush through it? Is there commentary on the experience you are having? Can you let yourself slow down and simply enjoy the experience of eating with your full attention?

Notice all that arises without needing to fix or change anything....

What Is Mindfulness? What is Mindful Eating?

A definition of mindfulness that I recently came upon is this: "Mindfulness focuses our attention and awareness on the present moment." This helps us disengage from habitual, conditioned, unsatisfying and unskillful habits and behaviors. Mindfulness helps us to see clearly, as old habitual ways arise, that we have the opportunity to make another choice. I will share examples of how mindfulness is something we can tap into and practice for the benefit of ourselves, others and the planet.

Benefits for ourselves:

To get present and simply enjoy our lives more

To cultivate our own sensitivity to our bodies and ourselves (which benefits all aspects of our life, starting with our own physical and mental well-being)

For others:

To cultivate our compassion for others

For the planet:

To cultivate compassionate self-discipline and care for the planet

Why practice mindful eating? Why bring mindfulness to our kitchens? In a sense, we could say that practicing mindfulness in our relationship with food is the core of sustainability. We begin to see that "ourselves, others and the planet" really come down to the same thing—LIFE. And by being mindful, we are simply experiencing our interconnection with life. Imagine how differently humans would live on this planet if we truly saw all of life as equal to ourselves.

Sensitivity to Ourselves

Do you ever wake up, start the day and then get caught in a stream of thoughts that lasts the entire day… of things to do, things to track, things to manage, things to fantasize about, things to get through, things to think about and plan for tomorrow, etc.? Are you familiar with this experience? You might make time or take a break for yourself (perhaps you exercise or watch your favorite TV show or go out for a drink with friends), but even that break feels only like a brief getaway from the nonstop stream of your life that keeps going, going, going.

How often do you sit down to a meal and it's sort of "just another meal"? You sit down, start eating, talk with whomever you're with, watch TV perhaps, but still remain caught in the nonstop stream of your day.

Or maybe you are someone who simply wants to enjoy the small moments of your life more fully? For example, is mealtime a time of peace and rejuvenation for you? Or are you lucky if you get enough time to sit down and eat your meal—at breakfast, between feeding the kids and getting them off to school, or at lunch, when it's hard to step away from the computer? It can be challenging to become more present, when we are so often used to distraction or multitasking, but it is absolutely possible to do—and mealtimes provide a great opportunity to do so.

If you make the effort to create a green kitchen, to make better choices for the planet and to cook healthy food, but you don't get to really be present and enjoy the meal (or the process of doing all that), is it really that worth it? What are we really serving here if we are leaving our own *joie de vivre* out of the picture? If we learn how to structure our lives according to "what is best for all?" what is the point if we don't include ourselves in that "all" and enjoy our time and our meals?

Sensitivity for Others

On one level, we can say, "of course, if I'm feeling interconnected and I'm experiencing more peace in myself, then it's easier for me to feel compassion for others." I would say, however, that compassion for others is simply a natural and effortless expression when we feel compassion for ourselves.

When I practice mindfulness, I experience a sense of being cared for unconditionally and, as the receiver of unconditional care, I also become the giver of unconditional care.

On another level, we can think about food and how unifying it is to human experience, just on a practical level. All of us, no matter what age, country, political leaning, or culture we are from, need food to survive. For all of us, food is one of the ways we sustain our lives.

For ALL of us, food brings up issues of money, need, hunger and our own vulnerability. But food is not available to all of us equally. Though 13% of the human population lives in starvation, we often neglect to think about this and ask ourselves how we can help.

Bringing mindfulness to our meals makes us more sensitive to our own bodies and our own vulnerability and gives us an appreciation for the food we eat on a deeper level.

Frugal Soup

When I lived at Arcosanti, the urban ecology experiment in Arizona mentioned earlier in this book, residents would come together for a special ritual every Friday at lunchtime. This ritual was called Frugal Soup. Someone would cook and serve a simple meal of frugal soup and homemade bread with butter and nothing else.

Members of the community brought their bowls and spoons and would serve each other. Everyone would eat in silence and then we would have a discussion about our experience and about our insights regarding food, both on a personal level and a global level.

People regularly brought up world hunger and their feelings—ranging from anger to despair—about this unacceptable phenomenon and how powerless they felt. Other people would talk about how much delight they received from the healthy food we grew in the gardens, while others would talk about small steps they were becoming inspired to take in their lives to address the world food crisis.

Just taking a break from our routine once a week and reflecting on the topic of food in the bigger picture can bring us together with other people in a profound way and help us to remember not to take the matter of food for granted. Sometimes simply creating a space for conscious appreciation of our food expands our awareness of the issue.

Sensitivity for the Planet

Since living sustainably is engaging in a new relationship with the earth, we need to be present for this relationship. If I am practicing mindfulness in my kitchen, I'm much more likely to turn off the kitchen lights or the running tap than if I'm unconscious. When we are present, we become sensitive. We become more aware of our immediate surroundings.

There is no magic in it; on one level mindfulness is very practical. I am more available to take good care of myself and the world when I'm present and centered. I become more available to do things like cook with energy efficiency in mind, or monitor my growing basil with sensitivity to the plant's needs, or sense the exact moment when the water I am heating is tepid so I can start preparing my bread sponge.

When I'm just following the chattering thoughts of the mind like a cat playing with a ball of yarn, I'm likely, just like the cat, to get into some trouble or leave a trail behind me.

It simply helps us to make less of a footprint on the planet when we are living in the present moment, rather than letting our bodies do their thing while our minds play video games or have conversations about the future.

Weaving it all together, we can see that it is a service to all, including ourselves, to be mindful. When I'm off in conditioned conversation in my head or letting my body do one thing while my mind does another, I completely miss out on what's in front of me. It may be a beautiful sunny day, I'm out in the garden harvesting sparkling purple beans for my meal, but I don't truly enjoy it if I'm not practicing mindfulness.

So think of mindful eating as using mealtimes as an opportunity to get more present and to experience a more centered and relaxed way of being. This is the world view of an earth steward.

Practicing Mindfulness

Here are some exercises to help you explore your own experience of mindfulness:

• Pick one meal a day or one meal a week to eat in silence. For this meal, let yourself sit in silence and eat without any conversation, no background music, no telephone…just you and the meal in front of you. As you eat, imagine that you are eating a meal for the first time and pay close attention to your physical experience. Put your utensil down between each bite and remember to breathe.

• Make it a ritual to sit down for "nothing but a cup of tea" now and then… not "tea while I work," or "tea while I watch TV," just a cup of tea…perhaps sitting outside on the porch. Allow yourself to do nothing but be present to sipping tea and being fully aware of whatever your experience is.

• Pick one meal to cook in silence and without distraction. Turn off the phone, turn off the computer and allow yourself an experience of interacting with the food you are preparing, the dishes you are washing, your body, your breath, yourself, with no distraction. If you are washing vegetables, just wash. If you are measuring flour, just measure. Take the time to enjoy each simple experience. See what you notice.

• When the weather permits, eat a meal outside, whether it is breakfast, lunch, or dinner and notice the different quality of your experience.

• After a meal, practice "mindful dishwashing." Set aside some time with no distraction to simply be present with yourself and the dishes you are washing. Notice the feeling of the water on your hands, the foaminess of the soap and take more care with each step of the process and with each dish than you normally do. Appreciate each of the items you are washing. Let go of any preconceived notions you have about washing dishes and just notice your overall experience and how you feel afterwards.

If you do these exercises, you might find that you taste or smell your food for the first time. You may find that your five senses are more vibrant during the meal and that the way you experience your food, your body, the bowl and spoon you are using and the room you are in becomes richer; you might find you notice things about yourself that you haven't before; you might notice your sense of time is a bit different; but most importantly, you might see how, with mindfulness, peace and interconnection can be a part of every mealtime.

Mindful Eating on Retreat

I can remember my first meal on a silent meditation retreat. This was a 10-day retreat at a silent meditation center. I felt awkward enough (though also strangely at home) learning to move about amongst 40 strangers in silence. I washed my hands in silence, stood in the slow-moving line of meditators, served myself from a table where our meal—handmade chapatis, brown rice, miso soup and a delicious stir-fry of tempeh and garden vegetables—was displayed and sat down to "simply eat."

The first thing I noticed was how relaxing and relieving it was to be able to sit in silence, without any noisy conversation or music, to enjoy my meal. I remember pausing to take a look at the colors on my plate, to smell the food, to be aware of my body and how I felt and the meal seemed to take on new dimensions of richness and satisfaction. This is how it was supposed to be!

I remember feeling surprised at how grateful I felt knowing that I would not be disturbed at this meal, no one would expect any conversation from me and I could just fully be with myself... with my emotional state, with my body and with the food in front of me. With every meal on that retreat, be it a simple breakfast of oatmeal, almonds and tea, or a more decadent Italian dinner, I recall that colors, tastes and textures seemed to only become more and more vivid and musical, as did my gratitude.

The Power of Sensitivity

Many of my clients have decided to go green out of a deepening sensitivity for life. Many of us have been taught to resist our own sensitivity, but when we embrace it, we are forever changed. It often takes experiences where we have to face our own vulnerability or the vulnerability of a loved one to change in this way.

For instance, one client's interest in sustainability stemmed from her care for her dog. Her beloved dog got very sick and for the first time it occurred to her that she no longer wanted him trampling around on the pesticides her neighbors used for the lawn, or eating foods that were bad for him, or having to endure a toxic flea application. She realized how much she wanted her dog to enjoy a healthy and natural life.

She made some changes for her dog and it got her thinking about her own life. She realized she no longer wanted to expose herself to toxins and chemicals in the same way. Thus began her engagement with holistic living and the path of sustainability.

Another client of mine developed an autoimmune disease and the situation triggered her to look more subtly, for the first time, about what goes into her system and about the toxins in her home—from the indoor air she breathes to the food she eats—and to take action. Another client remembers experiences as a child on her parents' farm of not wanting to eat animals, but never having the guts to go against the grain and speak up until she was much older, at which point she became vegetarian AND began the process of going green.

For all of these people, beginning to listen to their sensitivity and honor it rather than resist it, changed how they lived their whole lives and their sensitivity became a part of what makes them powerful people rather than something that isolates them from themselves and others.

Other Practical Benefits of Mindfulness

Mindful eating is beneficial not only in helping you to enjoy food more and experience a deeper connection to your body and the world around you, but we also know it has health benefits. The most obvious health benefit is that you are able to digest your meal well and consciously appreciate it. There are also obvious benefits to checking in with ourselves—noticing what is going on in our bodies, minds and energetic systems—before each meal.

Bringing attention to such things before and during eating takes us off of autopilot and supports us in making conscious choices that support our well-being. We're more likely to pick up that bag of chips or that pint of ice cream (just after vowing to eat healthier!) when we're not present to what's going on within us or around us.

When we are present and tuned in to ourselves, we can know what our body's needs are, when to stop eating, for example, and sense if there are other needs being brought to a meal that are not meant to be met through food. We can sense if there is stress building in our day and choose to consciously release it before eating.

Meditation: Getting Present to What Is

Take a moment right now to turn your attention within. What is your attention on right now? Take a moment to relax and bring your awareness to your body, simply feeling the sensations in your body, whatever they are in this moment. Now... become aware of your emotions... What feelings or emotions are you present to right now? Again, simply notice. And now... become aware of your mind. What is the quality of thinking you are present to right now? What thoughts are you aware of?

Now, letting your body, emotions, and mind be as they are, simply bring your attention to your breath... not breathing in any particular way, just breathing in and breathing out, and feeling the air as it enters your body, fills your body, and leaves your body. Let the breath be an anchor to the present moment and simply notice. Notice all that arises (body, emotion, and mind) to draw your attention out of the moment and notice where it goes. Keep your attention with your breath and allow the breath to anchor you.

How was that? What did you notice? Please take a moment to write about your experience.

Taking Transition Time Before Meals

One of the many things I'm grateful for regarding what the monastery taught me is how to be present to my life experience and practice awareness of what is going on inside of me as I go about my life activities. This gives me the opportunity to take care of myself and receive the richness of the simple moments of my life.

How can one practice mindful eating when not living in a silent monastery?

In every community I've lived in, mealtime has been a conscious and special break in the day. I always remember lunchtime at Green Gulch Farm. In the middle of an active full workday in the fields, no matter what, at noon we would pause, clean up our farm tools, set them aside and walk down a long path to get to the dining hall. That walk would serve as a transition time and, once there, we would clean off our work boots, wash our hands and step into the dining hall.

We ate together and, although there was no silence, every step we took could be taken with mindfulness. There would be a table of simple nourishing food, usually hot soup, salad and warm homemade bread. Mealtime was an opportunity to pause, to slow down and shift gears and replenish our energy in our active workday.

Though these meals were not eaten in silence, there was always a space where people had the option for eating in silence. I always knew that if I was having a hard time, felt stressed or entangled in my emotions, I could eat my meal in a more meditative way and take it as time for myself.

In contrast, when I moved to the city I was invited out to lunch with a friend my first week back in town. I was struck by how much of a rush my friend was in, having taken a brief break in a stressful workday and having her mind still be at work while she and I sat to talk and enjoy our meal. She would take a bite, barely taking time to chew and all the while she was talking about what someone had done to her at work that day. She didn't realize how fast she'd been going until her plate was mostly empty and I asked her how her meal was.

She paused, realized that she hadn't tasted any of it and at that moment she became present to the emotions she was actually feeling and burst into tears. At that point we were able to actually talk about the pressure she was experiencing at work and what was really going on underneath… and she was able to get some perspective on the situation and return to work feeling more centered.

Ways to Integrate Mindfulness Into Life in the City

Have you ever been on a camping trip and had the experience of the simplest meal—a pot of rice and beans or a bowl of oats—be the best meal you have ever tasted? When I'm camping out or even just enjoying trail mix on a hike, I often reflect on how easy it is to be awake to my senses when I am surrounded by nature, in a new environment, doing something active and in my body and tuned into the world around me. My passion at the moment is in how to integrate mindful living into urban existence.

Resistance to Mindfulness

The attitude of mindfulness can be brought to all activities in our kitchen and our general lifestyle to improve our quality of life. I've learned through teaching that people carry all kinds of misconceptions about mindfulness around, from "slow" to "careful" to "focused on the mind" to "relaxed and blissful." Why practice mindfulness, people ask?

In conversations we have had about mindfulness at workshops, here is some of what people have said:

"Being mindful helps me to become aware of my own habits around food... how I feel pressured to hurry through mealtime just like I feel pressured to hurry in my life."

"Mindfulness feeds the deep need for peace within each of us."

"It helps me to notice details I might not otherwise notice, like the subtleties in the taste of what I'm eating or the sensation of the water on my skin when I'm doing the dishes. When I'm not mindful, I miss out on those details."

"It gives me a choice other than autopilot."

"It makes a meal more interesting.

"It helps me to appreciate my food."

I'm motivated to practice mindfulness because I know through experience that, in life, so much more is available to me when I do so. I cannot even compare the two experiences actually. Regardless of one's spiritual, religious, or non-religious perspective, my interest is in how we all relate to the human experience and how we can each help ourselves to find more peace in life.

Face it, it's hard being human.

In today's world, there is simply so much out there pulling, calling and seducing our attention away from the present moment. I find it a necessity to pause throughout the day and anchor myself in the present moment so as to not get caught up in all of the distraction.

Pause and consider... what are your favorite distractions and ways of "dealing" with the world? Perhaps the Internet, TV, the telephone, smoking... what else? What is the life experience that these distractions give you? And what do these distractions keep you from?

Now take a moment to acknowledge your current approach to mealtimes.

When was the last time that you sat down to enjoy a meal with the focus being on relaxing, being present and enjoying the rich and subtle tastes and textures of your meal and your body while eating it?

On a typical busy workday, what is your approach to mealtime? What is your experience of lunch in the middle of a workday?

How about cooking? Are you generally in a rush to get the meal out? How long do you allow for cooking?

When is it easiest for you to be mindful? And when is it most difficult? Where do you go/what kind of experience are you having when it is most difficult?

But There is Not Enough Time!

Another reason I find it helpful to practice mindful eating is if you are interested in bringing meditation into your life but "can't seem to find time." Many people I work with feel drained by their work lives and want to find more time for themselves but can't see how to do so. You have to eat every day...why not make your meals a meditation? Why not practice staying present while you eat?

> *"There is no enlightenment outside of daily life."*
> Thich Nhat Hanh

Many people think that mindfulness is supposed to be about reaching (as quickly as possible) some heightened state of awareness and peace. We are used to instant gratification in our culture. What if, instead, meditation is meant to be an opportunity to simply sit and be with all that arises in each moment (and all that we habitually push away in exchange for instant gratification) and to be with ourselves in a much more intimate, grounded and peaceful way? What if it is simply an opportunity to be sensitive to our experience of life in each moment?

Whatever we are doing inside ourselves that is not compassionate will be reflected in our relationship with food (and everything else in our lives!). Giving ourselves a relationship with food that is kind, healthy and reflects our care for the world is a commitment that will help us to cultivate more compassion for ourselves in every aspect of our lives.

Here are Some More Ways to Practice Mindfulness:

If you often eat while watching the TV, pick one meal to eat away from the TV.

Approach meal preparation, eating and cleanup as a meditation, a time just for you and see what this experience gives you.

Make a commitment to never eat standing or driving or reading or multitasking. Take the time to sit and focus on your meal when it is time to eat.

Tips for Bringing Mindfulness to the Kitchen

Take care with how you store your groceries. Be aware of your body as it moves, be aware of holding the groceries with care as you put them away and stow each item one by one.

Be mindful of how you care for your knives. Have a place designated for storing knives. Use a sharpener regularly. See what it feels like to really take care of your knives rather than just use them without noticing them.

Try washing dishes as an act of thankfulness—gratitude for each dish, gratitude for the meal you just ate, gratitude for the water you are using.

Make it a practice to clean your kitchen at the end of every day. Again, be aware of your body, breath and state of mind as you complete the tasks at hand. Pay attention as you sweep the floor and as you clean the sink. Notice for yourself what the benefit is to mindfulness practice.

Mindfulness does not have to be limited to one exercise a day. You can actually practice it all the time, in every circumstance. Mindfulness in the kitchen doesn't mean you have to always be peaceful in the kitchen. It is more an invitation to stay present in the kitchen. If you are having a hard day or if you are in a foul mood, just be present to how it feels to have a hard day or be in a foul mood. Turn to your experience and see what you notice when you just allow your experience to be what it is and observe it. Allow whatever mood you are in to be held in a larger container of peaceful awareness.

If mindful eating and cooking appeals to you and you set out to begin this practice, you may find certain lifestyle changes would make it easier. For instance, is your kitchen/dining area set up so that you have the spaciousness and opportunity to turn your attention inward if you want to? Or is your eating space set up in the middle of your work space or by the television? Is there enough time around meals? Or are meals just tucked in between your commitments to work and other issues?

Perhaps you have a family who is very attached to their traditional ways of doing things, such as playing background music or eating while watching TV. Perhaps you should have a conversation to invite them to a night of mindfulness. Make whatever adjustments will support you in this intention and consider how you might invite family and friends to participate.

If you want some gentle ways to approach these ideas with family, sometimes just introducing something that's a bit out of the ordinary can encourage more presence (most of us don't go on autopilot when we are doing something new):

Choose one night per week for a candle-lit dinner, if you normally have lights on. Turn all lights off, light candles and see how it turns dinner into a new experience.

Choose one night per week to cook together as a family. Set up stations for everyone to work, i.e. cutting up different vegetables, etc., just to have everyone working together and involved in the creative preparation of their meal as a group.

Choose one meal to eat outside (if you normally eat inside and the climate allows).

Make one meal per week a new and "never tried" meal for your family. Even this can wake people up to their senses and to the moment.

If you live alone or have the luxury of eating certain meals alone, consider this idea:

I like to set aside an evening entirely for myself sometimes. I unplug my phone, turn the computer off, and meditate or go on a walk. Then I will simply take time to prepare a meal, simple or gourmet depending on my mood and energy level, and enjoy the slowness and sensuality of it. I set the table caringly for myself, light candles and I eat my meal bite by bite, taking a breath after each bite and setting my utensils down between bites. Even the cleanup process is a peaceful meditation. The world of distraction is turned off, my relationship with time changes, and I get to tune into the simple pleasure of being present and feeling grateful.

How Can I Practice This When I Have No Time?

We have the opportunity, when life is fast-paced and everything feels out of our control, to stay present and keep the focus of our attention on BEING MINDFUL—in our bodies, in the present moment, regardless of the pace of things. The question is, how can we be mindful when we are driving in traffic, preparing a meal, changing our baby's diapers, typing up a report, cleaning the windows, or getting dressed for a night out with friends? Integrating mindful eating into your daily or weekly routine is a perfect place to begin practicing this way of being.

Consider it.

Engaging in mindful eating meditation practices on a regular basis can help us discover a far more satisfying relationship to food—to eating, cooking, cleaning up and stowing the groceries—than we ever imagined or experienced before. These are activities that we all engage in every day. When we are mindful, sensitivity for ourselves, each other and the world at large emerge out of our everyday activities. The benefits of mindful eating are not restricted to physical and emotional health improvements; they can impact our entire lives through a better sense of interconnection and well-being. ●

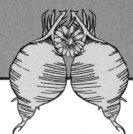

CHAPTER 14
COMMUNITY FOOD SHARING:
The Kitchen That Gives Back

"Good food should be a right, not a privilege."

—Alice Waters

Community: a group of people with a common characteristic or interest living together within a larger society

Food: something that nourishes, sustains, or supplies

Sharing: To participate in, use, enjoy, or experience jointly or in turns

YEARS AGO I SPENT TIME IN A SMALL VILLAGE IN Belize and experienced firsthand a "porch-visiting culture." In the village I stayed at in Belize, everyone had a porch. In the afternoon on hot days, free of the addiction to "somewhere to get to and something to do," people just sat on the porch and visited one another. Every day.

Visiting held an important place in the texture of Belizean culture. And porch visiting was also an opportunity for community food-sharing. Whenever you visited a neighbor, you would bring them herbs or flowers or vegetables from your garden, or fresh cashew fruit from your tree, and you might be served fresh coconut bread or iced tea.

I sometimes bring homemade treats with me to meetings in the city, just to offer a little nature-inspired delight to the unsuspecting colleague or client with whom I am meeting…maybe homemade raw chocolate balls, fruit from the garden, or a sprig of herbs. Gift giving, especially the gift of food, has a nourishing effect on people. This is different than the gift giving on special holidays, when gifts are expected and even sometimes a reason for stress. The kind of giving I am referring to is giving because we can, because gift giving is fun, and because we are fortunate people and giving gifts reminds us of what we have to give.

Nature's bounty is generous. When cultivating a garden, there is always extra harvest to share. It becomes second nature to offer friends and neighbors produce from your garden because it came to you as a gift from nature. It's natural to say, "Here, have this pumpkin," "please take a sprig of parsley," or "I don't know what to do with the outrageous abundance of apples my tree is producing… so please have some!"

In fact, in the summertime 80% of the work in a garden is harvesting the endless produce and finding people with whom to share. As my Zen teacher would say, "Gratitude wants to give"… and having a garden provides endless opportunities for gratitude—and for giving.

On the other hand, when we are dependent upon store-bought food, battling outrageous prices to fit our budgets, or feeling like it's an uphill struggle to try to follow the guidelines for healthy eating in our own lives, we can become a little less interested in sharing. Sharing can be an especially emotional topic in times of survival and economic distress.

But this is nothing we cannot shift with a subtle shift in perspective. I have shared more free meals with friends, neighbors, and strangers than I can recount, simply because as a grateful gardener and a lover of cooking, it brings me joy to share food with people. To share good food is to give an experience of peace, pleasure, satisfaction, and health. But I have also observed myself becoming stingy with food when I feel that my resources have become especially tight.

In my mind, a sustainable kitchen is founded on the principle of *community food sharing*, in alignment with the following principles from Chapter Seven:

- Cultivating a connection with a "sense of place" and "community" through food
- Being financially sustainable (or financially friendly)
- Giving back
- Through Community Food Sharing we can support ourselves better (both emotionally and physically), become closer to our friends and neighbors, and extend support out into our community and the world at large. A sustainable kitchen invites us to enjoy:
    - The exchange in sharing—being on both the giving end and the receiving end
    - The opportunity to go beyond the constraining beliefs tied into the monetary economy and support a bartering and gift-giving economy instead
    - Being part of a community of earth stewards that can make a difference and enhance the lives of everyone involved

Again, as we would say at the monastery, gratitude wants to give. The more we live in a world where we are THRIVING, practicing personal sustainability and environmental sustainability, the more we become ignited with the spirit of gratitude and the more we want to share with each other.

The more we remember that "we are in this together" rather than "it is up to me to survive alone," the more we thrive. By thriving, I don't mean we might have greater wealth or financial stability. Rather, I mean thriving in that we are out of our survival mode (always thinking there is not enough "for me," let alone for anyone else—and always listening to those limiting thoughts). Instead, we are taking care of ourselves and the world around us, practicing personal and planetary sustainability at the same time, so that we simply feel the joy and abundance in our world and want to share it with others.

Cooking for Others: Remembering that We Are All in this Together

I RECENTLY WOKE UP, A FEW MONTHS AFTER A RELATIONSHIP BREAK-up, feeling the loss and heartbreak as if it were yesterday. Some days we wake up feeling more tender and delicate than other days, and on that particular day, it felt like it took all of me to simply get out of bed and meditate. I looked at my work list for the day and activities for which I would normally feel enthusiasm and it all seemed terribly and horribly daunting.

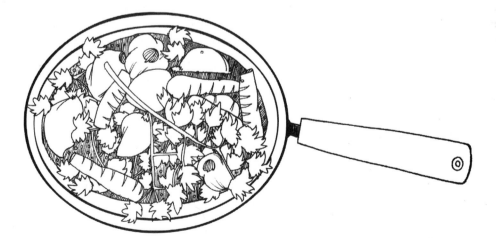

I thought about my options and felt frozen for a moment, realizing that it was not a choice to NOT work on this day. One of the items on the list, scheduled for lunchtime, was to prepare a special meal for a friend as part of a trade/barter for a service she had given me. I was bartering regularly with my cooking during this time, in response to the recession and in support of the alternative economy developing in Los Angeles. I heard the voice in my head saying, "Oh no, I can barely get my normal work done today, let alone put energy into creating a special meal for someone to delight in. There is no delight in my life today!"

Because I caught this voice of doom and glimpsed a preview of where that path would lead me, a shift occurred and I remembered that I had another choice. I washed my hands and began to prepare vegetables, choosing the dreaded task of cooking to attend to first. I slowly got into the *rhythm* of cooking and simply poured all of my feelings of love and heartbreak into preparing the meal.

I thought of the friend I was delivering the meal to, and the thought of bringing delight and love into her life in the middle of her workday completely transformed me. I then thought of another few friends and colleagues who I knew were also working hard today, up against deadlines like we all were and facing life's challenges and I decided to make enough food for all of them.

I was filled with the energy of gratitude and love that cooking provides for me and that cooking food for others gives to me too. I put each of the meals I prepared that day into travel containers, created an artistic menu for each friend, and placed each meal in a cloth bag for delivery.

Just then, my friend Peter stopped by unexpectedly and I had enough food leftover to send off with him after a brief but sweet visit. The meal that day was basmati rice, roasted vegetables, garlicky tempeh, and braised greens with a special nutty coconut sauce. Cooking that meal (in only an hour) and then spending an hour driving around town to deliver each one, which included brief visits with each friend, reminded me of how much I do have and how much I have to give… even on a day of grieving a lost relationship.

I arrived back at my home office that day filled with energy, turned on my computer, and began to go through my work list. Though I began my workday later than planned, I actually completed the tasks somewhat effortlessly and in much less time than expected. Later that day, I got to open my email inbox and received words of thanks and "aahs" and "ohs" from the happy recipients of my meal deliveries… but I had already spent the day in thanksgiving.

Sharing food with our community reminds us that "we are all in this together" and this is a spirit we can extend out into the world at large as well.

Free Farm Stand: Sharing Food with the Larger Community

MY FRIEND TREE RUNS AN AMAZING PROJECT IN SAN FRANCISCO CALLED Free Farm Stand. Tree has been my hero for years in the area of community food sharing. I met him when I lived in the Bay Area after college and I was a young urban gardener myself. Tree was an enthusiastic and humble gardener and revolutionary who grew wildly artful vegetable gardens. He embodied the spirit of generosity, simplicity, and creativity in his gardens; they were a reminder of the wild, free, and sensual nature of plants and of our natural selves.

Tree also ran No Penny Opera, one of the best examples of "community food sharing" that I have ever seen. On Fridays, volunteers would gather together and spend the day cooking and preparing a space at a local church to serve a free vegan dinner. Not only would amazing organic vegan food be served to a crowd of homeless and local people, but the servers would dress up in costume, play lively music, perform, and offer an experience of celebration, pleasure, and fun to all who came to dinner.

Tree's projects, like his gardens and No Penny Opera, model the nature of service where the giver and the receiver both benefit. Generosity is its own reward and Tree lives in generosity.

One day, Tree decided to start the Free Farm Stand. He set up a table in the small community garden where he worked and began giving produce away to neighbors and families with children. The project soon expanded to four tables and people lined up early to receive the gift of healthy produce. Last year the Free Farm Stand distributed over 6,000 pounds of produce that they either grew or gleaned from local trees. The 6,000 pounds does not account for all the produce they collected from farmers markets to give away.

The Free Farm Stand now has five gardens that mostly grow food for the stand. In Tree's words, "What is beautiful and really hard to describe is the excitement and good vibe that is stirred up by the neighbors gathering every week. People get to know each other and talk and share something of themselves. Every week, I meet someone that is doing something wonderful and inspiring. I personally get really excited when someone comes by with something to share, even if it is a handful of chervil grown by someone who wants to share her excitement about this herb with others.

"One day a man came by with a couple of fresh baked loaves of bread to share at the Free Farm Stand. He has a small business called Sour Flour and he taught himself how to bake five months ago last November. Now he bakes bread in his kitchen to give away. He was going to celebrate his 1000th loaf of bread baked and given away. So the stand is really more than just giving away free produce; it is about encouraging people to share and participating in a weekly neighborhood ritual or ceremony or theatrical event. We are promoting food growing and sharing to make sure everyone has access to healthy, locally grown food."

What a different world it would be if we all drew from this inspiration and grew some of our own food while also keeping our neighbors in need in mind. I appreciate projects such as Tree's because not only does it supply healthy food, but it builds community and creates a platform for people from all walks of life to come together in a joyful celebration of food and service. In every city there are gems like Tree and there are endless service projects to get involved in, if you make the effort to look for them.

Here Are Some Ways You Can Help In Your Own Neighborhood

SHARE FOOD FROM YOUR OWN GARDEN WITH FRIENDS AND NEIGHBORS.

Each time you go shopping for yourself, purchase at least one thing for a stranger or to donate to a food bank. You might buy one item for the food bank once a week and making a monthly donation OR buy a bag for the food bank once a week and make a weekly donation, depending on your financial capacity and what feels right for you.

Farmers markets tend to give out discounted or free food the last hour or so they are open. Consider going to the farmers market to collect (and deliver) produce for the local food bank. You might even create a sign that helps people to identify what you are doing and invite people to make offerings to your collection.

If you work at an office building, consider putting a weekly food bank box out for your co-workers to contribute to, and make a weekly delivery to a food bank or directly to organizations that help people in need.

Start your own version of Free Farm Stand... every city needs this!

Find other ways to support a gift-giving economy.

Tree's encouragement is to look for ways to reach out and get involved in the healing of your community and, I would add, get involved in the healing of the world food crisis as it manifests in your community.

In Tree's words, "First people have to get in touch with themselves and figure out what excites them, what they are passionate about, what they really want to do if they could do anything to help. In terms of repairing the damaged world we live in... one can start in one's own backyard or neighborhood to find good work to do. I recommend volunteering somewhere if they are shy about starting their own project or to get a sense of what they might be interested in doing.

"Visiting other groups that are doing similar work is always good to do to get inspiration and ideas about how to do something. Possibly look for ways to collaborate with others. If one wants to start one's own project, start small. Don't worry about the money at first; figure out how to do things for free using as little money as necessary. Recruit friends to help out. Don't buy new things unless necessary. Try to get things for free or used. Ask for in-kind donations. Make any project you do beautiful and exciting, filled with love and joy."

How to Support Ourselves and Each Other In Our Endeavor to Have a Sustainable Kitchen
Farmers Markets, Community Food-Sharing and Other Economical Strategies

DEPENDING ON WHERE YOU LIVE, IT CAN BE EASY OR A MAJOR CHALlenge to find affordable, local, organic whole foods. Along with shopping at farmers markets, which lowers the cost for you and supports your local community farmers, or joining a Community Supported Agriculture (CSA) group, consider creative ways you can work with friends and neighbors to save money sharing food. Some examples are:

- Start a food buying club (for cheaper prices in bulk).
- Start a food co-op.
- Garden strategically: plan with a few other gardeners what you are all growing and share with one another.
- Have regular green potlucks, where each person creates just one dish and you all receive the bounty of everyone else's cooking.
- Share resources such as a community compost, solar oven, or bicycle-powered blender. Save money by making these green investments as a group.

Poverty: Extending Ourselves Beyond

I WAS LUCKY TO GROW UP WITH A MOTHER WHO ALWAYS SOUGHT ways to help heal the world. She had been both an artist and a social worker for years, while raising three kids with my dad and struggling with money themselves. One day, after reading an article about children living with their families in the Skid Row area of downtown Los Angeles, only 20 minutes from our modest home, she said to herself, "Enough of this—someone has to help these people!" Within a short two months, she began an organization that eventually served thousands of children and families each year. Over the next few years, she reached out to others, bringing them into her work as it evolved.

Eventually she founded three nonprofit agencies and co-founded a fourth, all dedicated to intervening in the lives of homeless and low-income families and individuals—providing food, shelter, housing, jobs and opportunity, all from a humanitarian perspective and based on universal human rights. Three of the nonprofit charities she created have long been run by others, enabling her to focus her efforts for the past 20 years on innovative strategies to combat family homelessness and poverty on a national scale.

My mom's modeling of generosity continues to blow me away to this day. No matter what the circumstances are she will do whatever it takes to help a family or child in need. When I was in grade school, my mom met a young boy named Gabriel who was in an especially hopeless situation on Skid Row and, after conferring with my dad, she simply created a makeshift bedroom for him using dividers in our living room and brought him to live with us on and off for the next three years. People might look at my mom and think, "Oh, what a load to take on. What a lot of work!" But I look at my mother and recognize the energy, vitality and strength that giving so fully has given her. At 67, she is one of the most energetic and radiant women I know, because she knows that giving and receiving are inherently connected.

Aside from teaching her kids to always be aware of the person to whom just a little bit of our help, attention, or time would make a great difference, my mom has also taught me how to get past the lens that I think most of us in cities view the world through, without even being aware of it—the lens through which poor and homeless people are viewed as "different" from ourselves.

Doing so, even subconsciously, is a way of isolating ourselves rather than remembering that we are all in this together. Yet I know that it can be easy to forget and to turn away or feel that it is someone else's job to address poverty in the cities and communities in which we live. It can be so easy, when our own needs are taken care of, to forget that so many around us do not live with even the most basic of their human needs fulfilled.

Here is a practice to consider that I began after I moved back to the city:

Keep something in your car or day bag to offer to the homeless or to people in need. You pass homeless people many times a day if you live where I live and giving a simple piece of fruit or a protein bar is a small way to help out. If you don't want to give change, offering a healthy snack is a way of saying, "I see you and even though I may feel powerless to help you, I can at least offer you a smile and some simple nourishment." I can assure you that the recipient, in most cases, will experience a better day—and maybe benefit in other ways as well.

While this hardly addresses the larger issues of hunger, it is one simple way to impact someone's life through the sharing of food.

My sister, a photographer, describes a vivid memory of a group of hungry and ill-clad children she met a few years ago in a Zambian slum that she was visiting. She watched one of the children, a little girl about 10 years old, with a fruit roll she had been given. The girl slowly unwrapped the small roll and then carefully and meticulously divided it into over 25 tiny pieces to share with all of the other children that were circled around her, who in turn shared their pieces with other children. I can vouch that my sister will never forget the depth or the spirit of sharing that she witnessed in that moment. Moments like these can remind us of how rare it is for most people in this world to have all of their basic needs met and that we always have something to share.

A major part of the sustainability movement must be about reclaiming our connection to nature through FOOD (actually healing our relationship with nature through food) and, at the same time, RECLAIMING our connection to each other. Community food sharing is a way to step away from isolation and remember that we are all in this together. Urban community gardening, farmers markets, CSAs and service projects that reach out to those who do not have healthy food are all means to empower ourselves with this awareness and rebuild our sense of community in the spirit of sustainability. ●

CHAPTER 15
SUSTAINABILITY FROM THE INSIDE OUT

"The care of the Earth is our most ancient and most worthy and after all our most pleasing responsibility. To cherish what remains of it and to foster its renewal is our only hope."

—Wendell Berry

MY PASSION AS A SUSTAINABILITY COACH IS THE question: *How do we make long-lasting change for good in our lives?* What supports our good intentions and what sets us back? Even after reading a book that inspires and informs us, what's to keep us from going back to old ways or from getting bogged down by the vastness of the task at hand? If we want to create a sustainable kitchen in our homes, in my experience there are five areas we need to address:

• We need to learn about how nature works and to understand the basic principles of sustainable living. (Reading this book is a great first step.)
• We need to be willing to practice self-awareness and look at our internal landscape to see what our forms of resistance to making change are, so that we can learn to recognize resistance and let it go (thus freeing ourselves up to join the solution).

We need to understand that we are doing this for ourselves as much as for the world. If we are going green because we think we "should," while we may be successful, it will still just be another "should" or "duty" on our to-do list. There is a bigger opportunity here that involves taking passionate responsibility for the world in which we live. Taking passionate responsibility changes us while at the same time changing our world. Cultivating a sustainable world outside requires us to cultivate a sustainable world for ourselves.

We need to take it one step at a time and find community support for our efforts.

We need to understand that change is only possible if we are willing to enjoy it and to be fully alive, powerful, bold, and creative in the process of enacting change. When we bring joy into the process of doing anything we set out to do, we are much more likely to continue doing it.

CONSIDER:

What Is Motivating Your Choices?

Allow yourself to pause and relax… If you notice any area of tension in your body, take a deep breath into it and let it go, so you can simply be here, relaxed and present, in this moment.

Take a moment to mentally review the past 24 hours of your life and consider that over that time period you have had to make at least a few choices about food. Allow to arise in your mind one choice you made that was healthy and green or that you feel especially good about…Perhaps you walked to the market or remembered to bring your own shopping bag or took time to pack a healthy lunch for work… With whatever example arises, ask yourself what motivated this green choice? What supported you in making the green choice?

Now let that go and allow to arise in your mind an example of an unhealthy or NOT sustainable choice you made around food in the last 24 hours… What motivated that choice? What was going on for you in that moment? What does this simple example tell you about your own lifestyle?

What triggers you to make the not-so-green choice? What supports you in making the green choice?

Most people respond to this exercise by reporting that when they are centered, present, or experiencing well-being, they make greener choices, while stress or upset, laziness or inconvenience are behind their not-so-green choices.

What can you see about your own choices and motivations?

Self-Awareness and Breaking Old Patterns

THE FIRST THING I LEARNED AS A SUSTAINABILITY COACH IS THAT there is plenty of internal distraction that gets in the way of us changing old patterns and keeping new intentions. Each of us has our own good reason or believable argument for maintaining our old ways of doing things rather than embracing change. Let's call these "limiting thoughts."

Here are some examples of limiting thoughts that can thwart our attempts to go green. Are any of these voices familiar?

I don't have the time or money for this…

I'm too tired to make the extra effort right now…

I don't want to learn any more about what I shouldn't be eating and doing… I just want to enjoy my chocolate cake.

I know I'm not doing things right, but c'mon, I'm broke and this is all I can do, so let me off the hook.

My efforts are not going to make a difference anyway.

I already am doing the right thing… I'm following the rules… It's all of THEM out there who aren't doing it.

It's the fault of government and big business… Let them solve it!

If it's fashionable, I'll do it!

My friends aren't doing it, so why should I?

I'm too tired and overwhelmed today to do something for the environment.

I'm sick of the whole "green thing"…

CONSIDER:

- Do these cover the limiting thoughts that you fall into?
- What are your limiting beliefs around going green?
- What is your favorite form of resisting making change in your life?
- What limiting thoughts have you noticed while reading this book?

The good news is that we are not required to follow our limiting thoughts. They only have the power that we give them. Anyone who has made a change for the better in their lives knows that it takes commitment and vigilance to move beyond our mind's arguments for limitation and stay focused on whatever our heart's intention or goal is. We can bring the same kind of vigilance to transforming our relationship with food and committing to a sustainable lifestyle.

So how do we stay focused on our deepest intentions?

There is a term in Buddhism, "monkey mind," that refers to the wandering nature of the human mind that just jumps from thought to thought and sometimes takes wild leaps, while we follow blindly. That monkey mind is what we are up against in keeping our focus on our intention.

It helps to have a practice of self-awareness for staying present, noticing our thoughts for what they are and not being bound to them. Whether you already have a practice of this sort or not, knowing that our biggest challenge in sustainable living is our internal dynamic, here are some tools that can help to navigate the road to change.

Helpful Tools To Navigate The Way

THE GOAL OF THIS WORK IS TO: REEDUCATE OURSELVES, TAP INTO OUR passion and compassion for the world we live in, see resistance for what it is and be the change we wish to see. It is easy to get inspired by the idea of revolutionizing our relationship with food. We read the ideas presented in this book and they resonate with us; however, in order to actualize these changes we usually need to do some personal inquiry as well and really begin to see clearly what motivates our daily choices and actions. This personal inquiry is where the real work begins and where the fun and reward happen.

The basic tools to help us navigate our internal resistance to change—the voices of limitation in our heads—are the following:

- Non-judgment
- Beginner's mind
- Present-moment awareness
- Community support
- Taking it one "enjoyable" step at a time

Non-judgment

Most of us do NOT wake up in the morning plotting the ways we are going to make a negative impact on the earth. Correct? We are simply doing things the way we were taught to do them. We happen to be at a point in time, however, where it is evident that those ways are not sustainable, and a mind of non-judgment is CRITICAL in this transition. Sometimes the more we learn about environmental degradation or about "the green things we should be doing," the more we get caught up in judging ourselves… and the more we judge others.

Is judgment really necessary in the process of making change? Consider the amount of work we have ahead of us in helping to cleaning up our environment. Rising to the occasion is going to require our focused energy and commitment. Now consider the amount of mental energy that judgment requires.

In my experience, judgment works to keep us stuck in repetitive thought patterns that support limitation (or distract us from moving forward). Judgment drains the energy that we need for taking action and moving forward and distracts us from the task at hand. It might be more helpful to acknowledge that we are all doing the best we can, set up supportive accountability systems, and let the transition to sustainable living be an enjoyable process that changes our lives for the better, step by step. Why not be kind to ourselves as we are learning to be kind to the environment? I believe the spirit of kindness is our greatest teacher/asset in the endeavor to create a sustainable world.

We are all at different points with going green. Some of us (the lucky ones) have been raised by progressive parents who have been composting and gardening for years. Others grew up in families that offered no exposure to environmental education whatsoever. If we can accept this fact without judgment and acknowledge that every effort is a step in the right direction, we can appreciate ourselves for each effort we make, and we are then much more likely to hop, skip, and jump our way to our goal.

This is not to say there isn't a place for feeling anger or frustration about the environmental crisis. We need to acknowledge and accept all of the feelings that arise about this painful predicament we are in. See if you can acknowledge your feelings, however, with an open heart and without judgment.

Are you aware of any internal judgments about how green you are living? How green others are living? Do you meet the standards set up in your own mind? What if your job was to simply find enjoyable and interesting ways to lessen your environmental impact without constantly being compared to a standard?

Beginner's Mind

This book has offered fresh ways of doing things that you do every day. Be willing to relax the part of you that "knows the right way to do things already," and let yourself be an explorer, open to discovering new ideas and information about yourself and your relationship with food. Consider approaching all of your habitual tasks around food with a "beginner's mind." Pretend you are a kid in the kitchen learning how to do fun, creative projects involving food. This book is not here to preach a set of green "rules," but to inspire your own creativity based on an education in sustainability and a personal exploration of your relationship with food in the city. It also might encourage you to invent new ways of doing things.

Present-Moment Awareness

What does being present have to do with sustainability? In my experience, being present has everything to do with sustainability. The more present we are, the more we tend to experience compassion for ourselves and the world we live in. When we experience compassion, we naturally choose to take care of our world. There is no argument about "do I have time to pay attention to my water use while washing the dishes?" Rather, we choose to because we are sensitive on a more subtle level to the world around us and it is simply a natural expression of our sensitivity.

In addition, being present puts us in touch with our own experience. Someone telling you that organic carrots taste better than conventionally grown carrots is simply NOT going to sell you on the idea until you have your own visceral experience of eating an organically grown carrot.

Someone telling you that it is much better to wash dishes in an eco-friendly way is nothing compared to having your own experience of how rewarding (and easy) it is to have a low-impact, water-saving system for washing dishes. I encourage you to stay as present as you can and turn to your own experience as you try on the information presented in this book.

Present-moment awareness also gives us access to information and insight that comes from a different place than our "chattering mind/thinking mind." Our chattering/thinking mind tends to dwell in the past or future and tends to play and replay thoughts, rather than experience the present moment fully. Being caught up in our thoughts can actually distract us from the clarity of perception that comes naturally when we are simply more tuned in to our own present-moment awareness. When we are present, solutions to "problems" our chattering mind could never solve come to us naturally.

The Power of Community

It is much easier to adopt green ideas when you have some form of community support. Think about it: If you were going to take up running, it would be supportive to have a running partner to meet at a certain time each day. If you were learning to meditate, it might help to have a group you were committed to showing up for and meditating with. If you are on the path of revolutionizing your relationship with food, it can help to connect with other people who have joined this revolution.

On the practical level, for instance, it is more cost-effective to buy organic or other foods in bulk with a group of people, and more affordable to have a shared recycling and composting system. Community sharing is a vital ingredient in sustainable living. If your task is to turn a vacant yard into a garden, why not invite your neighbors over to help and make a party out of it? It is so much more uplifting to have the example and support of other people walking this path with you as you make these changes in your own life.

Recently, as I was walking down the street in my neighborhood, I noticed a sign that made me smile. In a well-populated area, a man had posted a colorful homemade sign with handouts informing people who walked by about the issue of leaf blowers and air pollution, and he offered simple ways to curb the problem. Leaf blowers in Los Angeles have become outlawed, and the public has been educated as to their harmful effects on the environment, yet everywhere you go, every day, there are more leaf blowers being used by gardening companies who take care of private lawns.

Every time I see someone making a personal effort, like the man who posted the information about alternatives to leaf blowing machines, I'm reminded that the task of cleaning up the environment is a task we share and this knowledge helps me to lighten up.

We are inundated by the news, both in our cars during work commutes and at home when we turn TV to the morning or nightly news. Unfortunately, in regards to the environment in particular, most of what we hear is the bad news. What would happen if we let go of bad world news and surrounded ourselves with good news for a change? How powerful would it be to connect every day with the heroic efforts people are making around the globe each day to heal the planet?

One Step at a Time

I emphasize again that it is helpful to make the changes prescribed in this book step by step. I find that my clients are most successful when they keep pressure out of their relationship with going green and let it be an enjoyable part of their lives. My hope is that reading this book has provided you with a radically honest education about food that most of us didn't receive while growing up, and that it has offered you the inspiration to see how life-affirming the proposed changes can be.

I hope you will integrate that education without judgment about the ways you may have been doing things in the past. Hopefully, you have learned how to reposition yourself from being a "consumer" to being an "earth steward."

Many people believe that the very fact that they live in a city or suburb means they can't be a steward of the earth. This is not true. It simply takes education, inspiration, practice, and patience. In the words of Cheri Huber,

"It doesn't matter how slow you go, just as long as you don't stop."

Remember, the goal of this book is not to add 50 more "shoulds" to your to-do list. So keep that in mind and go at your own pace. This is an invitation to join an urban food revolution for personal and planetary health. I invite you to adopt a new paradigm of sustainability—where you get to experience the joy and satisfaction that comes naturally from every step you take.

Stress and pressure have nothing to offer us in this revolution. Just as you are learning how to say NO to unhealthy toxins used in the kitchen, you will learn to say NO to unhealthy thought patterns. Instead, you are invited to feel the satisfaction at the end of every day that comes from being part of the solution, no matter how small the steps may be that you are taking.

The Sustainable Food Revolution: What is Our Role?

I'VE ALWAYS BEEN A HIGHLY SENSITIVE PERSON AND LONG AGO I FELT burdened by my sensitivity to the world around me. For me, sensitivity manifested itself in not being able to eat certain foods, not being able to be in highly synthetic environments, nor to partake in certain activities other people seemed to be able to tolerate, such as large crowds. Over time, I've come to see my sensitivity as a gift, because it serves as a guide to keep me connected to my heart, my body, and to my vulnerability, which I have come to learn is an authentically powerful place to reside.

The more we relate to the environmental crisis on a personal level, as in allowing ourselves to experience our sensitivity to, for example, the abuse of natural resources, the mistreatment of animals, the attack on ecosystems in the name of food production, and the pollution of pristine environments by trash created in the name of convenience, the more we become clear about how far we are willing to go to make a difference… and the more we acquire the tenacity to make that difference and to help others get in touch with their sensitivity too.

I believe that since we do not, as a society, hear directly from the fish impacted by our pollution, nor the once living soil degraded and depleted by poor farming practices, nor the honeybees whose entire species is threatened by our use of systemic pesticides, nor the traditional peoples whose cultures and livelihoods have been systematically destroyed by our Western agricultural practices, that there is a real need for our sensitivity. If you feel the call to speak up for cleaner water, cleaner air, an end to the use of toxins, and an end to practices that pollute and work against nature, please do so. Honor your sensitivity. It holds tremendous power.

Consider a world where we truly honor ourselves and all of the resources we use—a world in which we are not required to rape and plunder the planet in order to survive, but where we in fact "give back." When you act, notice if your actions are in alignment with this possibility.

It is vital to remember that we are all in this together. In terms of food, we must remember that beyond what we see on our plates is a web that connects us to the entire web of life on our planet.

For many common choices I make in my day around food, I ask myself if everyone were making a similar choice, would that choice be sustainable? When I am making a decision to use fresh or secondary water to water my plants, or to pick up packaged, take-out food versus cooking a one-pot meal at home, I ask myself if my choice will really make a difference. What if all my neighbors were choosing the more sustainable choice at the same time? How many of us would it take to change the world in which we live?

Do not undervalue the significance of your every action, and do not undervalue your power to make a beautifully positive impact with every action. You can begin by feeling the peace and empowerment in yourself that comes from letting your sensitivity guide your choices.

How Far Can We Go?

For starters, let us be done with polluting our world so that we can focus on cleaning it up. As individuals and as a society, if we redirect the energy that has created unnecessary trash and pollution and transform our resignation to the toxic chemicals that are in everything from our farming practices to our food packaging to our water supply, then perhaps we can put all that energy into the next phase of things: working with nature to design and create systems that improve on both the human supply/needs being met and the means by which these resources are provided.

We desperately need to reconnect to the spirit of "giving back"—to ourselves, to others, and to our planet.

In terms of how things could look, imagine a world in which all cities have thriving, local, organic food production systems, where every neighborhood has a healthy and affordable food supply, and where there are conscious waste disposal, recycling, and composting systems in place on a regional level.

Imagine bulk bins in every market, with the days of excessive packaging as a distant memory, and food co-operatives in every community. Imagine organic, edible fruit trees in parks, biodegradable materials replacing plastics, a cultural commitment to efficient energy use in kitchens, and restaurants that practice these principles in their design and operation. Imagine all children growing up eating healthy, organic food and with a sense of connection to their food system and pride in taking care of it.

Today there are farms, communities, activists, restaurants, chefs, concerned parents, schools, neighborhood groups, health practitioners, writers and many others pioneering this movement. Consider the health, well-being, and *joie de vivre* available to us all in joining this peaceful food revolution.

We need to embrace the spirit of an earth steward, one who lives in touch with his or her body and sensitivity, with awareness and with enthusiasm, and from a place of interconnection that honors all of life. An earth steward takes passionate responsibility for the world in which we live and finds joy in taking that responsibility.

Imagine using your kitchen as a laboratory and how this possibility might inspire and impact the rest of your life—starting today. ●

CHAPTER 16
A WORKBOOK AND RESOURCE LIST
To Support Your Success

Awareness/Writing Exercises

For this chapter, you will want to get out your pen and paper. Please find a quiet place and allow yourself 30 minutes or more for the following exercises:

1—A WRITING EXERCISE...
Personal Food Inventory

Most of my food comes from:

My basic diet consists of:

My diet on my "best days" is:

My diet on my "worst days" is:

Three things I do to eat healthfully are:

Three things I do to eat sustainably or to take care of planetary health in my kitchen are:

One way I already practice being a conscious consumer is:

My general feeling about "going green" is:

My staple foods are: (What do you always have in your pantry/fridge, no matter what?)

My favorite foods are: (Notice if your staple foods are different from your favorite foods.)

The main thing I'm aware of that is not so green in my eating/cooking patterns is:

I believe that if I go green (fully) I will have to give up eating/consuming:

The aspect of green living in relationship to food that I think will be most difficult is:
A way I admit that I am completely lax, lazy and careless regarding food choices is:
On a typical, busy workday, my general experience and approach to mealtimes is:
   (Rushed? Fast fuel? What else?)
My top three motivations in planning meals are:
My current economic situation is:
It determines my food choices by:
If I had all the time in the world or all the money in the world, I would eat differ-
   ently in this way:

Now, take a moment to look over your notes. See what you notice about your answers... Did anything surprise you? In what ways are you being guided by comfortable and familiar habits instead of making choices that are sustainable? What kind of "old habits" are you living by unconsciously? How are you letting the perceived limitations of time and money guide you?

Have you examined these beliefs and habits carefully or are you just running on autopilot?

Consider the ways you see yourself being motivated and directed by old habits that no longer serve you and that you feel ready to let go of.

2—An Awareness Exercise

Think of an experience you have had of a peaceful, nurturing meal.... Think big... a memory of wholesome, delicious food that inspired and soothed you. Perhaps it was at your favorite restaurant or on your last camping trip cooked over an open fire... It could have been a meal you ate today. What were the qualities of that meal? Perhaps nourishment... connection... joy... Write down a few of those qualities. Recall how it felt to be in your body enjoying that meal...

Think of a kitchen or restaurant that inspires a feeling of well-being in you...What
   are the qualities in this place that affect you so positively?
Remember that sustainable living invites us to tune in to our bodies and our
   present-moment awareness at a more subtle level than we might be used to.
What are the three most important values that you want to bring to your experience with food and cooking?
   1.
   2.
   3.
In what ways are you currently living in alignment—or out of alignment—with
   these values?
What would be one enjoyable and interesting way to bring each of these values into
   your kitchen?

3—Assessing Your Current Sustainability Practices:

The following questions are an assessment form for "How green are your current kitchen practices?" This is NOT a green report card. This is simply to give you more of a sense of where you are starting from and what aspect of the green kitchen you want to begin with. Pay attention to how your inner critic wants to make this about judgment—about passing (I'm doing everything right!) or failing (See, I am failing in going green). If you answer these questions with an open mind and non-judgment, you will simply be receiving helpful information that will help you to take the next peaceful step.

What do you currently do in your kitchen that reflects your concern for the environment? Take a moment to acknowledge/list the "green" choices you already make.

Are there any aspects of your relationship to food that you are particularly concerned with and feel might currently have a significantly negative environmental impact?

What about your daily diet nourishes you? What about your daily diet is "not working"? Be honest with yourself.

What is your worst, most environmentally unhealthy food habit? What drives this habit, to the best of your awareness?

For the following questions, please circle the number that best describes the degree to which you practice the following, 1 being the least degree and 10 being the most. (Note: This is NOT meant to be a "green" report card. It is simply an opportunity to acknowledge where you are now, as we begin this process.)

I recycle and try to be aware of creating minimum waste in my kitchen.

1   2   3   4   5   6   7   8   9   10

I make an effort to use green products and support conscious companies. I practice using my power as a consumer to make a difference.

1   2   3   4   5   6   7   8   9   10

I am aware of the CO_2 impact of my lifestyle and food choices, as it contributes to global warming, and try to reduce my CO_2 impact wherever possible.

1   2   3   4   5   6   7   8   9   10

I make an effort to stay informed about food issues and take action when I can.

1   2   3   4   5   6   7   8   9   10

I practice energy conservation/efficiency and use renewable energy in my kitchen.

1   2   3   4   5   6   7   8   9   10

I practice water conservation and efficiency in my kitchen.

1   2   3   4   5   6   7   8   9   10

Personal health is an important part of my life and I am actively engaged in maintaining and enjoying a healthy lifestyle.

1   2   3   4   5   6   7   8   9   10

My diet is based on local seasonal foods.

1   2   3   4   5   6   7   8   9   10

I buy in bulk and choose foods with minimum packaging.

1   2   3   4   5   6   7   8   9   10

I compost and practice avid creative reuse and recycling.

1   2   3   4   5   6   7   8   9   10

I cook without keeping in mind conservation of energy and food resources.

1   2   3   4   5   6   7   8   9   10

Do you feel that your current kitchen habits promote health, sustainability, and balance?

What do you believe/expect will be most challenging about the process of creating a sustainable kitchen? If you are already engaged in the process, what has been most challenging so far?

A Timeline

THROUGHOUT THE BOOK THERE ARE "NEXT STEPS" AND QUESTIONS laid out to help you actualize the principles being presented. For those of you who want more help with organization, here is an example of how to apply the ideas in this book over a period of either 12 WEEKS or 12 MONTHS, depending on your pace. I recommend that you first read the entire book and let yourself digest the information and then begin making changes as they arise organically. Then use this timeline to go deeper with your natural kitchen. If you choose to take 12 months, simply change Week to Month and follow this plan.

Week One: Take inventory of your kitchen and food habits in regard to sustainability (using the categories listed in Chapter Seven).

Week Two: Begin conscious green menu planning. Pick a day to use menu planning for the week as an opportunity to experiment and incorporate new, more sustainable food and cooking choices into your diet. Take notes about what works well and what challenges you face (internally and externally) as you explore this process.

Week Three: Prepare Your Urban Eco-Kit. Get yourself set for on-the-road sustainability by equipping yourself with the supplies listed in Chapter Eleven.

Week Four: Clean out your kitchen and dispose consciously of what does not belong.

Week Five: Prepare supplies shopping list. Consider any supplies you need to bring into your kitchen to make it sustainable, and budget accordingly. For instance, you may need a water purification system, healthy containers, pots and pans, or you may want to invest in more energy-efficient appliances.

Week Six: Set up your Radical Recycling Center as laid out in Chapter Four. As part of this process, access the most updated information online about the recycling guidelines for your neighborhood.

Week Seven: Prepare composting setup or find ways to improve your existing system.

Week Eight: Experiment with energy-efficient meals.

Week Nine: Develop an organic garden plan. This can be as simple as setting up a container herb garden in your kitchen window or taking the first step in growing your own food or making an existing garden even more sustainable.

Week 10: Menu Planning Phase Two—Bring mindfulness to your meals. Begin by picking a meal that is a special time just for you to eat in silence and experience mindful cooking and eating. Notice the effects of mindful eating and consider how to bring this element into your life more fully.

Week 11: Connect your food and product choices more deeply to the principles of sustainability. Take time to investigate the options that are most in alignment with your values and needs regarding local farms and organic produce, bulk shopping, co-operative and community support for affordable shopping, etc.

Week 12: Prepare a celebration meal. Make a plan to share the gift of your natural kitchen with friends, family, or your larger community in some way. Consider how you might want to bring the spirit of community food sharing into your life more fully. ●

GLOSSARY

Agave—A succulent plant that doesn't need much water to grow. It has many uses. The flowers are edible, the leaves can be used to make fiber or soap, and the nectar can be used as a delicious low-glycemic sweetener and be fermented for alcohol (tequila).

Barrel Effect—The "barrel effect" is a metaphor in which you imagine a barrel filling slowly with water. In this metaphor, the barrel is your body and the water is the toxins that enter your system day by day from various sources of exposure. One doesn't know when the barrel will fill completely and spill over. This is the same with the body. We are resilient bodies and we seem to do fine and handle it, until one day our body has too many toxins and our bodies begin to fail us.

Biodegradable—Material that will decompose when thrown out rather than remain trash in a landfill.

Biodiversity—The variation of life forms within a given ecosystem or on the entire planet. Biodiversity is used often as measure of the health of biological systems.

Body Burden—A process in which substances build up faster in the body than the body can eliminate. This is also known as "chemical load" or "bioaccumulation."

Brown rice syrup—A sweetener made from cooking brown rice with enzymes and then reducing it into a syrup.

Carbon footprint—The amount of carbon released into the atmosphere by a particular person, business, or activity; for example, you could measure/determine the carbon footprint of your last air travel, of your daily driving habits, or the amount of electricity you use in your home.

Closed cycle—A system that uses the resources from our land, our gardens, our kitchens in an intelligent conscious way so that our "waste" is being reused as a valuable resource elsewhere. For example, we can use the inedible parts of the vegetables we grow to create our own compost, instead of buying store-bought compost and sending the food waste to a dump. The compost can then be used to grow more vegetables.

Cob—A mix of mud or clay, sand, and straw often used to make wood-fired ovens because it is good for retaining heat.

Compassionate awareness—The practice of being present to what is happening in our lives, with no agenda other than to notice with non-judgment. This enables us to see how our conditioned mind works, so that we are not run by it and can make other choices. "Silent witnessing" is another term people sometimes use for this.

Compost—The nutrient-rich natural fertilizer that is the result of composting. Composting uses the natural process of decay and the interplay of carbon and nitrogen to turn our food scraps into nutritious soil humus for our gardens and farms.

Compost tea—A thick liquid created by steeping compost in water (ideally oxygenated). It is used to nourish plants and soil.

Community Supported Agriculture (CSA)—A way to support a small farmer directly by purchasing a seasonal share in a farm in your area in exchange for the delivery of a weekly pickup of fresh organic vegetables. This system gives the farm community support in advance for operating expenses, while giving the buyer a direct connection to a local farm.

Conditioned mind—The habitual thoughts and patterns that run in our minds and thus direct our life experience, if we are not practicing awareness. The "chatter" that runs in our heads, or the experience of "autopilot" are synonymous to the conditioned mind.

Consciousness—Consciousness comes from the Latin root "to know" and is synonymous with being aware or wakeful.

Conventional agriculture—Agriculture that is not organic or sustainable and relies on the use of pesticides, herbicides, and fungicides.

Cork—Spongy material made from the bark of the Cork Oak tree. When harvested properly, cork is highly sustainable because the bark grows back more quickly than other trees.

Creative reuse—Finding practical uses for resources that have been used once, ensuring that we get the most benefit possible out of an item. This cuts down on the need for new replacements and reduces the energy, water, and money needed to recycle something that's only been used once.

Earth Steward—Someone who recognizes the impact of our lifestyle on the earth and accepts joyful responsibility for both learning and modeling a more sustainable lifestyle now and for future generations.

Electromagnetic Radiation (EMR)—The rays of energy particles that travel from an electromagnetic source. Some examples of electromagnetic sources include the sun, cell phones, microwaves, and X-rays. These rays can be dangerous or harmless to humans depending on the level and duration of exposure.

FSC-certified—A certification for wood that meets sustainable harvest guidelines; created and monitored by the Forest Stewardship Council.

Giving back to the soil—Replenishing the soil after nutrients such as nitrogen have been leached by crops.

GMO—A Genetically Modified Organism. Also referred to as GEO, Genetically Engineered Organism. Seeds, crops, or animals created by cross-breeding and gene manipulation in order to ensure a characteristic that might be considered desirable to large commercial farmers. For example, some plants are bred to contain their own internal pesticides, others might have tough skins for easy harvesting.

Gray (Grey) water—A household's wasted water that comes from the laundry, kitchen sinks, showers, and baths. Greywater can often be reused as irrigation for trees and landscaping and sometimes for gardens.

Green manure—This is sometimes referred to as compost crop or cover crop and it is seed grown as nutrition for the soil (as opposed as for human harvest) and then plowed under the soil to enrich the soil with nutrients.

Green Revolution—A period of time after WWII when farming was changed immensely by the discovery and use of synthetic fertilizers and plant genetics, widely increasing food production. The Green Revolution is also known for the negative consequences of mass food production such as pesticides, pollution, loss of biodiversity, and foods depleted of nutrients.

Haybox cooking—A type of retained-heat cooking. Foods like soups and stews are boiled, sealed in pots, and then placed in an insulated box (traditionally using hay) to maintain heat.

Honeybee Disaster—The decline of the honeybee population around the United States. Also known as Colony Collapse Disorder, caused primarily by systemic pesticides.

Hughie Sink—This product, designed to help people save water in their kitchens, is a sink-sized container with handles and a spigot on the bottom that fits in your sink and allows you to collect excess water (from dishwashing, etc.). You can then use the spigot to easily water your plants.

Intentional community—These communities highly value cooperation and teamwork. The participants work toward the benefit of the whole community and not just the individual. These communities are sometimes referred to as ecovillages, co-houses, and communes.

Irradiation—The exposure of food to low levels of radiant energy to keep it from spoiling too fast. Unlike pasteurization, irradiation does not kill all bacteria so food still requires refrigeration.

Low- or non-VOC—VOCs are Volatile Organic Compounds that are found in drinking water, house paint, and industrial air. Low- or non-VOC paints are now available in most hardware stores. They contain less of these chemicals and make a lower carbon footprint on our world.

Keyhole gardening—These are often round or horseshoe-shaped gardens planted near the home. They allow easy access to plants that are used on a regular basis.

The Middle Way—In Buddhist philosophy this is the path to enlightenment. One finds the middle area or middle path between extremes. In this book, the Middle Way is also spoken of as the choice that is "best for all."

Mindfulness—The practice of focusing attention and awareness on the present moment. This helps us disengage from habitual, conditioned, unsatisfying and unskillful habits and behaviors. Mindfulness helps us to see clearly, as old habitual ways arise, that we have the opportunity to make another choice.

Molasses—A dark-colored thick syrupy substance made from the processing of sugar beets/sugar cane into sugar.

Monoculture—The growing and harvesting of a single crop or raising a single type of animal. This has become a common practice in corporate farming, leading to soil depletion, loss of biodiversity, and increased use of pesticides and hormones.

Organic—Refers to the certification that ensures something is grown and produced free of pesticides, herbicides and fungicides.

Outcrossing—The potential for non-GMO crops to be affected by GMO crops.

Peak hours—Time of day when energy is used the most.

Permaculture design—An approach to designing human settlements that mimics the relationships found in the natural world. It is a land use and community-building movement that strives to harmoniously integrate human dwellings, micro-climate, plants, animals, soil, and water into stable, productive communities. The word permaculture was coined in 1978 by Bill Mollison, an Australian ecologist, and one of his students, David Holmgren. It is a contraction of "permanent agriculture" or "permanent culture."

Pure soap—Refers to natural biodegradable soap such as Dr. Bronner's castile soap or 100% pure glycerin soap. This is in contrast to many of the mass-market soaps that contain chemicals and additives such as phosphates.

Quorn—The leading brand of mycoprotein, a popular vegetarian food protein derived from a fungus. Quorn uses egg white as a binder, so it is not a vegan food. It is available for purchase in health food stores.

Radical recycling—A system for taking recycling beyond the basic practice into the practice of reducing, reusing, and recycling every resource possible, to help reduce waste, create more of a "closed cycle," and shift toward zero waste.

Retained-heat cooking—A method of cooking that saves fuel and energy. Food in a liquid is brought to a boil then sealed tightly and placed in an insulated container to cook slowly for an extended amount of time. See also *Haybox cooking*.

Rocket stove—Named after the pipe that extends horizontally, these are simple, easy-to-assemble stoves that consume very little fuel and are often used for heating and cooking food outdoors.

Sheet mulching—The method of using mulch or compost to cover the ground before planting. A form of "no dig" gardening that prevents soil erosion and decreases water waste.

Slow Foods Movement—An international movement created in reaction to the "fast food culture" that promotes local fresh ingredients from farm to table.

Stevia—A flowering plant that is used as a sweetener and in teas.

Solar Tubes—Devices that conduct daylight into a room without any of the heat gain or loss that is associated with skylights.

Superfoods Diet—A diet based around densely nutritious foods—including raw foods, plants, and berries—that offer health and healing potential.

Sustainability—For this book, sustainability is defined as an approach to life that views environmental, human, and economic well-being as one and the same. Sustainability honors life, and the interconnections in the web of life, as far into the future as one can imagine. A system is only sustainable if it is designed to take care of all components of that system—now and into the future.

Vermiculture—The process of using worms and their by-products (created by the consumption of organic food waste) to add nutrients to a garden or plants. Common species of worms used are red worms, white worms, and earthworms.

Wildcrafting—The practice of harvesting plants from their natural, or "wild" habitat, for food, medicine, or other purposes.

Xylitol—A sweetener made from vegetables, mushrooms, berries, but most often birch. It is a sugar alcohol and is known to be good for the teeth.

Communities

Ampersand Sustainable Learning Center in Cerrillos, New Mexico, is an off-the-grid site demonstrating sustainable systems including permaculture, land restoration, organic gardening, passive solar design and wise water techniques. Ampersand residents build with natural and salvaged materials, cook with solar ovens and rely on rain catchment. For more information, please visit **ampersandproject.org**

Arcosanti is an experimental town in the desert of Arizona, built to manifest architect Paolo Soleri's concept of arcology—the fusion of architecture with ecology. For more information, please visit **arcosanti.org**

Aprovecho Institute is a nonprofit research and education center located on 40 acres in Oregon modeling and pioneering sustainable living techniques. For more information, please visit **aprovecho.net.**

Eco-Home is an ongoing living research center that demonstrates ecological living in an urban environment, based in Los Angeles. The Eco-Home is a restored and retrofitted California style bungalow circa 1911 that shows us how simple but wise property improvements can make your home warm and friendly yet environmentally sound and healthy. For more information, please visit **ecohome.org.**

Ear haven is an aspiring ecovillage in a mountain forest setting near Asheville, North Carolina, dedicated to caring for people and the Earth by learning, living and demonstrating a holistic, sustainable culture. For more information, please visit: **earthaven.org**

Free Farm Stand, in the San Francisco Bay Area, promotes home and local gardening through education and empowerment. By offering free starts/seedlings and produce to low-income families and a place for local farmers to share surplus crops, they support backyard and community gardens, nutrition and self-reliance via advice and opportunity. For more information, please visit: **freefarmstand.org**

Green Gulch Farm and Zen Center is a Soto Zen Buddhist community and thriving organic farm and garden located just north of San Francisco, nestled in a valley bordered by Mount Tamalpais, the Golden Gate National Recreation area and the Pacific Ocean. For 15 years they have offered apprenticeships, which emphasize meditation practice, study/instruction in Buddhist teachings and hands-on work experience and instruction in organic gardening/farming methods. For more information, please visit **sfc.org/ggf.**

Occidental Arts and Ecology Center (OAEC) is a nonprofit organizing and education center and organic farm in Northern California's Sonoma County. OAEC was founded in 1994 by a group of biologists, horticulturists, educators, activists and artists seeking innovative and practical approaches to the pressing environmental and economic crises of our day. For more information, please visit **oaec.org**.

The Zen Monastery Peace Center is an international center for the practice of peace and sustainability founded by American Zen teacher Cheri Huber. The monastery is set on 320 acres in the foothills of the Sierra Nevadas and offers workshops, retreats, and extended opportunities to deepen in the practice of compassionate awareness. The Zen Monastery Peace Center is a part of the nonprofit organization Living Compassion. For more information, please visit **livingcompassion.org**.

Resource List and Products

THE RESOURCE LIST FOR THIS BOOK COULD BE A BOOK IN ITSELF. Because there is so much information available, and product, I have simply provided some examples and some resources to help you begin taking the next steps.

Babies

(See Chapter Twelve for more information about how to make your own baby food.)

Books on How to Make Your Own Baby Food
The Petit Appetit Cookbook: Easy, Organic Recipes to Nurture Your Baby and Toddler, Lisa Barnes
Super Baby Food, Ruth Yaron

Stainless Steel Ice Cube Trays
thesoftlanding.com/onyx-stainless-steel-ice-cube-trays.html

Building Materials

(See Chapter Seven for more information about building materials.)
These are sources for green sustainable building and home-renovation materials. Visit these websites to find retailers in your area.

Cork and Bamboo Flooring
sustainableflooring.com

Energy-Efficient Light Bulbs
ledtronics.com
naturallighting.com

Energy Star Appliances
energystar.gov

Marmoleum
themarmoleumstore.com

Natural Wall Covering
American Clay americanclay.com

Non-VOC Paints & Finishes
bioshieldpaint.com
freshairechoicepaint.com
mythicpaint.com
olympic.com
americanclay.com

Sealants, glues, and finishes
greenguard.org

Clean 15/Dirty Dozen

(See Chapter Five for more information about the Clean 15/Dirty Dozen.)

Food News Wallet Guide

This is an application to download to your iPhone that offers information about the Clean 15/Dirty Dozen.
foodnews.org/walletguide.php

Cleaning Products

(See Chapter Seven for more information about non-toxic cleaning products. Many of these products are available in stores. Go to the company's website for the names of retailers in your area.)

Bleach Alternatives

Basic G
shaklee.net/naturally/product/00525
Nutribiotic (GSE)
nutribiotic.com/gse-liquid-concentrate-2oz.html
Oxygen based bleach
laundry-alternative.com/Oxygen_bleach_research.html

Hemp Kitchen Towels

rawganique.com/kitchenhkt1.htm

Laundry

Maggie's Soap Nuts
maggiespureland.com
Vermont Clothesline Company
smartdrying.com
Retractable clothesline
urbanclotheslines.com

Napkins & Paper Towels, Unbleached

ecolution.com

Non-Toxic Cleaners

7th Generation
seventhgeneration.com

Bio Pac (These household cleaners are environmentally friendly and not tested on animals)
bio-pac.com
Dr. Bronner's Soaps
drbronner.com
ECOVER
ecover.com/us/en/ (or herbtrader.com)
Oasis Soap Company
oasissoap.com
SHAKLEE Natural Products (Safe, clean, green household cleaners)
shaklee.com

Coffee/Tea

(See Chapter Seven for more information about eco-friendly coffee and tea products. Visit the websites to find retailers in your area.)

Books

Brewing Justice: Fair Trade Coffee, Sustainability, and Survival, Daniel Jaffee
The Story of Tea: A Cultural History and Drinking Guide, Mary Lou Heiss and Robert J. Heiss

Filters for Coffee/Tea

Cloth and Hemp Filters
nubiusorganics.com
Gold-Plated Tea and Coffee Filters
strandtea.com
swissgold.com
Organic cotton (for making your own bags/filters)
hyfab.com
Unbleached Filters
ifyoucare.com/coffee_filters.htm
French Press Coffee Makers
(available at many retail stores where coffeemakers are sold.)
bodumusa.com
Organic Fair Trade Coffee

Peace Coffee
peacecoffee.com
thanksgivingcoffee.com
Transfair USA
transfairusa.org
Pesticides on coffee farms
coffeehabitat.com/2006/12/pesticides_
used_2.html

Community Supported Agriculture (CSA)

(See Chapter Five for more information about CSA's.)
Local Harvest
Find CSAs in your community and learn about the important work some of these groups are doing.
localharvest.org/csa/

Composting

(See Chapter Three for more information about composting and vermiculture.)

Books on Worm Composting

Worms Eat My Garbage: How to Set Up and Maintain a Worm Composting System, Appelhof
The Worm Book: The Complete Guide to Gardening and Composting with Worms, Loren Nancarrow and Janet Hogan Taylor
Worms and Wormeries: Composting Your Kitchen Waste..and More!, Mike Woolnough

Compost Keeper

Ceramic or Stainless Steel Compost Crock
gaiam.com

Compost Bins

Garden Gourmet
gardengourmet.com

Happy Farmer
scdprobiotics.com/All_Seasons_Indoor_
Composter_Kit_p/kit1-1-1.htm

Inoculant

Dr. Earth Inoculant
drearth.com

Worm composting/Vermiculture

Find/buy local worms
findworms.com
worms.com
Make your own bin
whatcom.wsu.edu/ag/compost/
Easywormbin.htm
cityfarmer.org/wormcomp61.html

Cooking Products

(See Chapter Nine for more information about earth-friendly cooking products.)
Bambu Kitchen Products
(bamboo cutting boards, bowls, serveware and serving spoons, veneer ware, lacquer ware, nesting baskets, children's dishes and utensils, candles, bamboo nourishing cream)
bambuhome.com

Ceramic Cookware

Emile Henry
emilehenryusa.com
Felipe Ortega Earthen Pots
felipeortega.com

Energy-Saving Appliances

Barbara Kerr's Solar Center
azsolarcenter.org
Bicycle Powered Blender
bikeblender.com
rockthebike.com/blenders
instructables.com
Blenders
bulletexpress.com
buythebullet.com

Hand-cranked Blender
realgoods.com/product/63867.do?campaign=adwords&gcid=S31185x001&keyword=hand crank blender

Energy-Efficient Cookers/Ovens
Cob Ovens
lifeunplugged.net/greenbuilding/build-a-wood-fired-cob-oven.aspx
greeniacs.com/GreeniacsGuides/How-to-Build-a-Cob-Oven.html
Collapsible Solar Food Dryer
newdawnengineering.com/website/solar/dryer/
Crockpots/Slow Cookers (available at many retail stores where cookware is sold.)
crock pot.com
Haybox Cooking
instructables.com/id/hay-box-cooker/
selfsufficientish.com/hayboxcooker.htm
motherearthnews.com/Do-it-yourself/1980-01-01/Rediscover-the-Hay-Box-Cooker.aspx
Kerr-Cole Sustainable Living Center (for info on how to make your own solar oven)
solarcooking.org/bkerr/DoItYouself.htm
Rocket Stoves
rocketstove.org
off-grid.net/2009/05/04/rocket-stove-video/
Solar Cookers International
solarcookers.org
Silicone Baking Sheets
silpat.com
Vita-Mix
Vita-Mix.com

Low-Wattage Appliances
Magic Bullet Blender
buythebullet.com
Press Express Hand-Held Food Processor

Miscellaneous Green Kitchen
Cloth Crafters Sustainability Store (aprons, napkins, shower curtains, and more)
sustainabilitystore.com/providers/clothcrafters.htm
Cookbooks
Chez Panisse Cafe Cookbook, Alice Waters
The Monastery Cookbook (available through Keep It Simple Books)
Gaiam (yoga mats, pilates equipment, clothing, non-toxic cleaners, and more)
gaiam.com

Do-it-yourself
(See Chapter Six for more information on growing/making your own healthy ingredients.)

Books
The Urban Homestead, Kelley Koyne and Eric Knudsen
The Monastery Cookbook, Zen Monastery Practice Center

Growing Your Own Ingredients

Curing Your Own Olives
The Olive Harvest Cookbook: Olive Oil Lore and Recipes from McEvoy Ranch, Gerald Gass, Maren Caruso, Nan McEvoy, and Joyce Goldstein
The Food and Wine of Greece: More *Than 300 Classic and Modern Dishes from the Mainland and Islands,* Diane Kochilas
Olives: The Life and Lore of a Noble Fruit, Mort Rosenblum
Olives 101, "Cure Your Own Olives"
Drying Your Own Fruit
Preserving Summer's Bounty: A Quick and Easy Guide to Freezing, Canning, and Preserving, and Drying What You Grow, Rodale Food Center and Susan McClure

The Art of Confectionary: Showing The Various Methods of Preserving All Sorts of Fruits, Dry And Liquid (1761), Edward Lambert

How To Dry Foods—Enjoy Wholesome Dried Fruits, Vegetables, Meats & Fish With Over 100 Delicious Tested Recipes, Deanna Delong

Seasonal Chef, "How to Dry Fruit" seasonalchef.com/preserves21.htm

Fermenting Foods (Kim Chi, Sauerkraut, or Kombucha)

Good Morning, Kimchi!: Forty Different Kinds of Traditional & Fusion Kimchi Recipes, Suk-cha Yun

Wild Fermentation: The Flavor, Nutrition, and Craft of Live-Culture Foods, Sandor Ellix Katz and Sally Fallon

Making Sauerkraut and Pickled Vegetables at Home: Creative Recipes for Lactic Fermented Food to Improve Your Health (Natural Health Guide), Klaus Kaufmann and Annelies Schoneck

The Healing Crow, "Fermenting is Fun" healingcrow.com/ferfun/ferfun.html

Mushrooms

Mushroom Cultivator: A Practical Guide to Growing Mushrooms at Home, Paul Stamets and J.S. Chilton

Mushrooms For The Million-Growing, Cultivating & Harvesting Mushrooms, John Wright

The Better Days Books Organic Guide to Growing Mushrooms for Profit and Pleasure, William Falconer

Gardening Know How, "Learn How to Grow Mushrooms" gardeningknowhow.com/indoor/grow-mushrooms.htm

Sprouts

Sprout Garden, Mark Mathew Braunstein

The Sprouting Book: How to Grow and Use Sprouts to Maximize Your Health and Vitality, Ann Wigmore

Fresh Food from Small Spaces: The SquareInch Gardener's Guide to Year-Round Growing, Fermenting, and Sprouting, R.J. Ruppenthal

City Farmer (Canada's Office of Urban Agriculture), "Sprouting at Home" cityfarmer.org/sprout86.html

Making Basic Foods

Bread

Kneadlessly Simple: Fabulous, Fuss-free, No-Knead Breads, Nancy Baggett

The Bread Book: The Definitive Guide to Making Bread By Hand or Machine, Sara Lewis

Bread Matters: Why and How to Make Your Own, Andrew Whitley

BreadInfo.com, "Making Bread By Hand or with a Bread Machine" breadinfo.com

Condiments

The Balanced Plate: The Essential Elements of Whole Foods and Good Health, Renée Loux

The Candle Café Cookbook: More Than 150 Enlightened Recipes from New York's Renowned Vegan Restaurant, Joy Pierson, Bart Potenza, and Barbara Scott-Goodman

The Native Foods Restaurant Cookbook, Tanya Petrovna

The Fanatic Cook blog, "Gomasio (Sesame Salt)" fanaticcook.blogspot.com/2005/01/gomasio-sesame-salt.html

Granola

Variations on a Theme: Granola, Lori Butler Carter

Granola Madness: The Ultimate Granola Cookbook, Donna Wallstin

The Granola Cookbook, by Eric Miller

Joy of Baking, "Homemade Granola"
joyofbaking.com/breakfast/
HomemadeGranola.html

No-Bake Sprouted Crackers

Sprout man's Kitchen Garden Cookbook: 250 Flourless, Dairyless, Low Temperature, Low Fat, Low Salt, Living Food Vegetarian Recipes, Steve Meyerowitz, Beth Robbins, and Michael Parman

Rawsome!: Maximizing Health, Energy, and Culinary Delight With the Raw Foods Diet, Brigitte Mars

Living in the Raw: Recipes for a Healthy Lifestyle, Rose Lee Calabro

Ran Prieur, "Raw Sprouted Crackers"
ranprieur.com/misc/crackers.html

Raising Bees/Harvesting Honey

Keeping Bees And Making Honey, Alison Benjamin and Brian McCallum

The Backyard Beekeeper—Revised and Updated: An Absolute Beginner's Guide to Keeping Bees in Your Yard and Garden, Kim Flottum

Raising Healthy Honey Bees (Raising Healthy Animals Series), Randy Carl Lynn and Todd Cooney

BeeCARE
beecare.com

Soy Milk

How to Make Homemade Organic Oat Milk, Soy Milk, Rice Milk and Wheat Milk, Karen Peebles

The Practical Vegetarian, Mary Curtis

You Don't Need Meat, Peter Cox

Soya (Top Cultures), "How to Make Soy Milk"
soya.be/how-to-make-soy-milk.php

Sun Tea

Cooking for Healthy Healing, Book Two: The Healing Recipes, Linda Page

Renewable Energy Made Easy: Free Energy from Solar, Wind, Hydropower, and Other Alternative Energy Sources, David Craddock

Herbal Tea Gardens: 22 Plants for Your Enjoyment & Well-Being, Marietta Marshall Marcin

Simply Recipes, "Sun Tea"
simplyrecipes.com/recipes/sun_tea/

Tortillas

The Well-Filled Tortilla Cookbook, Victoria Wise and Susanna Hoffman

Family Feasts for $75 a Week: A Penny-wise Mom Shares Her Recipe for Cutting Hundreds from Your Monthly Food Bill, Mary Ostyn

1,000 Vegan Recipes, Robin Robertson
consciousshopper.blogspot.com/2009/11/
make-your-own-flour-tortillas-from.html

AllRecipes.com, "Tortillas from Scratch"
allrecipes.com/HowTo/Tortillas-from-Scratch/Detail.aspx

Yogurt

Making Cheese, Butter & Yogurt, Ricki Carroll

How to Make Homemade Organic Yogurt in Your Crockpot, Elizabeth Peebles

The Book Of Yogurt, Sonia Uvezian

"How to Make Yogurt"
makeyourownyogurt.com/

Double-Digging

(See Chapter Ten for more information about double-digging.)

Ecology Action
growbiointensive.org

Book and website

How to Grow Your Own Vegetables,
John Jeavons
johnjeavons.info

Eating On-the-Go (See also Food Storage)

(See Chapter Eleven for more information
about earth-friendly eating on-the-go.)

Bottles and Mugs
Kleen Kanteen
kleankanteen.com
SIGG Travel Mugs and Water Bottles
mysigg.com

Restaurants
Vegetarian restaurants
(Find restaurants in your area that follow
green guidelines for take-out food.)
vegdining.com

Reusable Utensils
SIGG
mysigg.com
Snackballs
booninc.com
**Stainless Steel Lunch Box from To-Go
Ware**
to-goware.com
Wrap 'n Mat
This is a reusable product created to
wrap sandwiches. It is literally a mat
that you wrap, which can be washed out
between uses. It is lined with PEVA,
which may not be as eco-friendly in its
production as a more natural material
like hemp, but PEVA is a non-toxic,
vinyl plastic, so it gets points for non-
toxicity. (There's a good description
of PEVA at healthybuilding.net/pvc/
SortingOutVinyls.html.)
wrap-n-mat.com

Energy Efficiency/ Conservation (See also Solar Energy)

(See Chapter Eight for more information
about ways to conserve and use energy
more efficiently.)

Appliance Comparison Charts
U.S. Dept. of Energy, "Energy Savers":
energysavers.gov/your_home/appliances/
index.cfm/mytopic=10040
U.S. Dept. of Energy, "Tips on Saving
Energy & Money at Home" www1.eere.
energy.gov/consumer/tips/appliances.html
**Federal Trade Commission, "Appliance
Energy Data"**
ftc.gov/appliancedata

Clotheslines
(You can tie string between two posts,
but these products will make your life
much simpler.)
Vermont Clothesline Company
smartdrying.com
Retractable clothesline
urbanclotheslines.com

Energy-Efficient Kitchen Appliances
energystar.gov
Friends of Gaviotas
(A nonprofit that works with South
America to increase sustainability and
use of solar power/wind.)
friendsofgaviotas.org
Kill-A-Watt Meter
killawattplus.com
Vegawatt
(Power your restaurant with waste
vegetable oil)
vegawatt.com

Fair Trade (Organic) Raw Foods Products

Cacao
essentiallivingfoods.com
ultimatesuperfoods.com
Coconut/Coconut Oil
ultimatesuperfoods.com
Creamy Coconut Bliss
coconutbliss.com

Farmers Markets

(See Chapter Five for more information about farmers' markets.)
Find a location for fresh seasonal produce in your neighborhood
localharvest.org

Food Co-Ops

Find a local co-op in your neighborhood
coopdirectory.org
localharvest.org/food-coops

Food Revolution
(These are communities and organizations working toward the affordability and accessibility of food for all.)
Affordable Food Co-op
mandelafoods.com
Free Farm Stand
freefarmstand.org
Grow Food Everywhere
seedsofsolidarity.org
Growing Power
growingpower.org

Food Storage Products (See also Eating On-The-Go)

(See Chapter Nine for more information about storing food healthfully.)
Ecobags
ecobags.com

Freezer Bags
Natural Value
naturalvalue.com
Soy Wax Paper
Natural Value
naturalvalue.com

Fruits And Vegetables

Bananas
mindfully.org/Pesticide/chiquita/chiquita11.htm

Gardening Organically and Sustainable Agriculture

Basic List of Companion Plants
en.wikipedia.org/wiki/List_of_companion_plants
Cover Crop
bountifulgardens.org/products.asp?dept=5
groworganic.com/cgy_365.html?welcome=T&theses=7031492
Pest Control
organic.lovetoknow.com/Organic_Pesticide
Seeds of Change
(Offers over 600 distinct varieties of 100% organically grown seeds for the home gardener)
seedsofchange.com
E.B. Stone Organic Soil
ebstone.org/ebstone.php

Organizations Addressing Global Sustainable Agriculture and Seed Sovereignty

Seed Savers Exchange
seedsavers.org

Sustainable Agriculture/Sustainable Food Revolution—Books to Deepen Your Education

Ancient Futures: Learning from Ladakh, Helena Norberg-Hodge

Bringing the Food Economy Home: Local Aalternatives to Global Agribusiness, Helena Norberg-Hodge

Coming Home to Eat, Gary Nabhan

Earth Democracy: Justice, Sustainability and Peace, Vandana Shiva

Food Not Lawns, H.C. Flores

The Food Revolution, John Robbins

From the Ground Up: Rethinking Industrial Agriculture, Helena Norberg-Hodge, Peter Goering and John Page

The Future of Progress: Reflections on Environment and Development, Contributors include Edward Goldsmith, Vandana Shiva, Sigmund Kvaloy, Martin Khor, Nicholas Hildyard, Gary Snyder and Helena Norberg-Hodge

Gaia's Garden, Poby Hemenway

Gardening at the Dragon's Gate, Wendy Johnson (gardeningatthedragonsgate.com)

How to Grow More Vegetables, John Jeavons (johnjeavons.info)

Monocultures of the Mind, Vandana Shiva

The New Organic Grower, Eliot Coleman

Plenty: Eating Locally on the 100-Mile Diet, Alisa Smith and J.B. Mackinno

Ripe for Change: Rethinking California's Food Economy, Katy Mamen, Steven Gorelick, Helena Norberg Hodge, and Diana Deumling

Shifting Direction: From Global Dependence to Local Interdependence, Helena Norberg-Hodge

Short Circuit: Strengthening Local Economies for Security in an Unstable World, Richard Douthwaite

Small is Beautiful, Big is Subsidised, Steven Gorelick, with a foreword by Helena Norberg-Hodge

Stolen Harvest: The Hijacking of the Global Food Supply, Vandana Shiva

Global Food Sustainability

(See Chapter Four for more information about global food sustainability.)
International Society for Ecology and Culture
isec.org
Navdanya International
vandanashiva.org
navdanya.org

Honeybees

Beekeeping
thefarm.org/charities/i4at/lib2/bees.htm
Save the Bees
ehow.com/how_2214229_help-save-honeybees.html
vanishingthebees.com

Meat snd Poultry

(See Chapter Five for more information on organic meat and poultry.)
Purchase Organic Meat Online
greenpeople.org/OrganicMeat.html
Find Stores Near You That Sell Organic Food and Meat
organicstorelocator.com
Non-GMO FOODS
(See Chapter 6 for more information on Non-GMO Foods.)
Seeds of Deception, "Genetically Modified Ingredients Overview"
seedsofdeception.com/Public/Buying Non-GMO/index.cfm

The Non-Toxic Kitchen

(See Chapter Two for more information on the Non-Toxic Kitchen.)
Debra Lynn Dadd's Website and Books
debralist.com
Home Safe Home
Really Green

Permaculture

Bill Mollison's Website
tagari.com
Permaculture Principles
permacultureprinciples.com
Regenerative Design Institute and Permaculture Design Institute of Northern California,
Penny Livingston-Stark
regenerativedesign.org

Pets

Biodegradable Waste Bags for Dogs and Cats
biobagusa.com

Plastics

Sea Studios Foundation: Think Beyond Plastic
greatgarbagepatch.org

Radical Recycling/Zero Waste

Biobags
biobagusa.com
Eco Plastics
eco2plastics.com
Plastic Bag Drying Rack
agoraconcepts.com
Pot Maker
potmaker.com

Recycling Bins

simplehuman.com
trashcansunlimited.com

Seafood

Monterey Bay Aquarium, "Seafood Watch"
montereybayaquarium.org/cr/cr_seafood-watch/sfw_health.aspx
Blue Ocean Institute, "Seafood Guide"
blueocean.org/programs/seafood/seafood-guide

School Lunches

Kids/School Meals
The Edible Schoolyard
edibleschoolyard.org

Slow Food Movement

Chez Panisse
chezpanisse.com/about/alice-waters
Slow Food U.S.A.
slowfoodusa.org
Slow Food (International)
slowfood.com

Soil Testing

National Sustainable Agriculture Information Service
attra.ncat.org

Solar Energy (See also Energy Effiency/Conservation)

Solar Living Institute
solarliving.org

Travel

Vegetarian Travel Guide (within the U.S.)
vegetarianusa.com

Water

Books
Rainwater Harvesting for the Drylands and Beyond, Brad Lancaster (Volumes 1, 2, and 3).
Water Follies: Groundwater pumping and the fate of America's fresh waters, Robert Jerome Glennon

Greywater
greywateraction.org
harvestingrainwater.com

Greywater Reuse
Art Ludwig's Website
oasisdesign.net
The Hughie Sink
hughie.com.au
Rainwater Catchment
harvesth20.com
Water-Efficient Faucets
niagaraconservation.com

Water Purification and Testing Systems
TDS Tester
tdsmeter.com
oxygenozone.com
aquasana.com
gaiam.com
purwater.com
watertanks.com/category/94/
culligan.com
gobeyondorganic.com
Water Quality In Your State, County, or City
epa.gov/safewater/ccr/whereyoulive.html
Water Saving Bucket
getngreen.com

ABOUT THE AUTHOR

DEBORAH EDEN TULL is a sustainability coach and meditation teacher who has been traveling to, living in, or teaching about sustainable communities internationally for the last 18 years, including seven years as a monk at the Zen Monastery Peace Center in Northern California. She has been organic gardening and farming for many years, including at Green Gulch Farm in Marin County, California, at Arcosanti in the Arizona desert, at the Zen Monastery Peace Center, and in urban gardens in the San Francisco Bay area and in Los Angeles. Certified in Permaculture Design, Bio-Intensive Organic Gardening, and Compost Education, she offers workshops throughout Los Angeles County and beyond, most recently at the Omega Institute in New York. Her approach to sustainable living is a unique combination of peace and environmentalism that emphasizes the interconnection between personal and planetary well-being.

Creative Green Sustainability Coaching
creativegreen@hotmail.com
creativegreen.net

CREATIVE GREEN SUSTAINABILITY COACHING combines practical sustainable living tools and skills with the practice of compassionate awareness to empower people in creating a sustainable world "from the inside out." Through workshops and consultations, Creative Green teaches the principles of sustainable living and guides people through the process of how to embody these principles in their homes, businesses, landscapes, or personal lifestyles. Through Creative Green, Deborah Eden Tull offers public workshops and is available for private workshops, consulting, and public speaking.

Creative Green workshops and coaching include the following:

- **Personal Lifestyle Coaching** to help bring peace, balance, and well-being into every day of your life.
- **Zen Meditation and Mindful Living Revolution** workshops and personal coaching, including workshops for activists and entrepreneurs on Mindful Leadership in Changing Times.
- **Home and Business Sustainability Consultations** to help create human-friendly and eco-friendly systems for sustainable living in your home, business, landscape, or lifestyle.
- **The Green Kitchen Transformation** to bring the principles of sustainability to your kitchen by addressing the areas of zero waste, home toxins, water and energy conservation, mindful eating, seasonal menus, and more.
- **Organic Gardening and Composting Workshops and Consultations** to give you the practical tools for cultivating a beautiful and life-affirming garden, growing your own food, and creating a "closed cycle" on your own property.
- **Green Schools Program** to offer consulting services and workshops to school classrooms, parents and PTA groups, and school administrators who want to go green.
- **Urban Sustainability Retreats** to offer city dwellers a day-long (or longer) retreat experience incorporating elements of meditation, transformational work, sustainable living, delicious healthy food, and community.

References

Danielle Seigle, "Fast Food and Obesity," October 14, 2009, articlesbase.com/nutrition-articles/fast-food-and-obesity-1338966.html (accessed November 20, 2009).

The Free Dictionary, "Consciousness," n.d., thefreedictionary.com/conscious (accessed November 20, 2009).

Jodi Ziesemer, "Energy Use in Organic Food Systems," August 2007, fao.org/docs/eims/upload/233069/energy-use-oa.pdf (accessed November 20, 2009).

Food and Agriculture Organization of the United Nations Media Center, "1.02 Billion People Hungry," June 19, 2009, fao.org/news/story/en/item/20568/icode/ (accessed November 20, 2009).

Colin Ingram, *The Drinking Water Book: A Complete Guide to Safe Drinking Water*. (Berkeley, California: Ten Speed Press, 1991).

David Goldbeck, *The Smart Kitchen: How to Design a Comfortable, Safe, Energy-efficient and Environment-friendly Workspace*. (Woodstock, NY: Ceres Press, 1989).

David Goldbeck, *The Smart Kitchen: How to Design a Comfortable, Safe, Energy-efficient and Environment-friendly Workspace*. (Woodstock, NY: Ceres Press, 1989).

Ruth Schwartz Cowan, *More Work For Mother: The Ironies Of Household Technology From The Open Hearth To The Microwave*. (New York: Basic Books, 1985).

David Goldbeck, *The Smart Kitchen: How to Design a Comfortable, Safe, Energy-efficient and Environment-friendly Workspace*. (Woodstock, NY: Ceres Press, 1989).

Godo Stoyke, *The Carbon Buster's Home Energy Handbook: Slowing Climate Change and Saving Money*. (Gabriola Island, B.C.: New Society Publishers, 2007).

Denise Knabe, "The Good Kitchen," February 2007, alive.com/5903a15a2.php?subject_bread_cramb=59 (accessed November 20, 2009).

Joseph M. Price, M.D., *Coronaries Cholesterol Chlorine*. (Panama: Rhino Publishing S.A., 2008).

Kathy Stein, *Beyond Recycling: A Reuser's Guide*. (Santa Fe, New Mexico: Clear Light Publishers, 1997).

Rome Neal, "Caffeine Nation: Is Coffee Beneficial or Bad for Americans?," September 7, 2003, cbsnews.com/stories/2002/11/14/sunday/main529388.shtml (accessed April 4, 2010).

Tim Kennedy, "Some Interesting Coffee-Related Statistics," n.d., docstoc.com/docs/27534697/Some-Interesting-Coffee-Related-Statistics/ (accessed April 10, 2010).

Tamara Straus, "Fair Trade Coffee: An Overview of the Issue," November 30, 2000, organicconsumers.org/starbucks/coffback.htm (accessed April 10, 2010).

Kathy Stein, *Beyond Recycling: A Reuser's Guide*. (Santa Fe, New Mexico: Clear Light Publishers, 1997).

Lynn Smythe, "How to Store Dried Herbs & Spices: Methods for Long-term Stockpiling," November 2, 2007, herb-gardens.suite101.com/article.cfm/storing_herbs (accessed November 20, 2009).

U.S. Environmental Protection Agency, "An Introduction to Indoor Air Quality," n.d., epa.gov/iaq/formalde.html (accessed November 20, 2009).

Encyclopedia Britannica, "Cancer-Causing Agents," n.d., britannica.com/EBchecked/topic/92230/cancer/224771/Cancer-causing-agents (accessed November 22, 2009).

Denise Knabe, "The Good Kitchen," February 2007, alive.com/5903a15a2.php?subject_bread_cramb=59 (accessed November 20, 2009).

U.S. Environmental Protection Agency, "Reduce, Reuse, Recycle, Buy Recycled," n.d. epa.gov/region09/waste/solid/reduce.html (accessed November 22, 2009).

Advanced Technology Environmental and Energy Center, Environmental & Energy Resources Library, "Sustainability and the Future of Humankind," n.d., eerl.org/SPT-eerl01-sustain.php (accessed November 22, 2009).

National Wildlife Federation, Eco-Schools USA Consumption and Waste Pathway, n.d., nwf.org/ecoschools/consumptionwaste.cfm (accessed November 22, 2009).

Heather Rogers, *Gone Tomorrow: The Hidden Life of Garbage*. (New York: The New Press, 2006).

Los Angeles County Department of Public Works, "Commonly Recycled Materials," n.d., dpw.lacounty.gov/epd/Recycling/crm.cfm#plastic (accessed December 9, 2009).

"A Balancing Act (Carbon-to-Nitrogen Ratios), n.d., composting101.com/c-n-ratio.html (accessed December 9, 2009).

"The Bokashi Bucket," n.d., bokashi.com.au/How-Bokashi-works.htm (accessed December 9, 2009).

Center for Earth Leadership, "Ten Stresses on the Planet: Loss of Topsoil," n.d., earthleaders.org/publications/stress_topsoil (accessed November 21, 2009).

Earth: A Graphic Look at the State of the World, "Food and Soil," theglobaleducationproject.org/earth/food-and-soil.php (accessed December 9, 2009).

Richard Drucker, Ph.D., "Depleted Soil and Compromised Food Sources: What You can Do About It," n.d., nutritionalwellness.com/archives/2006/jul/07_depleted_soil.php (accessed December 9, 2009).

Steve Meyerowitz, *The Organic Food Guide: How to Shop Smarter and Eat Healthier*. (Connecticut: The Globe Pequot Press, 2004).

BBC News, "Terminator Gene Halt a 'Major U-turn'," October 5, 1999, news.bbc.co.uk/2/hi/science/nature/465222.stm (accessed November 21, 2009).

The Center for Food Safety, n.d., truefoodnow.org/campaigns/genetically-engineered-foods/ (accessed November 21, 2009).

The Pew Initiative on Food and Biotechnology, "Factsheet: Genetically Modified Crops in the United States," August 2004, uwstudentweb.uwyo.edu/L/LPETER11/Factsheet%20Genetically%20Modified%20Crops%20in%20the%20United%20States.htm (accessed December 9, 2009).

"Do Genetically Modified Crops Reduce Pesticide Use? The Evidence Says Not Likely," World Wildlife Foundation-Canada Media Advisory (March 7, 2000).

Meyerowitz, Steve, *The Organic Food Guide: How to Shop Smarter and Eat Healthier*. Connecticut: The Globe Pequot Press, 2004, 42.

Jeffrey Kluger, David Bjerklie, Meenakshi Ganguly and Dick Thompson, "The Suicide Seeds, February 1, 1999, time.com/time/magazine/article/0,9171,990111,00.html (accessed December 9, 2009).

BBC News, "Terminator Gene Halt a 'Major U-turn'," October 5, 1999, news.bbc.co.uk/2/hi/science/nature/465222.stm (accessed November 21, 2009).

"What About Using Organic Fabrics in the carbon Footprint Calculation?," June 9, 2009, oecotextiles.wordpress.com/2009/06/09/what-about-using-organic-fabrics-in-the-carbon-footprint-calculation/ (accessed December 9, 2009).

Jeff Harrison, "Study: Nation Wastes Nearly Half Its Food," November 18, 2004, uanews.org/node/10448 (accessed November 21, 2009).

oecotextiles.wordpress.com/2009/06/09/what-about-using-organic-fabrics-in-the-carbon-footprint-calculation/

MSNBC, "U.S. Food Imports Rarely Inspected," April 16, 2007, msnbc.msn.com/id/18132087/ (accessed November 21, 2009).

The New York Times, "Bees Vanish, and Scientists Race for Reasons," April 24, 2007, nytimes. com/2007/04/24/science/24bees.html"nytimes.com/2007/04/24/science/24bees.html (accessed April 5, 2010).

"Loss of Bees Will Be a Disaster," n.d., honeybeecrisis.com/ (accessed December 9, 2009).

Organic Trade Association, "Industry Statistics and Projected Growth," n.d. ota.com/organic/mt/ business.html (accessed November 21, 2009).

ota.com/organic/mt/food.html

honeybeecrisis.com/

Cindy Burke, *To Buy or Not to Buy Organic: What You Need to Know to Choose the Healthiest, Safest, Most Earth-friendly Food.* (Cambridge, MA: Da Capo Press, 2007).

Cindy Burke, *To Buy or Not to Buy Organic: What You Need to Know to Choose the Healthiest, Safest, Most Earth-friendly Food.* (Cambridge, MA: Da Capo Press, 2007).

Pure Zing, "A Method to Help Identify Genetically Modified Foods," n.d., purezing.com.living/ toxins/living_toxins_id_gmo.html (accessed November 21, 2009).

Science Daily, "Arsenic In Chicken Feed May Pose Health Risks To Humans," April 10, 2007, sciencedaily.com/releases/2007/04/070409115746.htm (accessed December 9, 2009).

Monterey Bay Aquarium, "Seafood Watch: All Regions Guide," n.d., montereybayaquarium.org/ cr/SeafoodWatch/web/sfw_regional.aspx (accessed November 21, 2009).

Cindy Burke, *To Buy or Not to Buy Organic: What You Need to Know to Choose the Healthiest, Safest, Most Earth-friendly Food.* (Cambridge, MA: Da Capo Press, 2007).

Quamut.com, "Organic Food: Know What You're Getting When You Go Organic", n.d.kk

David Goldbeck, *The Smart Kitchen: How to Design a Comfortable, Safe, Energy-efficient, and Environment-friendly Workspace.* (Woodstock, NY: Ceres Press, 1989).

David Goldbeck, *The Smart Kitchen: How to Design a Comfortable, Safe, Energy-efficient, and Environment-friendly Workspace.* (Woodstock, NY: Ceres Press, 1989). .

Bureau of Labor Statistics, "Hedonic Quality Adjustment Methods for Microwave Ovens in the U.S. CPI," n.d., bls.gov/cpi/cpimwo.htm (accessed November 21, 2009).

Rock the Bike, Leif Bansner, Interview by Phone, April 2010.

Interview with Amanda Bramble, Co-Founder Ampersand Sustainable Learning Center, September2009.

The Solar Cooking Archive, "Solar Food Drying," n.d. solarcooking.wikia.com/wiki/Solar_food_ drying (accessed November 21, 2009).

Chris Roth, "The Haybox: Why Every Household Needs One," Spring 2003, lostvalley.org/ talkingleaves/node/142 (accessed December 9, 2009).

Rina Wolok, "How to Build a Cob Oven," July 22, 2008, greeniacs.com/GreeniacsGuides/How-to-Build-a-Cob-Oven.html (accessed November 21, 2009).

Harriet Kofalk, *Solar Cooking: A Primer/Cookbook.* (Summertown, TN: Book Publishing Company, 1995).

Harriet Kofalk, *Solar Cooking: A Primer/Cookbook.* (Summertown, TN: Book Publishing Company, 1995).

Harriet Kofalk, *Solar Cooking: A Primer/Cookbook.* (Summertown, TN: Book Publishing Company, 1995).

Fatfree Vegan Recipes, "Vegetarian Crock Pot Chili," n.d., fatfreevegan.com/crockpot/chili.shtml (accessed November 21, 2009).

Fatfree Vegan Recipes, "Vegetarian Crock Pot Chili," n.d., fatfreevegan.com/crockpot/paella.shtml (accessed November 21, 2009).

Oodora, "Safe, Healthy and Non-Leaching Cookware," March 15, 2009, oodora.com/health-and-food/product-reviews/safe-healthy-and-non-leaching-cookware.html (accessed November 21, 2009).

Greenversation: The Official Blog of the U.S. Environmental Protection Agency, "Lead in Pottery," July 16, 2009, blog.epa.gov/blog/2009/07/16/lead-in-pottery/ (accessed December 9, 2009).

Dr. Anita Pepi D.C., "Aluminum Poisoning," n.d., drpepi.com/aluminum-poisoning.php (accessed November 22, 2009).

Meredith A. Hickmann, *The Food and Drug Administration (FDA)*. (Nova Science Publishers, January 2004).

Dr. Anita Pepi D.C., "Aluminum Poisoning," n.d., drpepi.com/aluminum-poisoning.php (accessed November 22, 2009).

Consumer Affairs, "DuPont Agrees to Teflon Pollution Curbs," January 29, 2006, consumeraffairs.com/news04/2006/01/dupont_teflon.html (accessed November 22, 2009).

Debra Lynn Dadd, "Green Living Q&A," April 18, 2006. dld123.com/q&a/index.php?cid=97 (accessed October 2, 2009).

Ecology Action 2006, growbiointensive.org/grow_main.html (Accessed September 1, 2009).

Stein, Kathy. *Beyond Recycling: A Reuser's Guide*. Clear Light Publishers, 1997.

Stein, Kathy. *Beyond Recycling: A Reuser's Guide*. Clear Light Publishers, 1997.

Stein, Kathy. *Beyond Recycling: A Reuser's Guide*. Clear Light Publishers, 1997.

Environment California, "Bisphenol A Overview", n.d., environmentcalifornia.org/environmental-health/stop-toxic-toys/bisphenol-a-overview (accessed April 11, 2010).

americanchemistry.com/s_plastics/doc.asp?CID=1102&DID=4665

Wrap 'n mat

wastefreelunches.org/schools.html

wastefreelunches.org/schools.html

Journal of the American College of Nutrition, Vol 5, Issue 5, "Breast feeding and insulin-dependent diabetes mellitus in children," 1986, jacn.org/cgi/content/abstract/5/5/439 (accessed April 4, 2010).

Journal of the American College of Nutrition, Vol 5, Issue 5, "Breast feeding and insulin-dependent diabetes mellitus in children," 1986, jacn.org/cgi/content/abstract/5/5/439 (accessed April 4, 2010).

Cindy Burke, *To Buy or Not to Buy Organic: What You Need to Know to Choose the Healthiest, Safest, Most Earth-friendly Food*. (New York: Marlowe and Company, 2007).

ampersandproject.org

arcosanti.org

❧ process self-reliance series

Helping urbanites to live sustainably and self-sufficiently in the 21st Century

---

When There Is No Doctor

Preventive and Emergency Healthcare in Challenging Times

by Gerard S. Doyle, MD

A practical guide to preventative and emergency home healthcare, especially helpful during a financial downturn.

The fifth title in Process' Self-Reliance series demystifies medical practices with a practical, self-reliant approach to twenty-first-century health and home medicine. When There Is No Doctor is smartly designed and full of medical tips and emergency suggestions. At a time when our health system has become particularly susceptible to strain, it should be no further than an arm's reach away in your household.

• First home medical and emergency preparedness book for those interested in self-reliance and sustainable healthcare
• With issues like the Economic Crisis, Peak Oil, and Swine Flu, this is the first handbook to address the strains on our current health system and present sustainable, preventable home health and emergency preparedness solutions.
• Goes beyond other home medical books by addressing emergency situations involving doctor and drug shortages, the effects of economic crisis on health care, bioterrorism, and extreme weather.

Gerard S. Doyle, MD, teaches and practices emergency medicine at the University of Wisconsin, Madison, where he also plans the hospital's response to disasters.

6" × 9" • 200 Pages
ISBN 978-1934170-11-3 • $16.95
processmediainc.com

Urban Homestead

Your Guide to Self-Sufficient Living in the Heart of the City
EXPANDED AND REVISED EDITION

By Kelly Coyne and Erik Krutzen

This celebrated book, which The New York Timescalls "the contemporary bible on the subject," shows how to grow and preserve your own food, clean your house without toxins, raise chickens, gain energy independence, and more. Step-by-step projects, tips, and anecdotes will help get you started homesteading immediately. The Urban Homestead is also a guidebook to the larger movement and will point you to the best books and internet resources on self-sufficiency topics.

This copiously illustrated, two-color instruction book proposes a paradigm shift that will greatly enrich our lives, our communities, and our planet. By growing our own food and harnessing natural energy, we are planting seeds for the future of our cities.

New projects include:
- How to sterilize jars and bottles
- How to make infused oil
- Six ways to preserve a tomato
- How to make soda bread
- How to store grain with dry ice
- How to make a tomato can stove
- How to make a bike light

"The Urban Homestead... touches on vegetable gardening, poultry, DIY cleaning products and beer making—all outlined with a sense of play and fun. " —*Whole Life Times*

"...a delightfully readable and very useful guide to front- and back-yard vegetable gardening, food foraging, food preserving, chicken keeping, and other useful skills for anyone interested in taking a more active role in growing and preparing the food they eat." —*Boingboing.net*

6" x 9" • 336 Pages
ISBN 978-1934170014 • $16.95
processmediainc.com